HIS HOLINESS THE FOURTEENTH

DALAI LAMA

HIS HOLINESS THE FOURTEENTH
DALAI LAMA
AN ILLUSTRATED BIOGRAPHY

BY **TENZIN GEYCHE TETHONG**

WITH

GAUTAM PEMMARAJU

FOREWORD BY

TENDZIN CHOEGYAL (NGARI RINPOCHE)

PHOTO EDITOR **JANE MOORE**

Interlink Books

An imprint of Interlink Publishing Group, Inc.
Northampton, Massachusetts

CONTENTS

Facing page: Mural painting of the Fourteenth Dalai Lama by Amdo Jampa, at Samye Monastery, Central Tibet.

CHARTING A PATH FOR THE TIBETAN PEOPLE

BY TENDZIN CHOEGYAL (NGARI RINPOCHE)
BROTHER OF HIS HOLINESS THE DALAI LAMA

I was a vocal thirteen-year-old when my older brother, His Holiness the Fourteenth Dalai Lama, was forced to leave Tibet in the shadow of darkness. I traveled with my mother and sisters who, much to my amusement, were dressed as men to camouflage themselves. My mother was anxious that my behavior and outspokenness (a trait that has stayed with me) might reveal our identity. However, she needn't have worried as I was too enthralled by the Khampa rebels who traveled with us, by their weapons, and by the camera around my neck. In his book, *Freedom in Exile*, my brother writes about the dangerous escape and how tense he was on the journey. But for me it was the grandest adventure a young boy could have. I realize this may sound irreverent, but I firmly believe that had my brother remained in Lhasa and continued to follow the same trajectory of his predecessors, the world would not have had the fortune of knowing a comet of our times.

A single act of enormous bravery and kindness on the part of the Indian government, in giving the Dalai Lama and our people refuge, changed the course of our history. Seventy years on, we have carved out a small space that continues to instill, nurture, and protect Tibetan culture and spiritual practices. But it has come at a great price. Our people remain scattered, we are without a country, and since leaving Lhasa, I, like thousands of Tibetans, have not held a passport. Tibetans in exile are issued an Identity Certificate as their official document.

In the 1970s, I volunteered to join Establishment 22, or the Special Frontier Force, a secret elite regiment of Tibetan commandos that is a part of the Indian army. While it was raised to fight the Chinese army in Tibet, it fought in many theaters of war—except that one. At the time, there was a desperation among Tibetans in exile to do whatever we could to try and help reclaim our country. In the early years, volunteers would offer to enlist for no remuneration; just for a chance to fight the Chinese army. Some may find it surprising that the Dalai Lama's youngest brother had chosen a path that was not nonviolent. But for us it's not so unusual, as each member of my family has charted his or her own path, all serving the Tibetan cause.

Despite overtures and some encouraging developments, Tibetans within Tibet do not have the freedom to practice their religion and follow their culture. Yet, the human spirit endeavors.

Tendzin Choegyal (Ngari Rinpoche), on the right, with his older brother, the Dalai Lama, in lay clothes, during their harrowing escape from Lhasa, 1959.

Our single rallying point has been my older brother, His Holiness the Fourteenth Dalai Lama. His tireless efforts to fight for his people and lead us through the righteous path of dharma and human ethics has become an example, for even his detractors.

I have supported this book project from the day of its inception because the story of His Holiness is important for all humanity. And who better to tell it than my old friend, and a dedicated servant of the Tibetan people, Tenzin Geyche Tethong. His family has played an important role in the history of Tibet and has served successive Dalai Lamas.

He followed family tradition and was a part of His Holiness' Private Office for almost four decades. Through these years, we have shared life's greatest joys and deepest sorrows as friends, colleagues, and now retired men. In one of my darkest moments, when I suffered from depression, Tenzin Geyche-la would visit, goading me to accompany him for a walk or a swim. On one such occasion, I continued to ignore his request and turned around to find him doing a handstand to catch my attention. He was still a monk at this time and was wearing his robe—I burst out laughing and surrendered to his request.

The making of this book has allowed us to spend hours discussing, reminiscing about many such stories, and me pulling his leg, which has been the nature of our relationship for over fifty years. Through these stories and treasured photos, I hope we can provide an enduring record of the Tibetan experience, guided by our spiritual leader, my older brother, His Holiness the Fourteenth Dalai Lama of Tibet.

—TENDZIN CHOEGYAL (NGARI RINPOCHE)

HIS HOLINESS AS I CAME TO KNOW HIM

BY TENZIN GEYCHE TETHONG

This book was written in the hope of inviting people to understand what His Holiness the Fourteenth Dalai Lama means to us as Tibetans, and what it means to be a refugee community. It tells a story of how His Holiness' life changed after 1959, with the Tibetan uprising, and how hard he worked so we could retain our sense of identity, our culture, and our social systems, even in exile. It also tells about the valuable contributions His Holiness has made, not only for Tibet and the Tibetan people but also for the wider world, contributions not given attention in other sources.

I first came to Dharamsala, in northern India, in the winter of 1962–1963 on a bus from Pathankot. I was exhilarated at the first sight of the mountains as we entered the Kangra Valley. McLeod Ganj, or Upper Dharamsala as it was called then, was a small, deserted town, almost extinct. As we drove to the upper reaches from the old market of Kotwali Bazaar, there was little to see except a few buildings on the north side of the road, including the Nowrojee shop—the "storehouse of curiosities"— and a few British-built homes that remained. There was but one bus a day to Delhi and just a few others going down to Kotwali Bazaar from McLeod Ganj. Dharamsala seemed tucked away, with little or no communication with the outside world.

A steep fifteen-minute climb above McLeod Ganj led to Swarg Ashram, the home allocated to His Holiness, where he lived with his immediate family and with the Masters of Robes, Ceremonies, and Food; secretaries, translators, and personal attendants until 1967. This was to become my home, too.

As the youngest member of his Private Office, I was given "staff housing" on the premises. At the time, this was a room no larger than seven by ten feet, which I shared with with Venerable Lobsang Gawa, His Holiness' senior attendant. Since there was not enough space for two beds, we shared a bunk bed, with me on the top bunk. Our toilet was a small structure, a short distance away, which was shared by others who lived in Swarg Ashram. There was little time to complain about the lack of creature comforts since there was so much to be done, and after all, His Holiness,

The Fourteenth Dalai Lama with his prayer beads, or mala, in the prayer room of his private residence, Dharamsala, 2004.

who had once lived in the grand Potala and Norbulingka palaces, adjusted to his new home (which left a lot to be desired) without complaint.

When I joined the Office, there were only four of us working there—Venerable Kungo Tara, who was the principal secretary and a former colleague of my father; Kungo Rinchen-la (Sadutshang), who helped with the English correspondence; and Champa Yonten-la and myself, the two clerks for the Tibetan and the English sections. Champa Yonten-la was nicknamed "the Tibetan Typewriter" on account of his exceptionally good handwriting. Also keeping us company were His Holiness' pet dogs, two Lhasa Apsos called Sangye and Tashi (gifted by the Everest mountaineer Tenzin Norgay), and later, a cat that had made itself at home. Our circumstances were modest, but we were charged with passion and dedication to our jobs. His Holiness was only twenty-three when he had to flee his own country. But he had the foresight to know that the 80,000 refugees who escaped Tibet into India before the Chinese sealed the border would need rehabilitation and resettlement.

Our focus in those early years of exile was to establish systems, institutions, and organizations. The Indian government had been welcoming and gracious in allowing us to set up our own schools to keep children well-versed in Tibetan studies, and settlements where Tibetans could farm and find ways to be self-sufficient. India herself was a young nation, only twelve years old, and His Holiness has never forgotten the counry's generosity and kindness in giving us refuge. He has even called himself a "Son of India."

Alongside education, he established several institutions to preserve Tibetan culture, the first of these being the Tibetan Institute of Performing Arts (TIPA), which continues to thrive today. Around 1968–1969, TIPA (known as the Drama School at the time) almost closed down because of various problems, including infighting among its members. At that time, I volunteered to try and save the institute. Fortunately, I was successful. It was at TIPA that I met my future wife, Kalsang Chukie, who is a well-known singer. We married in 1980, eight years after she had left TIPA, and after I had given up my monk's vows.

In this photo, taken in Bodh Gaya, I can be seen crouched to the bottom right of His Holiness' throne.

Our role in the Private Office was to support His Holiness in any of his endeavors—be it appealing to the international community to support the Tibetan cause or giving our time to the various organizations and settlements within India. His Holiness would write countless letters to world leaders and seldom receive a response. Those were tough days.

During the next four decades that I spent at the Private Office, I traveled extensively with His Holiness as his private secretary and translator. Over the years encompassing three popes, three US presidents, and numerous heads of states, diplomats, scientists, artists, followers, and

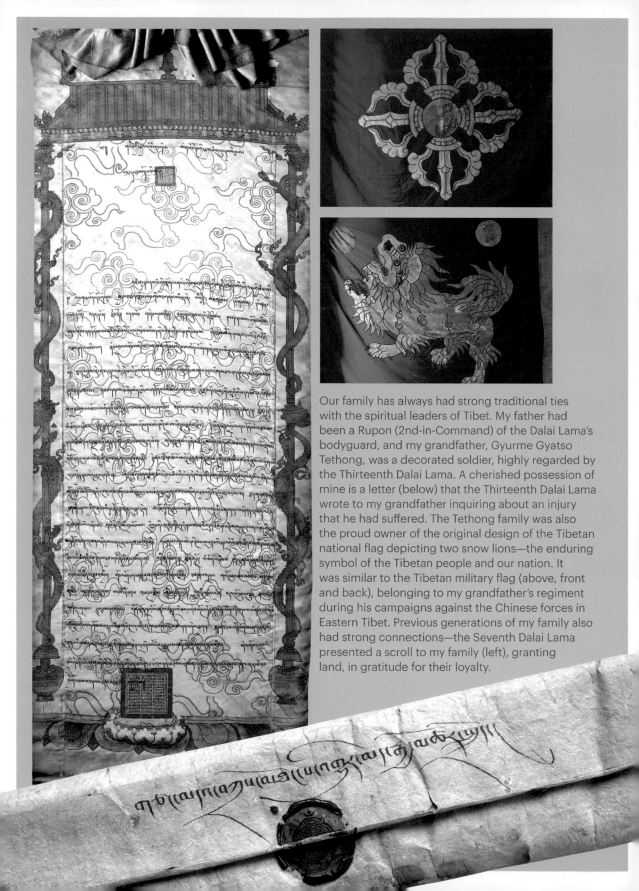

Our family has always had strong traditional ties with the spiritual leaders of Tibet. My father had been a Rupon (2nd-in-Command) of the Dalai Lama's bodyguard, and my grandfather, Gyurme Gyatso Tethong, was a decorated soldier, highly regarded by the Thirteenth Dalai Lama. A cherished possession of mine is a letter (below) that the Thirteenth Dalai Lama wrote to my grandfather inquiring about an injury that he had suffered. The Tethong family was also the proud owner of the original design of the Tibetan national flag depicting two snow lions—the enduring symbol of the Tibetan people and our nation. It was similar to the Tibetan military flag (above, front and back), belonging to my grandfather's regiment during his campaigns against the Chinese forces in Eastern Tibet. Previous generations of my family also had strong connections—the Seventh Dalai Lama presented a scroll to my family (left), granting land, in gratitude for their loyalty.

dissenters, I was by his side. Because of my position, which I believe was a stroke of luck of being at the right place at the right time, I was able to get a ringside view of world affairs as they unfolded. But most importantly, I was able to serve our spiritual and temporal leader, a living, breathing bodhisattva who guides us in all matters. But I am getting ahead of myself.

My family came to India in the winter of 1949, ten years before the Dalai Lama had to flee Tibet. My father, Sonam Topjor Wangchuk Tethong, born in 1924, was a Tibetan government official with the supplies office in Lhasa. He joined service at sixteen but continued studies and scholarly pursuits. He was a man of progressive thinking, widely read in Western literature and history, a genuine scholar of Chinese, and a very keen photographer. Sensing Chinese aggression, my father sought a transfer to Kalimpong, a small hill town in West Bengal, and was granted leave to join the Tibet Trade Mission there. Several Tibetans lived in Kalimpong and Darjeeling; both places were frontier towns with diverse populations.

Before leaving Tibet for good, we spent some time at our family place in Shigatse, which I recall as

a very happy and idyllic setting. My memories are sparse, mostly of picking peas in the fields near the house and being scared of the person in charge; of swimming in the river, and riding a donkey. The workers in the fields used to offer me *chang* (Tibetan barley beer), even though I was quite young, as this was common in the Tsang area. We also had a residence in Lhasa where we stopped at times.

Following the 1959 occupation, the Chinese requested my father to return to Tibet as the principal of their new school in Lhasa. He refused and decided instead to work with exiled Tibetans, particularly with the leaders, including former Prime Minister Lukhangwa, His Holiness' older brother Gyalo Thondup, W. D. Shakabpa, and others involved in Tibet's freedom struggle. My father was a staunch patriot; the loss of Tibet and the violent suppression of the people troubled him deeply. He was a shy, timid man with a melancholic disposition. The burden of his responsibilities perhaps took a toll on him.

I was six when we arrived in Kalimpong. I first attended St. Joseph's Convent and in 1955 began studies at St. Augustine's boys' school. I later

Left: My father, pictured above when young, was a man of letters and in 1959 served at the first institution started by His Holiness in exile, a school in Mussoorie. He continued to be a part of many educational endeavors associated with the Tibetan community in exile and passed away in Dharamsala in 1997.

Right: My mother, Sonam Peldon, of the Samdrup Phodrang family, photographed at a studio in Kalimpong.

I am the eldest of four brothers. We were all very close growing up. Tenzin Namgyal Tethong, who comes right after me, is a well-respected member of the Tibetan government. He has served as prime minister and led a delegation to Tibet in 1980. Kunga Namgyal Tethong lives in Switzerland with his family. Unfortunately our youngest brother Phuntsog Namgyal passed away in 2015.

moved to Mount Hermon School in Darjeeling. In the winter of 1959, my father, along with our family, moved to Mussoorie, where the Dalai Lama was temporarily residing. My father taught history at the first Tibetan school that was set up in exile but changed jobs a few times. Due to these moves, from Darjeeling to Mussoorie, and then later to Simla, my three brothers—Tenzin Namgyal, Kunga Namgyal, Phuntsog Namgyal—and I lost three years of studies. In 1962, I rejoined school, at the insistence of Mrs. Buxton, an English lady helping Tibetan refugees. I completed my schooling (Senior Cambridge) in 1963 and later that winter came to Dharamsala to work for some months in what was then called the Council for Tibetan Education.

Following that, I was asked to join the Private Office as a replacement for a friend who had moved to the US for further studies. The next year, I took my ordination as a monk. I was twenty.

My English education came in handy, and I rose through the ranks. By 1977, I was Private Secretary to His Holiness, and I would serve as *kalon* (minister) from 1983 to 1985.

However, my first encounter with His Holiness had been in the winter of 1956, at the Buddha Jayanti celebrations in Sarnath—though I have no great memories of that trip except being very excited. I do, however, vividly recall my first private audience with His Holiness in Swarg Ashram during the monsoon of 1963. I was called into a room with a leaking roof where a bucket had been placed underneath the leaky spot. The room had none of the grandeur or pomp of the famed Potala and Norbulingka palaces in Lhasa, but for me, it was the grandest and most important one I had ever stepped into. His Holiness inquired about me, my interests, and about my intention to serve the Tibetan government in exile. He praised my father's loyalty and dedication, and said that I should follow in his footsteps. This encounter, in all its simplicity and banality, is imprinted in my memory forever.

As his translator and private secretary, I accompanied His Holiness on his first trip abroad to Japan in September 1967, and to the West, an eleven-country trip to Europe, in 1973. In the early years, we sometimes stayed at monasteries and relied on the generosity of our well-wishers. His Holiness had boundless energy to meet as many people as possible, to interact with those from other cultures and faiths—all the while reminding others of the plight of the Tibetan people. As any young, curious man, I enjoyed my travels with him despite our often hectic schedules (which His Holiness has a penchant of deviating from quite often!). Like most of us, His Holiness' temper was most often tested when we traveled. I remember his impatience when something went wrong with the planned program, or the luggage took too long to arrive in the evening, especially because he usually retires early, in order to wake up at 3 or 4 am. I had the good fortune to have been with him in California when we learned he had been awarded the Nobel Peace Prize, and I had the great honor of traveling to Norway for the ceremony. Over

time, he began receiving a large number of visitors in Dharamsala. My role as his private secretary was to manage these meetings, and to be a gatekeeper of sorts—a tough task, but a rewarding one, as I had the opportunity to meet such an extraordinary range of people.

My time at the Private Office brought me into close proximity with other members of His Holiness' family. Perhaps I was destined to serve His Holiness, as my ancestors had once served his predecessors. His mother, Diki Tsering, lovingly known as Gyalyum Chenmo—the Great Mother of the Dalai Lama—was an exceptional woman. Wise and kind, she served as a maternal figure for us Tibetans. I was very fond of her and would like to believe she of me. She would often invite me when she cooked one of her legendary dishes.

His Holiness' youngest brother, Tendzin Choegyal (Ngari Rinpoche), and I are close in age and have had the fortune of sharing a warm friendship for sixty years. We were colleagues briefly at the Private Office, and later at the Tibetan Youth Congress, but our camaraderie goes beyond, and today we meet often to reminisce and carp about current world affairs. It was on his insistence and help that I began writing this book.

In 2006 I retired. His Holiness granted me two extensions, after which I wanted to leave to make room for the younger colleagues who were very ably managing the growing demands of the Private Office; but also because after over forty years, I was not as productive anymore and was also extremely stressed from the job. His Holiness' popularity and stature in the world had grown exponentially. People were gravitating toward his humility, selfless compassion, his mantra that "as human beings we are all the same," and his teachings to help comprehend suffering and contemplate the spiritual pathway to eternal deliverance.

The Nobel Peace Prize of 1989 was only one such affirmation of the world's recognition and admiration of his peaceful resistance to the

In 1964, at the age of 20, I became a monk. In 1976, when I decided to give up my robes, the person I was most anxious to tell was His Holiness. As I had suspected, he was not happy with my decision and asked me to think it over carefully. No matter how much I thought it over, I felt I could not remain a monk. His Holiness was obviously not happy but accepted my decision.

occupation of our country, of his dedication to leading by example, by living a life of compassion and kindness. In a 2008 poll conducted by the *International Herald Tribune*, His Holiness was voted the most respected world leader—an incredible feat for a Tibetan leader.

Now I spend time on my own dharma studies, meeting old friends, and giving my time to Tibetan causes. There are few of us left—those who came from Tibet. Perhaps we provide the last link to a way of life, to an older, more arcane world. There are roughly 150,000 Tibetans in diaspora, of whom about 100,000 live in India. Now there are second- and third-generation Tibetans born there.

My reason for writing this book is to leave a record of what it was like to create a nation from nothing in exile. Of how His Holiness rallied endlessly for his people, and continues to do so. The chances of me seeing a free Tibet are slim. But through this book I hope to show a younger generation that it is an ongoing struggle during which we have achieved a great deal. There is only an eight-year difference between His Holiness and I. The relative closeness in age does not adequately capture the vastness of his presence for me. I hope my efforts do justice to his stature and love of humankind, and also serve our common cause of striving for peace, harmony, and happiness.

When addressing certain prominent people in this account, such as His Holiness' brothers or sisters, I wanted to use the proper way of addressing them in our Tibetan society. For example, I would typically address His Holiness' elder brother as Kungo Gyalo Thondup, or his elder sister as Yabshi, Lhacham Tsering Dolma, and so on. However, I feel that this will become too confusing for non-Tibetan readers. So I am opting to address them as they would be by non-Tibetans: simply by their names.

It is difficult to encompass His Holiness' life, beliefs, teachings, and impact within the confines of this book. It was my endeavor to provide a narrative history of his life that is infused with my observations and experiences in the years spent with him. The photographs in this book are remarkable—some from the albums of His Holiness' family have

I learned many things during my years of working closely with His Holiness. Probably one of the most important things is to have a balanced and holistic view of things, especially in matters and issues that are controversial and contentious.

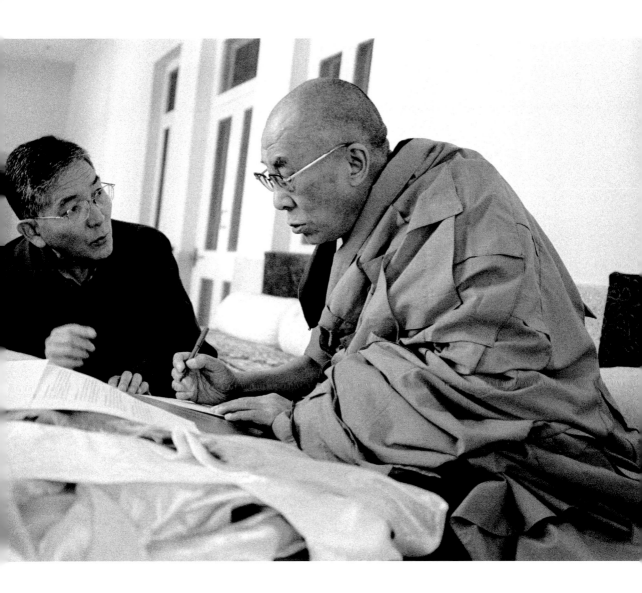

never been published before. Jane Moore has been a dedicated friend to the Tibetans and brings with her decades of experience in photo editing and research. She has unearthed gems for our book, at times coercing people for months for just that one photo!

—TENZIN GEYCHE TETHONG

"The Dalai Lama is like a ray of sunshine,
which is impossible for any one group of people
to obscure. The ray of Buddhist faith will
shine on everyone through him."

MANCHU EMPEROR K'ANG-SI TO THE SEVENTH DALAI LAMA

Prologue
The Bodhisattva of Compassion

BUDDHISM AND THE DALAI LAMAS OF TIBET
(605-1933)

The story of His Holiness the Fourteenth Dalai Lama of Tibet, Tenzin Gyatso, is inseparable from the recent history of the Tibetan people. But these two stories are also interwoven with older narratives reaching back in time, which shed light on many twists and turns of this chronicle. So it may be helpful first to reflect briefly on the story of Tibetan Buddhism, the lineage of the Dalai Lama as Tibet's spiritual and temporal leader, and the consequential presence of one earlier Dalai Lama in particular, the Great Thirteenth.

BUDDHISM IN TIBET

Tibet is deeply connected to Buddhism. The Tibetan people's way of life has been completely influenced by it. It is no exaggeration to say that before the invasion of Tibet by China in 1949, ninety-nine percent of the population were practicing Buddhists. In the past in Tibet, it was not uncommon for a young child of four or five to pick up an insect to save it from being stepped on, because of the Buddhist teaching that every living being is sacred. It has been fairly common even for lay people, let alone monks and nuns, to be engaged in serious spiritual practices several hours a day.

Avalokiteshvara, Tibet's patron saint, is regarded as the Bodhisattva of Compassion. Bodhisattvas are realized beings, inspired by the wish to attain complete enlightenment, who have vowed to be reborn in the world to help all living beings. This deity, also referred to as *Chenrezig*, is revered as the most glorious of bodhisattvas in the Buddhist world. He is said to have left the celestial realm and emanated in Tibet in order to transform the nation from warmongering and barbaric ways to a peaceful land where Buddhism could truly flourish. *The Lotus Sutra* is considered the earliest classical Buddhist text to provide details of the many manifestations of Avalokiteshvara, including several female forms.

In Sanskrit, *avalokita* means seeing or gazing down, and *esvara* means Lord, suggesting a being who looks down unwaveringly from above upon sentient beings with the continual wish to help them. His most elaborate

Map showing the
boundaries of the
Tibetan Empire
between the 780s and
790s.

Songtsen Gampo
moved the capital
from Yarlung to Lhasa.
After consolidated
his power by unifying
tribal kingdoms
throughout Tibet,
a Chinese princess
traveled from
Chang'an, capital
of the ancient Tang
Dynasty, to Lhasa to
marry him.

Facing page: A
twentieth-century
painting of the Potala
Palace and sacred
monuments of Lhasa.
The Jokhang Temple
(bottom, right) built
by Songtsen Gampo,
houses Tibet's most
sacred statue, the
Jowo Buddha. Ground
mineral pigment on
cotton.

form is represented with eleven heads, a thousand arms, and a thousand eyes on his outstretched palms. A *mani*, or jewel, is clasped in his hands in the shape of a *padme*, or lotus. His mantra, *Om Mani Padme Hum*, essentially means the purification of our gross body, mind, and speech through the union of compassion and wisdom.

The Dalai Lamas and several of our ancient kings are believed by Tibetan Buddhists to be manifestations of Avalokiteshvara. The present and Fourteenth Dalai Lama is considered a pure manifestation; the omnipresent six-syllable mantra *Om Mani Padme Hum* therefore indirectly invokes him. Often uttered by Tibetan Buddhists millions of times during the course of a life, the qualities of wisdom and compassion are, in this way, encouraged to arise within the mind.

THE FIRST DHARMA KING AND HIS LEGACY

Buddhism in Tibet became widespread during the reign of Songtsen Gampo, thirty-third king of the Yarlung dynasty. Born circa 605 AD in the northeast of Lhasa and enthroned at the age of thirteen, he is revered as the first of three divine Dharma kings (Choegyal) of Tibet. Songtsen Gampo unified several Tibetan kingdoms. After which, he moved his seat from the

Yarlung Valley to Lhasa in the Kyichu Valley, "place of the gods." From there, he conquered parts of neighboring Nepal and Western China. The political and cultural foundations he established in Tibet, and his enlightened leadership, opened the way for Buddhadharma, Buddhist teaching, to flourish throughout Tibet and to spread across his empire.

The Jowo Buddha statue, portraying Buddha Shakyamuni at the age of 12. It was brought to Tibet from China by Princess Wen-ch'eng as part of her dowry and is housed in the Jokhang temple.

Two of Songtsen Gampo's wives are credited with significantly influencing this emperor's cultural awareness. His Nepalese wife, Princess Bhrikuti, daughter of King Amshuvarman, was a devout Buddhist who introduced valuable artistic traditions of Himalayan Buddhism to Tibet. His Chinese wife, Princess Wen-ch'eng, daughter of the Tang emperor Taizong, brought with her a treasure trove of ancient Chinese wisdom in the form of books and manuscripts. The most sacred temple in Tibet, the Jokhang in Lhasa, was built during this king's reign. It eventually housed the venerated Jowo Buddha statue, brought by Princess Wen-ch'eng from Chang'an, ancient capital of the Tang dynasty, as a wedding gift. This precious statue had been crafted in Bodh Gaya, India, and later presented to a previous emperor of the Tang dynasty. Princess Bhrikuti also brought a statue with her, of Buddha Akshobya. This was placed in Lhasa's other holy temple, the Ramoche.

For several years, Songtsen Gampo meditated in a cave on Lhasa's Marpo-ri, or Red Hill. Centuries later, this site became the location of the vast Potala Palace, for three centuries the palace of the Dalai Lamas. A progressive reformer, inclined toward scholarship and meditation, he was responsible for the creation of a new Tibetan script, enabling translation of the ancient Sanskrit Buddhist treatises of India into the new literary language of Classical Tibetan. He also adopted sacred codes of conduct from Buddhist scripture, leading to a more just society. Celebrated in Tibet as an emanation of Avalokiteshvara, it is from this near-mythic, unifying seventh-century emperor that each successive Dalai Lama may claim spiritual descent.

Tibetan Script and Scriptures

For millennia, the Tibetan language had been purely oral. But circa 632, Songtsen Gampo sent court minister Thonmi Sambhota, along with sixteen other students, to India to learn Sanskrit and to devise a Tibetan written script. Thonmi Sambhota is said to have gained great knowledge under the tutelage of a Brahmin named Lipikara. Some claim this court minister went to South India. It seems more likely that he studied in Kashmir, and possibly at the prestigious Nalanda University in Bihar, founded in the fifth century. Following Thonmi Sambhota's return, Songtsen Gampo secluded himself for several years to learn from him all the knowledge he had brought back. He then commissioned the translation of several hundred Buddhist texts into the new Classical Tibetan script.

Two principal styles of script developed: *U-chen* (with a head), for the printing of manuscripts; and *U-med* (without a head), for cursive handwriting used in daily life. As a result, translated manuscripts were often copied in pure gold ink by expert calligraphers. Calligraphy today still holds an honored place in the spiritual traditions of Tibet. It is studied as part of the monastic curriculum, and some monks dedicate their lives to mastering the subtleties of the art, attaining great heights of aesthetic achievement. The Fourteenth Dalai Lama himself studied calligraphy, and he signs his name in traditional *U-med*.

Top: Exceptional linguist, calligrapher, and scholar Thonmi Sambhota, who laid the foundation of the Tibetan writing system in the seventh century AD.

Script: Signature of His Holiness the Fourteenth Dalai Lama, in one form of *U-med* script.

We would not have all the Tibetan treatises we have today, which have helped to preserve Buddhism in a pure form from the time of Buddha Shakyamuni in the sixth century BCE, if it were not for Thonmi Sambhota's great efforts. The Tibetan Buddhist canon comprises the Kangyur, the translated words of the Buddha, in over a hundred volumes, and the Tengyur, translations of commentaries on these works written by Indian Buddhist masters, in over 200 volumes. Originally printed from woodblocks and traditionally wrapped in silk covers, these volumes are kept in monasteries, nunneries, and large temples for the purposes of study and constant reference.

The extraordinary contribution made to general scholarship and experience, thanks to the devising of a Tibetan script, is inestimable.

THE DALAI LAMAS OF TIBET

The lineage of the Dalai Lama began with Gedrun Drupa, born in the fourteenth century to a nomadic family. He was later recognized as the First Dalai Lama when the institution was established in the sixteenth century. Since then, the position has grown in spiritual authority. In the seventeenth century, it gained temporal—or political—authority, starting from the time of the Great Fifth Dalai Lama.

Today, the Fourteenth Dalai Lama is the most powerful spiritual and political symbol of his land and people. As the Tibetan warrior Aten wrote:

"The connection of every Tibetan with the Dalai Lama is a deep and inexpressible thing. To us the Dalai Lama symbolizes the whole of Tibet...he is the living embodiment of the eternal principles of Buddhism."

1. Gedun Drupa, 1391–1474
2. Gedun Gyatso, 1475–1542
3. Sonam Gyatso, 1543–1588
4. Yonten Gyatso, 1589–1617
5. Ngawang Lobsang Gyatso, 1617–1682
6. Tsangyang Gyatso, 1683–1706
7. Kelzang Gyatso, 1708–1757
8. Jamphel Gyatso, 1758–1804
9. Lungtok Gyatso, 1805–1815
10. Tsultrim Gyatso, 1816–1837
11. Khedrup Gyatso, 1838–1856
12. Trinley Gyatso, 1857–1875
13. Thubten Gyatso, 1876–1933
14. Tenzin Gyatso, 1935–

Frescoes at the Norbulingka Institute,
Sidhpur, Himachal Pradesh.

THE THIRTEENTH DALAI LAMA: SOCIAL REFORMER

The Thirteenth Dalai Lama, Thubten Gyatso, was destined to become an important and enduring figure in Tibetan history. He guided us skillfully, progressively, and often impetuously, through a period of turbulence into a new era during which the idea of Tibetan independence gained currency. My grandfather served the Thirteenth Dalai Lama as a successful soldier, and later as an administrator, so from a young age we were aware of our familial links and of stories about events of the past.

Born on 27 May 1876, he was recognized as the Thirteenth Dalai Lama in 1878. The previous four Dalai Lamas had all died prematurely. When the Twelfth Dalai Lama, Trinley Gyatso, died in 1875 at the young age of twenty, his face is said to have turned toward the southeast. It was taken as a sign that the new incarnation would be born in that direction.

This was confirmed by the Nechung Oracle and by the Eighth Panchen Lama, which overrode the favored practice of Manchu emperors—of selecting the final candidate by picking a name from a golden urn. Manchurian leaders had tried to enforce the urn system in an attempt to undermine Tibetan tradition. Charles Bell, an officer in the British Indian colonial government and scholar who would become a great friend to Tibet, wrote that the setting aside of the urn system reflected the decline of Manchu influence over the Tibetans.

Thubten Gyatso was formally enthroned on 1 August 1879 in a ceremony titled "The Prayer for the Power of the Golden Throne." Thereafter he lived in the Potala and Norbulingka palaces under the care of servants, monks, tutors, and the regent. The Thirteenth Dalai Lama took on temporal power in 1895 and would become a great reformer. His efforts at administrative discipline and reform, and international diplomacy, demonstrated his vision and intelligence. He transformed into a skillful and successful political and spiritual leader, fiercely advocating Tibetan independence. A "serious and tough" leader, he was responsible for introducing a number of monastic reforms.

First photograph of the Thirteenth Dalai Lama in Lhasa at Norbulingka Palace, 14 October 1921, taken by Charles Bell. He worked to improve and increase the military, introduce modern education, make social reforms, revive discipline in the monasteries, take a firm stance with the often intriguing, corrupt government, and generally move forward to meet the challenges of the times.

THE DRAGON, THE LION, AND THE BEAR

At the turn of the twentieth century, the ambitions of three empires converged on Tibet. For millennia, China had been expanding from its cradle, the basin of the Yellow River, or the "Mother River," and it had long hungered for, and claimed authority over, Tibetan lands and waters as its manifest destiny. As the Thirteenth Dalai Lama assumed leadership, border conflicts with Tibet kept erupting, and Chinese presence continued to grow.

During the same time, a power struggle in Central Asia between Great Britain and Tzarist Russia, known as "the Great Game," was intensifying. Britain aimed to protect the "crown jewel" of its imperial wealth—India, while Russia was determined to expand its enormous lands and influence. Tibet now found itself to be a strategic geographic prize where this rivalry could play out.

Potala Palace, Lhasa. The winter palace of the Dalai Lamas situated atop Marpo-ri, or Red Hill. The construction of this magnificent structure was begun in 1645 by the Fifth Dalai Lama. The layout of the palace includes the rooftop shrines of some of the earlier Dalai Lamas. While the White Palace served as the seat of the Tibetan government and the main residence of the Dalai Lamas, the central structure (Red Palace) housed chapels, sacred statues, and the tombs of eight Dalai Lamas.

Unhappy with the Chinese presence there, the British had been insisting that Tibet's lands be opened up for trade. British news reports suggested that the Russians were negotiating a secret deal with the Chinese. A trigger point was the Dalai Lama's close ties with Agvan Dorjiev, a Buryat-Mongol monk, who had become His Holiness' debate partner, trusted political advisor, and friend. It was a relationship between an energetic young Dalai Lama in his twenties, committed to Tibetan aspirations for independence, and a youthfully mature Siberian monk, committed to Buryat nationalism. Sensing a threat, the British suspected that the Dalai Lama intended to build alliance with the Russians, threatening British agendas in the region. British goods were already coming to Lhasa through existing trade routes. The British Indian government decided to send a political mission to Tibet, led by Francis E. Younghusband. The Dalai Lama saw these moves as British territorial ambitions.

This was Pargo Kaling, the ancient entrance to Lhasa, taken from the east in 1921. Colonel Francis Younghusband marched with his men into Lhasa through this magnificent stone gateway in 1904. The large chorten (Buddhist stupa) with sacred relics over the gateway, created a majestic entry to the capital city of Tibet.

In November 1903, to counter Russian intentions, the British made plans to invade Tibet. That December, British forces under the command of General David Macdonald and Colonel Younghusband crossed the border, ascending the Tibetan plateau, and by summer 1904 had reached Lhasa, overwhelming all Tibetan resistance along the way. Nearly one-third of Tibetan forces died fighting the British.

The Dalai Lama was forced to flee to Mongolia. It was the first time he would leave his own country. At the end of July 1904, he reached Ulan Bator (then called Urga) in Mongolia after an arduous journey of three months. He remained there in exile for two years. In August 1907, Great Britain and Russian signed the Anglo-Russian Convention, in which the two countries recognized "the principle of suzerainty of China over Tibet"—Chinese political authority. The game board was reset for new interventions to come.

Tibetans protectively standing at the entrance to the Jokhang Temple when British forces came marching into Lhasa.

The Buryat Monk and the Thirteenth Dalai Lama

The Tibetan episode of "the Great Game," and Tibet's precarious vulnerability to external forces are illuminated by the story of the Dalai Lama's relationship with Agvan Dorjiev, his debate partner, trusted advisor, and faithful friend. Also known as Ngawang Dorjee, or by his monastic title Tsenyi Khempo, tales are legendary of this fascinating Buryat-Mongol monk, who rose to be such an influential figure. Actively involved in Buryat nationalism, his support for Tibet and his role in Tibetan history deserve to be more fully acknowledged.

Born in 1854 in a Siberian village east of Lake Baikal, Dorjiev was an ethnic Buryat, an indigenous group of semi-nomadic people from the Russian Far East province of Buryatia. He grew up in a Buddhist household, studied at a monastery close to his home, and married at the age of fourteen. But he soon took a vow of celibacy from his mentor, Pelden Chopel Pelzangpo, in order to continue religious studies. At the age of nineteen, he accompanied his mentor to Lhasa and enrolled in studies at the Gomang College of Drepung Monastery. His studies were briefly interrupted when he had to leave Tibet for Mongolia, due to Tibetan policy of restricting a foreigner's stay.

Above: First-ever representation of the Thirteenth Dalai Lama, created in Ulan Bator, Mongolia, during his exile in 1905.

Facing page: Agvan Dorjiev, Buddhist scholar and diplomat, 1898, St. Petersburg.

There, he took full monastic vows, and five years later, at the age of twenty-six, returned to Lhasa.

Arriving in Lhasa during the New Year's celebrations of 1880, Dorjiev immersed himself in studies and precociously attained his Geshe degree—roughly equivalent to a doctorate in Buddhist studies—in the short span of eight years. It was during this time that, through his mentor, he became close to the young Dalai Lama as an assistant debate partner, or *tsenshap*.

As the world beyond Tibet was changing, so, too, were many things shifting wthin Tibet. Dorjiev became involved in establishing diplomatic relations between Tibet and Russia after convincing the Dalai Lama that it was in Tibet's interest. The Russians indicated to Dorjiev on his diplomatic visits there that they could consider military assistance to the Tibetan army. On the instructions of the Thirteenth, Dorjiev also established monasteries in Russia.

While Dorjiev was in the thick of negotiations with the Russian government, the British were growing uneasy with these efforts and saw the developing relationship between Tibet and

Agvan Dorjiev was instrumental in the signing of the Tibet-Mongolia Treaty of 1913 of friendship and recognition of each other's independence. As Dalai Lama's personal envoy, he made several visits to St. Petersburg (then Petrograd). He is seen here leaving Peterhof Palace after an audience with Tzar Nicholas II in 1901, seeking support from Russia.

Russia as a threat. The Chinese, too, were not happy. This led to the armed British expedition in Tibet in 1904.

On 30 July 1904, the Thirteenth Dalai Lama appointed a prime minister to oversee the affairs of Tibet, and he fled into exile. Dorjiev, along with the Dalai Lama's close associates, accompanied him on this three-month-long journey to Mongolia. During their stay, Dorjiev effectively acted as his emissary and political advisor. In 1905, he successfully lobbied the Russian government for permission to establish a Buddhist temple in St. Petersburg. In 1907, following the Anglo-Russian Convention, effectively removing Tibet from the "Great Game," the Dalai Lama returned to Tibet.

Dorjiev met with the Thirteenth for the last time in Tibet in August 1912, before he left for Mongolia. His successful campaign led to the signing of the Tibet–Mongolia Treaty in 1913, in which both countries recognized "each other's independence and promised to strengthen their mutual friendship." He also established a center for Tibetan traditional medicine in the monastery in Atsagat in Buryatia.

After the Russian Revolution in 1917, Dorjiev was arrested and sentenced to death. He received a pardon on the promise of collaborating with Bolsheviks. He was arrested again during Stalin's purges and died in 1938 in a prison hospital.

OPENING TIBET TO THE WORLD

Upon his return to Tibet in 1906, after two years of exile in Mongolia, the Thirteenth chose to spend time in Kumbum Monastery. A British Indian government delegation visited him there, urging him to return to the capital and resume his duties. But the Great Thirteenth had other plans.

The first official contact between Tibet and the United States took place soon after the Dalai Lama's return. While in exile, he had come in contact with the US diplomat and Tibetan scholar in China, William Woodville Rockhill. In early 1908, the Thirteenth Dalai Lama left Kumbum Monastery for China in an effort to ease tensions on the eastern frontier in Kham. The idea of consolidating an independent Tibet was now firmly entrenched in his mind, and he hoped to garner support through personal diplomatic efforts. Wishing to make a pilgrimage, he proceeded to Wutai Shan (Five-Peaked Mountain) on his way to Peking. The most prominent Buddhist site in China, Wutai Shan is considered the home of the Bodhisattva of Wisdom, Manjusri. It comprises over fifty-three monasteries and temples.

On 13 June, William Rockhill left Peking and trekked for five days to Wutai Shan to meet with the Dalai Lama. At their first meeting, the American's ability to speak Tibetan fluently pleased the Dalai Lama very much. Their second meeting veered toward more serious matters. Rockhill suggested that the Dalai Lama build good relations with his neighbors, particularly India.

Afterward, on 30 June, the US diplomat wrote with excitement to Theodore Roosevelt, "Dear Mr. President: I have just had such a unique and interesting experience that I cannot forbear writing to you at once about it." The meeting with Rockhill in Wutai Shan was the beginning of Tibet opening itself up to the world, initiating relations that broke with tradition.

Left: William Woodville Rockhill (1854–1914), once US diplomat to China, was the first American Tibetologist.

Below: The first two folios of the sutra, *Perfection of Wisdom in Eight Thousand Lines*. A gift from the Dalai Lama, it was presented to Rockhill during his stay at Wutai Shan in 1908. The sutra is wrapped in yellow silk.

ENCOUNTERING THE DRAGON

In September 1908, after his fruitful five-month stay in Wutai Shan, the Dalai Lama reached Peking, now called Beijing. His first task was to seek an audience with the Manchu Emperor. Following a welcome with due pomp and ceremony, the Dalai Lama proceeded to the Yellow Temple, where the Great Fifth had stayed in 1653. Well aware that political equations had changed, he knew that the tensions with the Chinese would dictate terms.

Sure enough, he was informed that at the audience with the Emperor, scheduled for 6 October, he would have to prostrate and would be seated at a low couch near the throne. This was unacceptable, and so the audience was postponed. Following talks, the terms were made somewhat less humiliating. Also, he was to meet the Emperor and the Empress Dowager separately, since she was the one who actually wielded power. But the Manchu plan to subordinate the Dalai Lama went further. He was given

Mural in Norbulingka Palace of the Thirteenth Dalai Lama meeting Emperor Kuang-hsu and the Empress Tzu-hsi in Peking, in 1908.

the title, "Sincerely Obedient, Reincarnation-helping, Most Excellent Buddha of the West."

Meeting with the foreign ministry, the Dalai Lama reminded them that the Sino-Tibetan relationship had always been one of religious cooperation. He then asserted that Chinese officials were overstepping their position in Eastern Tibet. Chinese officials agreed to curb their forces in Kham but asked His Holiness to accept the 1906 Anglo-Chinese Agreement. No documents, however, were signed. It was clear that the decline of the Manchu Empire was nearly complete. The Empress Dowager was now widely unpopular, even among her own officials.

Both the Emperor and the Empress Dowager died in November 1908. In his role as priest to the Manchu emperors, the Dalai Lama conducted religious ceremonies for them and also attended the enthronement of the heir, the two-year-old cousin of the departed Emperor, destined to be the last Manchu emperor of China.

The Dalai Lama left Beijing on 21 December 1908, making his way back home beset by tumult and confusion. During his stay, the Chinese press and officialdom had vilified him as "a proud and ignorant man." W. W. Rockhill was witness to all these events. In a letter to President Roosevelt, he wrote:

> He [the Dalai Lama] must take the bitter with the sweet, and the only suggestion I could make was he should not delay too long... His pride has suffered terribly while here and he leaves Peking with his

On the Thirteenth Dalai Lama's return to Lhasa, a ceremony was held at the Potala Palace marking the formal handing back of the government to him. This new gold seal presented to him by the National Assembly in 1909 described his authority over Tibet as "indestructible as a diamond." Seals were traditionally pressed in red cinnabar, as seen above.

On his way back from China, the Great Thirteenth halted at the Shardzong hermitage in the Tsongkha region of Amdo. He was received by the Rinpoche there and also the local people—among whom was a nine-year-old boy whose son, years later, would be recognized as the Fourteenth Dalai Lama. The Thirteenth left a pair of boots behind and even gazed out and commented on the beauty of a particular house in Taktser, a village nearby—the house in which his successor was to be born twenty-seven years later.

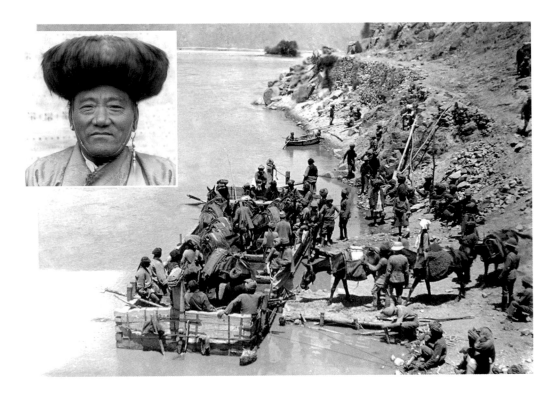

dislike for the Chinese intensified. I fear…serious trouble may yet be in store for my friend the Dalai Lama…if not for China…

With his return to Lhasa early in 1909, after an absence of almost five years, people were overjoyed. The Thirteenth set about introducing needed reforms, particularly regarding the functioning of monasteries, as discipline had severely lapsed.

"THE BUTCHER OF KHAM"

During his absence, a Manchu general, Zhao Erfeng, had been actively pursuing ways to expand Chinese influence in Tibet. In 1903, the murder of a deputy ambassador by a monk had led to retribution by Chinese forces. In 1905, Zhao Erfeng led troops under the pretext of investigating the murder and unleashed such brutal force that he earned the nickname "the Butcher of Kham." Several monasteries were sacked.

Flat-bottomed ferry boats at Chaksam on the Tsangpo river transported heavy loads.

Inset: Chensel Namgang held off the greater force of Chinese troops with just a few men, enabling the Dalai Lama to escape after the troops caught up with him near Chaksam.

In 1912, Namgang was appointed Commander in Chief of the Tibetan army. In 1913, he married into the Tsarong family, becoming Dasang Dudul Tsarong.

The residency in Yatung, home of David Macdonald, where the Thirteenth Dalai Lama stayed in 1910. Macdonald offered the Dalai Lama his own sleeping quarters, gave him chicken soup, and made it possible for him to reach India by diverting the Chinese who arrived the following day.

Following the Dalai Lama's return, the Chinese deputy ambassador issued a letter assuring no interference in religious affairs. But it said nothing about political affairs, clearly revealing Chinese intentions.

In February 1910, Chinese forces attacked local security personnel in Lhasa, killing several of them. They also fired at the Jokhang Temple and Potala Palace. The Dalai Lama saw no choice other than to flee again. He appointed a new prime minister, and later that night he left for Yatung near the state of Sikkim, on India's northeastern border, clearly placing hope in the British. The Chinese sent troops in hot pursuit, but the Dalai Lama pressed on. Reaching the British residency, he was warmly welcomed by David Macdonald, the British trade agent at Yatung.

On 21 February, the Dalai Lama crossed over into India, leaving a letter with Macdonald to be forwarded to British officials in India.

> …I now look to you for protection, and I trust that the relations between the British government and Tibet will be that of a father to his children. Wishing to be guided by you, I hope to give full information on my arrival in India.

EXILE IN INDIA

Entering Sikkim, the Dalai Lama and his entourage traveled via Jelep Pass, the very one through which Colonel Younghusband had led British troops into Tibet and forced the Dalai Lama and the Tibetan government into compromise. He proceded onward to Kalimpong, in Darjeeling district, a small town at the time, on the important trade route between India and Tibet. There he was welcomed by Raja Ugyen Dorji, an influential Bhutanese trade official and political figure. He stayed as a guest of Dorji for several days before leaving for the town of Darjeeling. It was there that he first met Charles Bell, the British officer who was destined to become his good friend and advisor for twenty-three years. Of his initial impression of the Dalai Lama, Bell wrote:

> At first sight he did not look like a king...His kingdom gone, he
> was without the trappings of royalty. No palaces, no priesthood, not
> even the proper clothes; so sudden and rapid was his flight. Yet he
> was the god-king of Tibet, the Incarnation of Chen-re-zi himself.

In a house placed at his disposal by the British Indian government, officials had "hurriedly contrived [a] throne in one of the largest rooms." The Dalai Lama and Bell conversed in Tibetan; the British official was a serious scholar of all things Tibetan. In their conversations, the Dalai Lama insisted that the British should intervene on Tibet's behalf, but Bell had been instructed to maintain neutrality.

Continuing on to Calcutta, the Dalai Lama called on the Viceroy, Lord Minto, on 14 March. He criticized Chinese excesses and also sought to allay their fears about his advisor, Dorjiev. Chinese territorial ambitions were not restricted to Tibet, he pointed out to Lord Minto. Following the Younghusband expedition, the new trade agreements between the British and the Tibetans were now under threat because of Chinese aggression.

EXPELLING AN INVADER

Meanwhile in Tibet, a resistance movement was building in response to violent Chinese incursions. Realizing that the situation would not be easy to control, the Chinese sent word requesting the Dalai Lama to return to Tibet. Rejecting their placatory overtures, he replied:

> You are fully aware of this inexcusable illegal action taken by your troops. Yet, you inform me and my ministers that the situation in Tibet is peaceful and that status quo is being maintained. I know that this has been said to persuade me to return and I also know that it is false.

During the winter of 1910, the Dalai Lama visited important Buddhist sites in India, including Lumbini, Bodh Gaya, Sarnath, and Kushinagar. Later in 1911, as meetings with Bell continued in Darjeeling, the Dalai Lama was informed that the British Government in London had decided not to intervene. Greatly upset, he petitioned the British again, but to no avail. He then secretly appealed to the Russian tzar, again through a letter delivered personally by Dorjiev. The tzar's reply was polite and noncommittal. Tellingly, it was sent to the British and not directly to the Dalai Lama.

Facing page: The Thirteenth Dalai Lama in Darjeeling, 1910. As a guest of Charles Bell, the British political agent of Sikkim, Tibet, and Nepal, all courtesies were extended to His Holiness' stay in India.

From Left: Sir Charles Bell, the Maharaj Kumar Sidkeong Tulku of Sikkim, and the Thirteenth Dalai Lama, at Hastings House, Calcutta, 1910.

Above: Medal presented to Sir Charles Bell by the Thirteenth on 19 February 1912, before returning to Lhasa.

A Friend to Tibet: Sir Charles Alfred Bell

In the early twentieth century, Sir Charles Alfred Bell was widely acknowledged as the primary Western authority on Tibet. A gifted diplomat and a friend of the Dalai Lama, he was fascinated with Tibetan culture and history. Born in Calcutta in 1870, Bell joined the Indian Civil Service in 1891. His posting to Darjeeling in 1900 brought him close to the region and led him to write a grammar and dictionary of the Tibetan language.

He first met the Dalai Lama in Sikkim in 1910 during His Holiness' exile. Involved in the Simla Convention negotiations, Bell had helped repair the damage caused by British armed aggression in Tibet in 1904–1905. The turnaround was so remarkable that the Dalai Lama offered troops to the British when World War I broke out.

After resigning from service in 1919, Bell devoted himself to Tibetan studies, but he was called back in 1920 as an advisor to the Dalai Lama for a year. It was during this visit to Tibet that he found that British-Tibetan relations had weakened. He also observed the rivalry between the Dalai Lama and the Panchen Lama, noting in particular the latter's proximity to the Chinese. A singular figure in Anglo-Tibetan relations, he paved the way for Britain's forward policy in the Himalayan region, which would have "far-reaching consequences for Tibet and India in the future." Bell recognized that historically, the Dalai Lama was Tibet's spiritual and temporal leader whose power and position were "supreme and unassailable" since they were not limited to this life: "The Ruler in this life; the Uplifter in the hereafter."

In the meantime, the Qing dynasty was deposed by the Chinese nationalist and founding figure, Sun Yat-sen. Chinese garrisons in Tibet mutinied and clashes broke out between Tibetans and Chinese troops. The Dalai Lama moved to Kalimpong and stayed at Bhutan House, built for him on the vast property of Raja Ugyen Dorji. He sent instructions to his government to set up a war department and prepare to attack the Chinese. It was November 1911.

In the following weeks, hostilities increased and continued well into the next year. But by June 1912, all remaining Chinese troops had been expelled from Tibet, and Manchu rule had ended. The Dalai Lama began preparing to leave India. The time had come for him to resume direct leadership of his country and people. But as Charles Bell noted, "They had learnt well the bitter lessons of adversity," which the following Tibetan proverb summed up: "Better than a hundred precepts is a single press on the nose."

Bidding farewell to Charles Bell, the Dalai Lama left Kalimpong in June 1912. He reached Lhasa in January 1913, returning from a second exile in a world on the brink of a great war.

Here, His Holiness, shaded by an umbrella, at the British residency in Yatung, Chumbi Valley, blesses Tibetans lining up to see him. Returning to Lhasa in 1912 after two years of exile in India, the Dalai Lama was coming home with a new resolve and farsighted dreams for Tibet, known as the Land of Snows.

Proclamation of Independence of Tibet

Issued on 13 February 1913 by the Thirteenth Dalai Lama, the Proclamation of Independence was presented to the people of Tibet, affirming the Dalai Lama's authority to rule. With an acknowledgment that Tibet and China had always lived in mutual support of each other through the former "Preceptor-Patron" relationship, it stated:

> "I have returned safely to my rightful and sacred land, and we shall drive out the remaining Chinese troops from Kham. The Chinese evil scheme to enslave Tibet under the pretext of a Preceptor-Patron relationship instantly fell apart like sand clumps, fading in a moment like a rainbow in the sky. As a golden age has been ushered in and sentient beings can now enjoy religious and material prosperity once more..."

Contemporary re-creation of the Proclamation of Independence.

DRAWING BOUNDARIES

Following years of turmoil, by 1913 it was clear to the British that an autonomous Tibet was more conducive to the region than any form of control by the Chinese. A conference was convened in Simla, India, to bring much-needed stability to the region, settle the issue of Tibet's independence, and contain Chinese expansion.

Sir Henry McMahon, the foreign secretary of British India, was the British representative. While Archibald Rose was to assist the Chinese, Charles Bell was to present the Tibetan position. China sent its representative, Ifan Chen, and Minister Paljor Dorje Shatra was the delegate of the Thirteenth Dalai Lama.

The negotiations were long-winded, lasting over six months. It was only on 27 April 1914, that an initial tripartite agreement was signed and sealed by the three parties. The Tibetans had provided documents to prove that Tibet had functioned as an independent state for centuries. The understanding between the Fifth Dalai Lama and the

British, Tibetan, and Chinese delegations at the Simla Convention. Sir Henry McMahon (seated, center), between (left) Chinese delegate Ifan Chen and (right) Tibetan Minister Paljor Dorje. Standing behind McMahon are (left) Archibald Rose and (right) Charles Bell.

Map labels:
N
TIBET
Nye Chu
LHUNTSEDZONG
Chayul Chu
Boundary proposed by the Indian General Staff in June 1912
Loro Chu
LHAKHANG DZONG
28°
28°
Final version of McMahon Line, March 1914
TSONADZONG
Nyamjang R.
B H U T A N
First draft McMahon Line, November 1913
TAWANG
Se La
SENGEDZONG
Kur R.
Dangma R.
DIRANGDZONG
Bomdi La
TALUNGDZONG
RUPA
SHERGAON
Kameng R.
27°
27°
Outer Line
AMATULLA
Old
Old Outer Line
DEWANGIRI
Dhansiri R.
ASSAM
0 16
MILES
91°
UDALGURI
A.L. 1963
93°

McMahon Line proposals regarding the Tawang region. According to many historians, the most far reaching result of the Simla Convention was the delimitation of 850 miles of boundary between India and Tibet.

Manchu emperor at the time had been purely religious, and not of a political union, as the Chinese claimed.

The Simla Convention eventually reached its conclusion in late February, when McMahon presented a formula for a two-zone division of Tibet into Inner Tibet, the regions of Amdo and Eastern Kham; and Outer Tibet, U Tsang and Western Kham. The autonomy of Outer Tibet was recognized, and it was suggested that China would refrain from interfering with it. The entire Simla Convention saga was a complex game of intrigue in which the British gained the upper hand.

In August 1914, a month after the final signing by Tibet and India only, as China refused to ratify such a document, Britain entered World War I. The world would change dramatically, and so would Tibet's fate.

MODERN EDUCATION AND REFORMS

Below: One of the most progressive Dalai Lamas, the Thirteenth recognized the need to change with changing times. After his return to Lhasa in 1913, at Charles Bell's suggestion, four Tibetan boys, between the ages of twelve and fifteen were selected to be sent to England for higher education. They would benefit from outside exposure and bring back their training to Tibet. They came to be known as "the Rugby Boys."

Left: Cars first arrived in Tibet in mid-1920 when Sir Charles Bell presented to the Thirteenth a blue-colored Baby Austin, with the licence plate TIBET 1. A second Baby Austin, with the licence plate TIBET 2, was photographed at the British Mission in 1933.

Left: One of the first telegraph poles erected in Tibet, between Gyantse and Lhasa. The first post and telegraph office was opened in Lhasa in 1920. The earlier British line from India to Gyantse was extended to Lhasa in the 1920s to serve the Tibetan capital.

Below: The new national flag of Tibet, designed by the Thirteenth Dalai Lama, was based on the seventh-century snow lion standard of Emperor Songtsen Gampo.

LAST TESTAMENT OF THE GREAT THIRTEENTH

The Proclamation of Independence by the Thirteenth ushered in a new era in Tibet. From his personal experience of twice having had to flee his country, the Thirteenth Dalai Lama learned how important it was for a country to be truly independent. He realized how the agendas of other countries are driven by their own interests. Through his travels to India, China, and Mongolia, he came to recognize the need for Tibet to change.

Over the next decade, the Dalai Lama initiated reforms. Tibet's small army was modernized, and a police department was established in Lhasa. The Tibetan postal system was launched, and a mint was built to issue Tibetan-made coins and currency. In 1923, the first school in Tibet for learning the English language was opened, in Gyantse, supervised by British officer and naturalist Frank Ludlow. As well as sending Tibetan students to England to study, he paid much attention

First parade of soldiers with the newly designed Tibetan national flag in 1916, in front of the Norbulingka summer palace in Lhasa.

to the quality of Buddhist learning in the monasteries. Western-style dress began to be adopted by some.

Convinced that Tibet should not remain isolated, he made attempts at building relationships with the British, the Russians, as well as the Chinese, despite their differences and the risks involved. The Thirteenth Dalai Lama foresaw what would happen to Tibet if it did not guard itselves against foreign invasion.

Even amid change and receptivity to new ideas, factional rivalries in the political elite began to grow as well. In 1931, the Nechung oracle informed the government that the Dalai Lama was not well and that he would "depart soon to the Honorable Field." Consequently, the Dalai Lama wrote his final political statement and testament, in 1932, during a visit to Reting Monastery. A kind of advisory, it suggested steps Tibetans should undertake in the future. Tibetans refer to it as Shel-chem, his Last Testament. It was printed and widely distributed in Tibet. Its text was ominously prophetic.

> *It may happen that here, in the centre of Tibet, religion and government will be attacked both from without and from within. Unless we can guard our own country, it will now happen that the Dalai and Panchen Lamas, the Father and the Son, and all the revered holders of the Faith, will disappear and become nameless. Monks and monasteries will be destroyed. The rule of law will be weakened. The lands and property of government officials will be seized. They themselves will be forced to serve their enemies or wander the country like beggars. Everyone will be forced to live in misery, and the days and nights will pass slowly, and with great suffering and terror.*

Therefore, now, when the strength of peace and happiness is with us, while the power to do something about the situation is still in our hands, we should make every effort to safeguard ourselves against this impending disaster. Use peaceful methods where they are appropriate; but where they are not appropriate, do not hesitate to resort to more forceful means. Work diligently now, while there is still time. Then there will be no regrets.

A year later, on 17 December 1933, the Precious Protector passed away. He was fifty-eight. With the passing of the Great Thirteenth, the idea of Tibetan independence began to gain currency around the world, and a next chapter of Tibet was ready to unfold. The mantle of Tibetan leadership, and a path of reform, would be passed forward. But history would pass forward conflicts of the past, as well.

Fortunately for the Tibetan people, the Thirteenth Dalai Lama would choose to be reincarnated in His Holiness the Fourteenth Dalai Lama, Tenzin Gyatso.

Above: Thirteenth Dalai Lama, on low throne in his audience room at the Chensel Lingka, his favorite place within the grounds of Norbulingka, the summer palace of the Dalai Lama in Lhasa.

Facing page: One of the last photos taken of the Thirteenth Dalai Lama, in September 1933, in his garden at the Chensel Lingka. He was very fond of his garden and plants, which he tended with care.

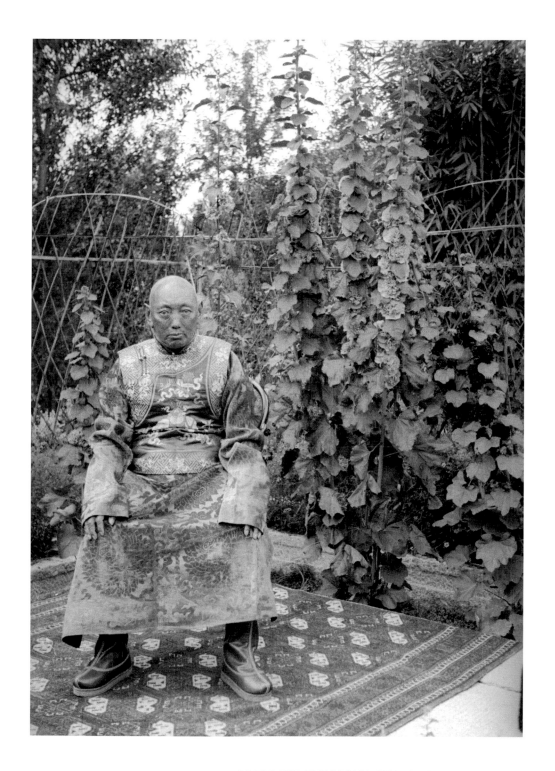

"Old friends pass away, new friends appear.
It is just like the days.
An old day passes, a new day arrives.
The important thing is to make it meaningful:
a meaningful friend—or a meaningful day."

HIS HOLINESS THE FOURTEENTH DALAI LAMA

Part 1:
The Precious Protector in the Land of Snows

THE FOURTEENTH DALAI LAMA, CHINESE INVASION,
AND THE PEOPLE'S UPRISING IN LHASA

(1934–1959)

"A favorite occupation of mine as an infant was to pack things in a bag as if I was about to go on a long journey. 'I'm going to Lhasa, I'm going to Lhasa,' I would say. This, coupled with my insistence that I be allowed always to sit at the head of the table, was later said to be an indication that I must have known that I was destined for greater things."

THE FOURTEENTH DALAI LAMA

THE DISCOVERY OF
THE FOURTEENTH DALAI LAMA

Immediately after the Great Thirteenth's death, a bitter power struggle erupted between four warring aristocrats. However, none of them were able to secure sufficient individual support from the Tibetan National Assembly. Finally, the issue of appointing a regent was resolved by divination, and the charismatic twenty-four-year-old Reting Rinpoche was selected. He was to become a significant, if not controversial, figure in Tibetan history. One of his first tasks was to investigate all the various signs to identify the successor of the Great Thirteenth.

In April 1935, according to existing tradition in seeking out the Dalai Lama's reincarnation, Reting Rinpoche and Trimon, a powerful member of the Kashag (cabinet), visited Chokhorgyal Monastery and the sacred lake of Lhamo Lhatso nearby. The monastery, founded by the second Dalai Lama, Gedun Gyatso, is about 15 kilometers from the lake. The guardian of the lake, goddess Palden Lhamo, protects Tibet, the Dalai Lama, and Panchen Lama as "The Victorious Queen who Turns Back Enemies."

W. D. Shakabpa, a twenty-three-year-old government official in the Treasury Department, was among the group at the lake. He recounts that upon arrival the party dispersed individually in complete silence. Reting Rinpoche and the officials with him were in deep meditation in the hope of a vision. Although Shakabpa did not see anything, the Regent did—three Tibetan syllables *Ah, Ka,* and *Ma,* and a village scene. He saw other signs as well: a three-storied monastery with turquoise and gold roof tiles, a winding road from the monastery to a small hill, and a modest house opposite the hill. In their interpretation of the syllables, it was concluded that *Ah* referred to the province of Amdo, and *Ka* referred to Kumbum Monastery. Prior to these visions, there had been other signs. The head of the embalmed body of the Thirteenth Dalai Lama had turned direction at the Norbulingka—from the south to the northeast (where Amdo was)—to where the incarnation would be found.

On his return to Lhasa, the Regent submitted a report. Soon after, three more search parties were put together and sent to different parts of eastern Tibet. Basil Gould was in Lhasa at the time and would later write an account of the events. Kewtsang Rinpoche of Sera Monastery was the head of the search party who eventually identified the Fourteenth Dalai Lama. He was given several objects to test candidates for the reincarnation. Nechung Oracle, the state oracle of Tibet, presented to Kewtsang Rinpoche a ritual-mirror. The other objects given to them were three personal items of the Thirteenth Dalai Lama: a rosary, a ritual ivory hand drum (*damaru*), and a cane walking stick. The team eventually reached Jyekundo, a town under Chinese occupation.

In the meantime the second highest spiritual authority in Tibetan Buddhism, the self-exiled Ninth Panchen Lama, had also arrived in Jyekundo with a Chinese military escort. While the Panchen Lama and the Thirteenth Dalai Lama had had political differences driven by Chinese interference, the deep spiritual link between them remained strong. Kewtsang Rinpoche's group met the Panchen Lama with their credentials, and he in turn gave them a list of three possible candidates.

Left: Reting Rinpoche (Jamphal Yeshe), Regent of Tibet in 1940. He would become Senior Tutor to the young Dalai Lama who remembers him as a man of "relaxed mental disposition, a man who took things easily."

Right: Lobsang Namgyal, medium for the Nechung oracle, in a trance, confirmed that Lhamo Thondup was the true reincarnation of the Thirteenth Dalai Lama.

The team set out for Kumbum Monastery. The monastery matched the vision the Regent had seen in the lake. After formalities and meetings, the group resumed their search. Traveling in disguise, the group found that the first candidate on the list had died, and the second, when shown the personal items of the Thirteenth Dalai Lama, shied away.

Months later, they arrived in Taktser Village, where the final candidate on the Panchen Lama's list lived with his family. They were welcomed warmly. The young boy was delighted to see Kewtsang Rinpoche—who was disguised as a servant—and wanted to sit on his lap. He asked for the Thirteenth's rosary which was around the lama's neck. When asked to identify him, the boy told Kewtsang Rinpoche that he was "an Aka (elder) from Sera." To the monk's amazement, the boy also identified his colleagues without hesitation. Kewtsang Rinpoche spent most of his time observing the boy who seemed very attached to the rosary.

The remaining members of the group had been looking at other possible candidates. None seemed to fit the bill. They sent a message to the government with details of all candidates and received a reply

The young Lhamo Thondup identifying past belongings of the Thirteenth Dalai Lama (top of mural). Once recognized as the Fourteenth Dalai Lama, he is escorted to Lhasa in a golden palanquin (bottom of mural). From Norbulingka Palace.

that Lhamo Thondup, the young boy in Taktser, seemed promising and that he should be shown the personal objects of the Thirteenth Dalai Lama. A few days later, they left for Taktser, encountering many auspicious signs along the way and when they arrived were welcomed with evening tea. The house and surroundings reminded them of the Regent's vision at the lake.

After seeking permission to test the boy, they placed the personal items of the Dalai Lama in front of him. When two rosaries were shown to the child, one authentic, and the other a duplicate, he immediately grabbed the authentic one and put it around his neck. Object after object, the boy picked out the items belonging to the Thirteenth. Sonam Wangdu, one of the four members of the group, recalled that when offered two *damaru*, a worn, plain one used by the late Dalai Lama and another more ornate *damaru*, the boy picked up the first one and played with it joyously. The next morning as the search party prepared to leave, the boy insisted on accompanying them, and his parents had to hold him back.

The team sent a coded message to Lhasa and waited for a response. Months later, in the autumn of 1936, they finally received instructions asking them to bring the boy to Lhasa. But the seemingly simple task of taking the boy to Lhasa was not quite that straightforward.

The Dalai Lama's parents with a sibling who died in infancy and his brother, Gyalo Thondup, at Kumbum monastery, 1939.

Facing page: One of the earliest photographs of His Holiness, at the age of four, at Kumbum Monastery, 1939. He is holding in his lap a Gospel of St. John card presented to him by a visiting missionary.

These photographs were taken by Archibald Steele (inset), an American foreign correspondent who was living in China. He traveled to Kumbum to see the four-year-old child candidate for new the incarnation of the Thirteenth Dalai Lama. He later wrote that, of all his travels and assignments, the trip to Tibet and meeting the Dalai Lama were the most exciting.

Kumbum Monastery

Kumbum Monastery near Lake Kokonor, located in the historical Tsongkha region of northeast Amdo, is the birthplace of Je Tsong Khapa, the great fourteenth-century reformer of Buddhism in Tibet and founder of the *Gelug* (virtuous) School of Buddhism to which the Dalai Lamas all belong. The monastery was founded in 1583 by the Third Dalai Lama, Sonam Gyatso (1543–1588) and has four colleges for Debate, Tantric, Medical, and Kalachakra studies, built one after the other over a few centuries. Kumbum means "one hundred thousand holy images" or "enlightening bodies" which refers to the magical number of images of the Buddha Simhananda that are said to be on the leaves of a legendary sandalwood tree planted at the spot of Tsong Khapa's birth.

Historically, Kumbum was the frequent residence of previous Dalai Lamas and Panchen Lamas. The Thirteenth Dalai Lama took refuge here for many months, during which he made a visit to a nearby hermitage from where he saw Taktser Village, home of his future incarnation. His successor spent two years sheltered in Kumbum while ransom negotiations for his safe passage to Lhasa were taking place. Kumbum is also where the Fourteenth Dalai Lama's older brother, Thubten Jigme Norbu (Taktser Rinpoche) began his training as a monk and in 1949 at the age of twenty-seven, became abbot.

The monastery, containing several precious artifacts, was one of the first to come under Chinese attack and suffered greatly.

Kumbum Monastery, in Amdo.

Inset: A painting of Je Tsong Khapa, born 1357, founder of the Gelug School of Buddhism, to which the Dalai Lamas belong.

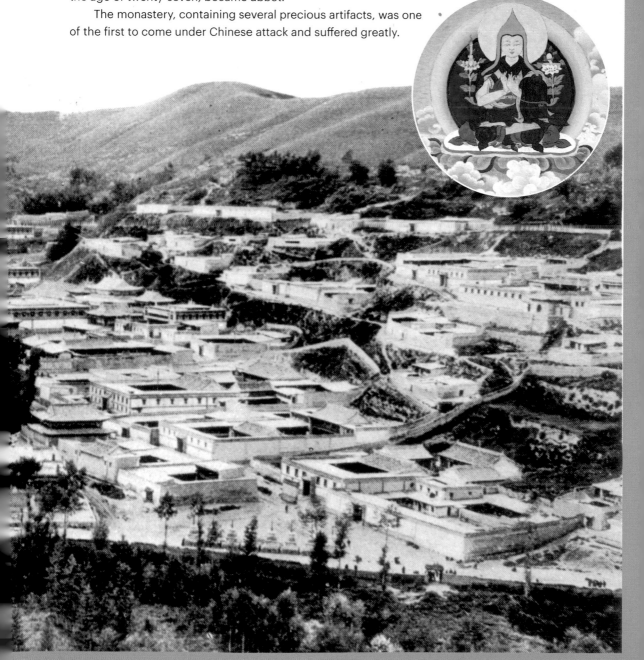

THE RANSOM

Kewtsang Rinpoche was aware of the threat that Ma Bufang, the Hui Muslim warlord, posed for the safety of the young Dalai Lama. In 1932, Ma Bufang had successfully campaigned against the Tibetan forces with the support of the Kuomintang government. He had become the Governor of Qinghai Province, which included Amdo, with his capital at Sining. Kewtsang Rinpoche tried to keep the identity of the chosen boy a secret, but Ma Bufang made his presence known immediately. At a formal examination at the regional government headquarters, he personally questioned all the candidates, including the future Dalai Lama, who was in the meantime housed at Kumbum Monastery along with his two brothers, Lobsang Samten, and the sixteen-year-old Taktser Rinpoche, already studying at the monastery.

On meeting the young Dalai Lama, Ma Bufang was certain that he was indeed the reincarnate. He demanded a ransom of 100,000 *dayangs* ($15–20,000 at the time). Unfortunately, the matter did not end there. They were asked for another 300,000 *dayangs* from the officials in Sining, who used this as an opportunity to inflate the expenses incurred by the

The newly discovered Fourteenth Dalai Lama, with Chinese officials, shortly before leaving Amdo for Lhasa, a caravan journey of three months.

轉 坐 達 賴 喇 嘛 十 四 年 岁 方 五 歲

local authorities, Kumbum Monastery, and other monasteries in the region (Kumbum Monastery also asked for some personal items of the Thirteenth Dalai Lama). The shocked search party had not anticipated this. They tried to negotiate, but the governor was adamant—unless all his demands were met the young boy could not travel. By this time, the young future Dalai Lama, nearly four years old, had spent over a year and a half at Kumbum.

At long last an opportunity presented itself. A group of wealthy local Muslims were preparing for a pilgrimage to Mecca through India, and they agreed to escort the boy and his parents to Lhasa. It was now the summer of 1939. True to his unscrupulous form, the governor demanded an additional 5,000 *dayangs* for the cost of a security escort for the young boy. Finally, having endured Ma Bufang's larceny, it was time for the young boy's departure to Lhasa.

Nearly fifty years later, during a visit to the University of California, His Holiness was introduced to a Chinese student during a tea break— she turned out to be Ma Bufang's granddaughter. His Holiness enjoyed a warm, friendly conversation with her.

The young Dalai Lama with officials, Kumbum Monastery, 1939. His brothers Taktser Rinpoche and Lobsang Samten were also at Kumbum during this time, training as monks.

THE JOURNEY TO LHASA

In July 1939, a large caravan set out for Lhasa. Sonam Wandu, one of the search party members recalls that it was "...a fine sunny day with white clouds dotting the sky and forming into various auspicious shapes, occasionally punctuated by light showers." The date and time of departure had been set by astrologers beforehand. Having been elevated to nobility, the little boy's family was allowed to travel with him, much to his relief. The party comprised his parents, uncle, and two older brothers, Gyalo Thondup and Lobsang Samten. As the caravan traveled, they were joined by Tibetan merchants and Muslim pilgrims on their way to Mecca. On occasion, the party was stopped by groups of Tibetan and Mongolian nomads seeking blessings.

The caravan often encountered rough terrain, making it difficult for all, including the animals. Tellingly, one of the places the party stopped at was called No Grass No Water. Of the journey, His Holiness recalls being captivated by herds of wild yaks and wild asses on the plains, and small deer. Often, the two young siblings, Lobsang Samten and Lhamo Thondup, would squabble and get into physical fights that threatened to topple the palanquin over and their mother would be called to set

Kumbum Monastery courtyard, as the caravan of the four-year-old Dalai Lama prepared to leave for the three-month journey to Lhasa. The large caravan included members of the Dalai Lama's family, pilgrims, government officials, members of the search party, and scouts whose knowledge of the incalculable route made them indispensable for such a challenging journey.

The party, which had now grown into a cavalcade, stopped at the historically important Reting Monastery, which was a week's journey from Lhasa. The Regent, who hailed from here, briefed the Dalai Lama's family about what to expect in Lhasa. It was here that the Dalai Lama's father and the Regent forged a friendship over their common passion, horses.

things right. Occasionally, the young boy would break out into tears.

The journey required crossing several rivers, and Sonam Wangdu writes that the Dalai Lama was most delighted by his ride in a traditional yak-skinned coracle. Often he would be carried on the shoulders of one of the men in the party across turbulent waters and difficult terrain.

The travelers were vastly relieved to reach the borders of U–Tsang province, where Lhasa was located. The party had crossed over into the Tibetan-controlled area, which allowed the government in Lhasa to formally announce that the reincarnation had been found. An elaborate blessing was conducted accordingly. Thereafter, the young Dalai Lama would stay in a yellow tent. The travelers were asked to break their journey at Nagchu, where a welcome ceremony was awaiting the new incarnation. The delighted people gathered there shouted out: "A happy sun now shines on Tibet."

A huge encampment was erected on the Doeguthang Plain, a few miles outside Lhasa, where the Dalai Lama was formally welcomed in 1939.

Inset: At the center of the encampment was the *Macha Chenmo* (The Great Peacock), exclusively used as a reception tent for a new Dalai Lama. During the course of a few days, thousands of Tibetans came to pay their respects to their new leader.

The Tibetan government had organized a "state-level reception camp" on the Doeguthang Plain, a few miles from Lhasa. At the very center of the formation was the special marquee reserved for the Dalai Lamas, known as the *Macha Chenmo*, or "Great Peacock," with a lining of "superfine yellow brocade." Surrounding this main tent were rings of smaller tents for officials. Amazed onlookers described it as, "magnificent, resembling rings of heavenly bodies twinkling in a starry night." The regent and the prime minister conducted mandala offerings, and then the young Dalai Lama met numerous officials. Representatives from India, China, Kashmir, Ladakh, Nepal, Sikkim, Bhutan, and the British Mission were present. A few days later, the entourage left for the capital city of Lhasa. Lhamo Thondup, now officially the Fourteenth Dalai Lama, entered Lhasa in an elaborate procession with a remarkable display of pageantry. He would recall "a great sense of homecoming and endless crowds of people." The city

Horsemen in ceremonial dress and conical hats, carrying banners and standards surmounted by tridents. Part of the Dalai Lama's escort on the final leg of his journey to Lhasa, 1939. His mother writes in her autobiography, "As soon as I saw the city of Lhasa from a distance, there was a lump in my throat. I had heard so much about this city and had so often dreamed of it, and I now saw my dreams coming true."

streets were lined with people seeking the young boy's blessings. From oracles in trances, dancers in animal costumes, monks, and commoners alike, the streets were filled with thronging crowds. The Dalai Lama's mother recollects, "Many people were weeping tears of joy. I was close to tears. Here I was, a peasant woman, now raised to the highest position a mother could hold." After the Nechung Oracle officially welcomed him to Lhasa, the Dalai Lama was taken to the Jokhang Temple in a palanquin, where he consecrated the central statue of Avalokiteshvara. The journey came to a conclusion when the four-year-old, along with his brother Lobsang Samten, were taken to the summer palace Norbulingka, "which stood amidst a wonderful rich environment of orchards and beautiful flower gardens."

It was 8 October 1939. The young Dalai Lama had come home.

Exuberant crowds lined the streets of Lhasa as the palanquin of the Dalai Lama approached the Jokhang Temple, Lhasa, 1939.

ENTHRONEMENT

As the year progressed, the new Dalai Lama was inducted into his role, although formal education as a monk had not yet begun for him. He saw his parents every day, as the Regent turned a blind eye to such transgressions. The young boy particularly savored the forbidden foods he was able to eat at his parents' home, such as eggs and pork. In the winter of 1939, he was taken in a state procession from Norbulingka Palace to the Jokhang for the *utra taphue* ceremony, the ritual cutting of his hair in preparation for him becoming a monk. This was performed by Reting Rinpoche, who had become his Senior Tutor. On 24 November he was formally renamed by Reting Rinpoche, as Jetsun Jampel Ngawang Lobsang Yishi Tenzin Gyatso—"The Holy One, The Tender Glory, Mighty in Speech, of Excellent Intellect, of Absolute Wisdom, Holding the Doctrine, The Ocean-wide."

As dawn broke the day before the official enthronement ceremony, people lined the streets to watch the elaborate procession in which the Dalai Lama was taken from Norbulingka to the Potala Palace. On 22 February 1940, the ceremony, known as *Ser-Thri-Nga-Sol,* "The Return to the Golden Throne," which marked the continuation of the lineage of the Dalai Lamas was held at the Potala Palace. The young Dalai Lama was placed on the Golden Throne, where he greeted and blessed all those who had come to pay their respects. The British Political Officer Basil Gould was in attendance and wrote a detailed account of the ceremony, "(he)…sat quietly and with great dignity, completely at ease in these strange surroundings giving the proper blessing to each person."

The Dalai Lama, age four, seated on the Golden Throne.

Facing page: A story on the enthronement ceremony in 9 March 1940 edition of *The Illustrated London News.*

THE NEW DALAI LAMA: A CHILD ENTHRONED IN EASTERN SPLENDOUR.

"TENDER GLORY, MIGHTY IN SPEECH, EXCELLENT INTELLECT, ABSOLUTE WISDOM, HOLDING THE DOCTRINE, OCEAN-WIDE": THE FIRST PICTURE TO REACH ENGLAND OF THE ENTHRONEMENT OF THE NEW FIVE-YEAR-OLD RULER OF TIBET.

Scenes of exceptional magnificence characterised the enthronement on February 22 in the vast Assembly Hall of the Potala, the Monastery Palace of Lhasa, of the new Dalai Lama of Tibet, a five-year-old child who was discovered last year in a remote village in China. Describing the installation, which was attended on behalf of the British Government and the Government of India by Mr. B. J. Gould, C.M.G., C.I.E., Political Officer in Sikkim and British Representative for Tibet and Bhutan since 1935, a special "Times" correspondent said that the fourteenth incarnation of the Dalai Lama wore a golden robe and a yellow hat and "briskly and confidently climbed the lower steps of the throne," from where he was lifted to his place by the Lord Chamberlain and carefully wrapped in red and golden robes. "The scene was one of magnificence and solemnity," added the correspondent. "To the right of the throne, 7 ft. high, stood the Dalai Lama's golden food table, inset with great rubies, pearls, and turquoises. To the left . . . sat the Dalai Lama's father in a robe of gold brocade, embroidered with green, and with a skirt of rainbow-striped silk. His mother was in a stiff brocade and purple robe." (Associated Press.)

Delegations from China, British India, Nepal, and other parts of Tibet came bearing gifts. The British delegation presented "a gold clock with a nightingale that pops out and sings, a pedal motor car, and a tricycle to the Dalai Lama." Following a ceremonial tea service an hour before dawn, a loud voice ordered silence, and the gathering stood up. As Basil Gould writes, "The door was opened and there entered at a brisk pace a small figure, in golden robes and pointed yellow hat with long flaps over the ears…he was then lifted by the Chikyab Khenpo to the top of the throne, and made warm and comfortable in his wrappings."

The Dalai Lama moved to the Potala, the magnificent palace and the traditional seat of authority. But in his own words the palace was "not a nice place to live in…it was ancient and decrepit, and behind the drapes that hung across each of the four walls lay deposits of century-old dust." The idyll had ended. It was time for the young boy to transition into the role for which he was destined.

Above: Black hat dancers in the eastern courtyard of the Potala Palace celebrate New Year, 1937. In 1940, the audience would have considerably swelled as the festivities were opened to the public.

Facing page: Monks of Namgyal Monastery in ceremonial costume gather in the eastern courtyard of the Potala, prior to the entrance of ritual dancers, New Year, 1937. A similar scene would have greeted visitors who attended the festivities here a few days before the Dalai Lama's enthronement in 1940.

FAMILY IN LHASA

Life for the family of the young Dalai Lama changed dramatically in Lhasa. His father attended government meetings, although he had no role, and his mother, Diki Tsering, became Gyalyum Chenmo, the Great Mother. Their first house was near the Norbulingka, where the Dalai Lama was settling in. This allowed his family to see him regularly to ease the pain of separation. At Norbulingka, the young Dalai Lama felt a connection with his predecessor for the first time. In his autobiography His Holiness writes: "She (mother) told me that we entered one room and I pointed to a box and said to open it. My teeth would be there. And they were…"

They were formally inducted into Tibetan nobility, and the family's name was changed to Yabshi Taktser. The family was given several large estates—one near Lhasa and two near the border of India. The aristocratic Phala family gifted an estate to the Dalai Lama's family, located between Shigatse and Gyantse. Each estate came with a retinue of staff. The family became quite wealthy from the income they generated. In the winter, the Dalai Lama traditionally moved to the Potala. Reting Rinpoche built a house below the palace so that the family could be close to him. As the Great Mother noted, they "were escorted in a grand procession of two hundred men and musicians" when they moved in. Much to his happiness, the Dalai Lama's older brother Lobsang Samten was allowed to live with him at the Potala Palace, sharing lessons, meals, and playing together.

The family's first home in Lhasa was near the Norbulingka Palace. The Great Mother recalled, "When we entered our rooms, we found many sacks of rice, flour, butter, and tea that had been sent as gifts. Silks, brocades, and carpets were brought in…the next day the government supplied us with staff members…"

A few years later, the Regent built them a new home, visible from the Dalai Lama's living quarters at the Potala. This was Yabshi Taktser, seen below. *Taktser* means "roaring tiger."

The Dalai Lama's mother learned to assimilate in Lhasa and deal with Tibetan nobility and high society, despite her longing for her old life which allowed "freedom and privacy." On important occasions such as the New Year, the family would entertain several officials, monks, and others. Large banquets became a part of their lives, but the Great Mother was "a novice in matters of diplomacy and had much to learn about Lhasa society." Gyalo Thondup remembers that the family would have to borrow plates and dishes, since they did not have enough for such occasions. The Dalai Lama's mother remained the simple peasant woman who continued to follow Amdo customs and festivals, alongside Lhasa ones, thus winning many hearts. It was only on ceremonial occasions that she would wear elaborate dresses, choosing instead to wear the simple chuba dress. His Holiness' father however, was affected by life in Lhasa. Quick to anger, his newly acquired status caused him to be abrasive in dealings, and on a few occasions he was reprimanded by the National Assembly for his actions.

A year later His Holiness' sister, Tsering Dolma, and her husband came to Lhasa to stay with the family. Taktser Rinpoche soon followed her, and the entire family was reunited. Gyalo Thondup was admitted to

Members of the Fourteenth Dalai Lama's family and servants outside their home near the Norbulingka Palace, 1940–1941. The Dalai Lama's parents are wearing new silk and brocade robes. The Great Mother later wrote, "My husband and Gyalo Thondup were influenced by the local fashion and had their right ears pierced for turquoise earrings." She herself returned to wearing her beloved traditional Amdo headdress, or *hari*, rather unfashionable in Lhasa, and continued to bake her traditional Amdo bread.

The Dalai Lama's parents at a children's party at the Dekyi Lingka, home of the British mission, in 1940.

Tarkhang, an elite, private but traditional school that groomed students to enter government service. Despite the Thirteenth Dalai Lama taking great initiative in promoting modern education, it was not prevalent in Tibet. One notable exception was the school Gyantse, started by Frank Ludlow of the Indian Educational Service, which only survived three years. The only option was to send students outside of the country. It was decided that the Fourteenth Dalai Lama's older brother, Gyalo Thondup, would go to China for further education.

Reting Rinpoche foresaw that good relations with China should be a part of Tibetan foreign policy, and this idea shaped Gyalo Thondup's education, as he was the only one among the brothers to not become a monk. He was groomed to assist his brother. The delegation sent by the Chinese Kuomintang government to the Dalai Lama's enthronement remained in Lhasa and opened an informal mission; reciprocally the Tibetan government set up an office in Chonqing and later in Nanjing. The strengthening of ties and the need for someone who could assist the Dalai Lama further propelled the plan to send Gyalo Thondup to China. Consequently, he began studies in Chinese under the tutelage of the Regent's interpreter, a Muslim man named Ma Baoxun. In the

A rare photograph of the Great Mother with her eldest daughter, Tsering Dolma (top right), son-in-law, Phuntsog Tashi Taklha and their children, Tenzin Ngawang, far left and Khando Tsering, far right at their family home in Lhasa. Jetsun Pema and Tendzin Choegyal can be seen on either side of her.

autumn of 1945, Gyalo Thondup moved to China for further studies. The Great Mother was not happy with the decision, which led to many family arguments, but eventually the men of the household prevailed. In 1948 Gyalo Thondup married Zhu Dan, the daughter of a Kuomintang general who was close to Chiang Kai-Shek.

Soon there were additions to the family. A girl, named Jetsun Pema, was born in July 1940. Three years later a son, Tendzin Chota, was born. However, he passed away at the age of two because of a severe bronchial infection. In 1946, the youngest sibling, Tendzin Choegyal, was born. He would be recognized as the reincarnation of Ngari Rinpoche of Chomo Lungnga some years later, even though his mother had wanted to "make him a monk scholar to serve His Holiness." The oldest sibling, Thubten Jigme Norbu (Taktser Rinpoche), was almost twenty-four years old and was preparing for an important monastic examination.

It was a happy time for the growing family and for the young His Holiness, "a whole year free from any responsibility, happily playing with my brother and seeing my parents quite regularly. It was the last temporal liberty I was ever to know."

Left: Lobsang Samten, photographed at Yabshi Taktser, was three years older than the Dalai Lama, and his immediate elder brother. The two were very close as they lived together for a few years at the Potala Palace when the Dalai Lama had first come to Lhasa. Later, Lobsang Samten was sent away to a private school.

Right: The Dalai Lama's youngest brother, Tendzin Choegyal (Ngari Rinpoche), in the arms of a servant, in front of a tent in the garden of Dekyi Lingka, 1948–1949. The man on the right is holding the little boy's brocade hat.

LIFE IN LHASA

Despite their tender age, the two brothers were put through a rigorous traditional system of Tibetan monastic studies. In his book *My Land, My People* the Dalai Lama writes, "The basic purpose of the Tibetan system is to broaden and cultivate the mind by a wide variety of knowledge." Some may question why the Dalai Lama, himself an earthly manifestation of Chenrezig, Tibet's patron deity, would have to go through a process of "learning." In *The Dalai Lama: An Extraordinary Life*, Alexander Norman writes, "It is true, that from the perspective of Buddhist tradition, learning for the Dalai Lama…is to a large extent a question of relearning…His earthly manifestations are not subject to the usual constraints of embodied existence."

The Dalai Lama remembers two horsewhips that hung in the room—a yellow one for himself and a leather one for his brother. Unfortunately, Lobsang Samten was at the receiving end of the leather whip, mostly to instill fear in both students.

But His Holiness took a great liking to both his main teachers, Reting Rinpoche and Taktra Rinpoche. He grew especially fond of a third tutor appointed to instruct him, none other than Kewtsang Rinpoche, the head of the search party who had identified his incarnation in Taktser. It appears though that the Dalai Lama took advantage of this affection, for he would often insist on his tutor reciting the lesson himself.

During this time, the young boy also came in contact with someone who was to become his closest confidante and most extraordinary mentor—Ling Rinpoche, the assistant tutor, about whom the Dalai Lama was to later write a very heartfelt biography. Ling Rinpoche was a very special and revered person for His Holiness for a number of reasons. The vows of a monk, a fully ordained Gelong (Bhiksu), are held in great regard by His Holiness. He received his full Bhiksu ordination from Ling Rinpoche. On many occasions during teachings I have heard His Holiness say how strongly he feels about being a Gelong, so much so that often in his dreams he sees himself as a "simple monk" rather than

Facing page: The Fourteenth Dalai Lama, age seven, photographed by Ilya Tolstoy, grandson of Leo Tolstoy, and American explorer Brooke Dolan, at the Potala Palace, December 1942. Tolstoy and Dolan visited bearing gifts from US President Franklin Delano Roosevelt.

the Dalai Lama. My friend, Thubten Tsering Lingtsang, who had served Ling Rinpoche for many years, told me that it was Ling Rinpoche who persuaded His Holiness to return to Lhasa from Yatung in 1950 in spite of strong opposition from Gyalo Thondup and Shakabpa. According to Thubten Tsering, Ling Rinpoche told His Holiness to blame it on the old monk! His Holiness received many important tantric initiations and teachings from Ling Rinpoche, including the Kalachakra initiation in 1952. Finally, Thubten Tsering told me how His Holiness cut short a visit to Europe to be at Ling Rinpoche's bedside when he had taken

ill suddenly. As His Holiness entered the room he performed the full-body-stretched prostration—that is how deeply His Holiness revered Ling Rinpoche.

A retinue of personal attendants took care of the young ruler—the *Chöpon Khenpo* was Master of the Ritual, the *Sölpon Khenpo* was the Master of the Kitchen, and the *Simpon Khenpo* was the Master of the Robes. His Holiness became very attached to the Master of the Kitchen whom he called "Ponpo," and describes the attachment in an endearing fashion, likening it to the bond between a kitten or a small pet with the master who feeds it. His Holiness adds, "I sometimes think that the act of bringing food is one of the basic roots of all relationships."

The brothers' classes alternated between periods of stay at the Potala and Norbulingka Palaces. The boys were not allowed friends of their

The two young brothers: His Holiness (left) with Lobsang Samten, and staff at the Potala Palace. Standing behind the Dalai Lama is his favorite, "Ponpo."

Facing page, above: Ling Rinpoche, senior tutor, and below: Trijang Rinpoche, junior tutor of the Fourteenth Dalai Lama.

own age, but within the palace complexes, the staff members became their friends. Much like other boys, the days were often filled with an aversion to learning lessons and squabbles between the siblings. His Holiness occupied the bedroom of the Great Fifth on the seventh story of the Potala. It was not only a palace but also contained several government offices, storerooms, and chapels—including the one that contained all the embalmed bodies of the previous Dalai Lamas, and housed the Namgyal Monastery, which had numerous monks and students. He remembers his personal chamber being very cold and poorly lit. The daily routine was more or less the same at both Potala and Norbulingka. Following morning prayers the Dalai Lama would have a typically Tibetan breakfast of tea and *tsampa*, ground roasted barley, which was sweetened with honey or caramel. His Holiness has vivid memories of these early days in Lhasa. His childlike humor is very much intact in the way he recalls the Master of the Ritual nodding off while reciting morning prayers in the classroom. This gave His Holiness the opportunity to observe the curious birds perched in the trees outside. He describes the comic way in which the Master of the Ritual's voice would sound like a gramophone record slowing down as he fell asleep—only to wake up with a start. Having lost his train of thought, the old man would get confused and often repeat himself.

Two years later, Lobsang Samten was sent to a private school which saddened his younger brother deeply. "I remember standing at the window watching, my heart full of sorrow, as he disappeared into the distance." It was far from fun and games for the young boy, who was required to sit for meetings with members of the Tibetan government after his morning

lessons. This was to groom him for his eventual assumption as the temporal leader of the nation. The Lord Chamberlain helped him with his official ceremonies and duties, which were conducted in a formal manner. Following further studies, the Dalai Lama would eagerly await the best part of the day—playtime. He fondly remembers his many toys, including the gifts from the many visitors and foreign officials who had attended his enthronement. A favorite was a Meccano set gifted to him by Basil Gould. Over time, much to his delight, he acquired more until he had all of the Meccano sets. He also recalls the gifts he received from the US President, Franklin Roosevelt—which he valued greatly—a pair of singing birds and a gold watch.

His Holiness vividly recalls disliking the later half of the day, when the sun began to descend and his quarters darkened. He hated the moment when the light in his room rapidly darkened "as the room sank back into shade, a shadow fell across my heart." His Holiness remarks that he

Left: The Dalai Lama, aged 9, at the lakeside pavilion within Norbulingka Palace, an area of parkland with animals, birds and exquisite plants, 1944. He often sat and studied here.

Right: The Lukhang (Serpent Temple) on lake, 1921. The pavilion is in the foreground with the Lukhang temple roof visible behind, to the right.

was a reluctant student and disliked studies. His curriculum was similar to that taught to other monks—logic, Tibetan art and culture, Sanskrit, medicine, and Buddhist philosophy. A very important element of Tibetan monastic education is dialectics. Debate sessions were often viewed by the public who saw them as a source of blessing.

Life as a young monk in training, and as the Dalai Lama, was quite regimented. Yet His Holiness' disposition seemed one of great curiosity. It is this trait that comes to the fore in his memories of early days at the Potala and Norbulingka. Much like any other young boy of his age, His Holiness often would ignore his studies and prayers, and instead would lose himself to stray thought—conjuring up stories and eagerly waiting for his bedtime ones. But as he confesses, several of the stories would be "of a supernatural nature" which would cause him fright when he eventually retired for the night. The young Dalai Lama, having ascended the throne at the tender age of four, seemed in ways like other young children. But as those who witnessed his discovery and enthronement were aware, he was no ordinary child. He was their Dalai Lama, the bodhisattva of compassion, who kept returning to serve the Tibetan people.

The bronze lion in the foreground was a gift from one of the emperors of China. Photo by Archibald Steele.

While visiting Sweden in 2011, decades after fleeing Lhasa, His Holiness points to a familiar room in the Potala Palace depicted on a tapestry.

"In here was a meeting hall which I peaked into as young boy."

Inset: View from the upper thirteenth floor of the Potala Palace, where the Fourteenth Dalai Lama had his quarters. Left, the Kyichu River and Valley. Top right, the roof of the Thirteenth Dalai Lama's tomb. This photo was taken in November 1936, a year after the Fourteenth Dalai Lama was born.

A Gift from President Franklin Delano Roosevelt

THE WHITE HOUSE
WASHINGTON

July 3, 1942

Your Holiness:

Two of my fellow countrymen, Ilia Tolstoy and Brooke Dolan, hope to visit your Pontificate and the historic and widely famed city of Lhasa. There are in the United States of America many persons, among them myself, who, long and greatly interested in your land and people, would highly value such an opportunity.

As you know, the people of the United States, in association with those of twenty-seven other countries, are now engaged in a war which has been thrust upon the world by nations bent on conquest who are intent upon destroying freedom of thought, of religion, and of action everywhere. The United Nations are fighting today in defense of and for preservation of freedom, confident that we shall be victorious because our cause is just, our capacity is adequate, and our determination is unshakable.

I am asking Ilia Tolstoy and Brooke Dolan to convey to you a little gift in token of my friendly sentiment toward you.

With cordial greetings, I am

Very sincerely yours,

Franklin D. Roosevelt

His Holiness
The Dalai Lama,
Supreme Pontiff of the Lama Church,
Lhasa.

In late 1942, two agents of the OSS, America's wartime intelligence agency, traveled to Tibet on a special mission "to survey a possible supply route from India to China via Tibet to replace the Burma Road that had two months earlier fallen to the Japanese." But their secret mission was to evaluate Tibet in strategic terms for US purposes. The two men were the accomplished naturalist Brooke Dolan, who had led two important expeditions to China, and Ilya Tolstoy, the grandson of the renowned Russian literary figure. On 20 December, they presented a letter and a Patek Phillipe gold chronograph watch to the seven-year-old Dalai Lama on behalf of President Franklin D. Roosevelt. It was the first official visit of US representatives to Tibet. The Tibetans received the two visitors warmly and gave them a letter stating it was "the first time that friendly relations were established." Prior to the meeting, Princess Kukula of Sikkim came to the rescue of the two Americans who needed appropriate wrapping for the gift box. She offered the red ribbon in her hair.

Having fixed it several times himself, the Dalai Lama eventually had to send the watch to Switzerland for repair in 1959, where it remained safe. With his characteristic humor His Holiness once remarked, "It seems that this watch has made the prayer that it will never be in the hands of the Chinese!" It has steadfastly kept him company, including during his visit to the US in 2007 to receive the Congressional Gold Medal from President George W. Bush. His Holiness has had a lifelong love affair with watches and has been generous in gifting them to others as well. I am the proud recipient of at least two watches which he gifted me during my time at the Private Office.

UNITED STATES GOVERNMENT
COORDINATOR OF INFORMATION
WASHINGTON, D.C.

June 9th, 1942

MEMORANDUM TO LT. COL. GOODFELLOW

FROM - COLONEL WILLIAM J. DONOVAN

This will authorize you to purchase a watch which
will cost in the neighborhood of $2,800.00 to be
given to the Dalai Lama by the President.

"…I have always enjoyed repairing watches. But I can remember a number of occasions as a boy when, completely losing my patience with those tiny, intricate parts, I picked up the mechanism and smashed it down on the table. Of course, later I felt very sorry and ashamed of my behavior—especially when, as on one occasion, I had to return the watch to its owner in a condition worse than it was before!"

DALAI LAMA

The seven-year-old Dalai Lama was too enthralled by the pocket watch when he received it, and he paid little attention to the letter that accompanied it from Roosevelt. The letter was misplaced, until 2010 when President Barack Obama gave him a copy during their closed door meeting in Washington.

TWO TRAGIC DEATHS

While the Dalai Lama's spiritual education continued, political intrigue plagued his inner court. In February 1941, Reting Rinpoche resigned as Regent and planned to go on a pilgrimage to India. He had faced opposition regarding an official allotment of estates for himself, and there were rumors of him breaking his vow of celibacy. He felt that temporarily resigning might help assuage the antagonism. The Dalai Lama's senior tutor, Taktra Rinpoche, replaced him. As an older man, he seemed a lesser threat than an ambitious youngster, however he was stricter out of the two. It was on Taktra Rinpoche's authority that Lobsang Samten was sent away to private school, and with him in control he limited the Great Mother's visits to her son as he felt she may be "misinforming" him.

The Dalai Lama's family was close to Reting Rinpoche. His older brother Gyalo Thondup recalls that they tried to persuade the Regent to reconsider but he retired to his estates away from the politics of Lhasa. However in December 1944, under the influence of friends and monastic staff, he returned to Lhasa hoping to regain his position. To his shock, Takta Rinpoche refused to vacate the office for him. At the time, Gyalo Thondup was preparing to leave for China. He claimed that Reting Rinpoche gave him a missive for President Chiang Kai-Shek, to persuade Taktra Rinpoche. Gyalo Thondup says he never delivered it.

During this time, the Dalai Lama's father, Gyalyab Chenmo, took ill, and after struggling for forty-four days, passed away in 1947 when the youngest child (Ngari Rinpoche) was only a year old. The circumstances surrounding his death became a controversy. It is

Gyalyab Chenmo, father of the Dalai Lama, at home in Lhasa, 1944.
About him, the Great Mother writes in her autobiography, "My husband was an upright and honest man, straightforward, but powerful and domineering, with a hot temper. He was fond of gambling and having a good time, and he loved riding swift horses."

widely believed that he was poisoned, though his death was officially ruled as death by natural causes. He was an open supporter of Reting Rinpoche, and many aristocrats, including supporters of Taktra Rinpoche, believed that His Holiness' father's actions were unbecoming of his position. At the time of his death, Gyalyab Chenmo was only forty-eight years old.

Reting Rinpoche's attempt to return to office ended in grave tragedy. In February 1947, Taktra Rinpoche canceled plans to participate in the Monlam butter sculpture festival after learning of a threat to his life. A few weeks later, Ngawang Namgyal, the Dalai Lama's Chief of Staff (Chikyab Khenpo), received a package with a hand grenade inside which exploded. He was close to the Regent. Having received information that Reting Rinpoche had approached Chiang Kai-Shek, the Tibetan Government placed the former Regent under house arrest in Lhasa on 18 April 1947. He died in custody shortly after. The monks of Reting Rinpoche's monastery, Sera, took to arms, and troops were sent to quell the disturbances. His Holiness remembers hearing gunshots during a debate. Government troops had clashed with the Sera monks, and some had been killed.

Following his death, Reting Rinpoche's home was razed to the ground, parts of the Reting monastery were destroyed, and his estates confiscated.

His Holiness expresses a sense of regret about this episode. He was very fond of his first guru and often wondered if he could have intervened directly. The first two names originally given to the Dalai Lama by Reting Rinpoche in 1939 were dropped but years later, His Holiness restored them on the advice of the Nechung oracle. This was twelve-year-old Dalai Lama's first taste of the complex and often ugly side of politics.

Born to a humble family, the charismatic Reting Rinpoche became Regent at a very young age.

He forged a friendship with the Dalai Lama's father over a common love of horses. The Dalai Lama's mother writes in her memoirs, "The arrest and assassination of Reting would not have been so simple if my husband had been alive, since he had more resources at his disposal than I had and would at least have prevented the arrest and imprisonment from occurring so smoothly. "

AN UNUSUAL FRIENDSHIP

Lhasa, often known as the "Forbidden City," was difficult to reach and closed off to foreigners. Tibetans valued their isolation and did not welcome outside influence on their way of life. There were few foreigners in Lhasa in 1946, which is why when in mid-January two raggedy Europeans—Heinrich Harrer and Peter Aufschnaiter—arrived, they were an enigma. People flocked to see the foreigners, and I heard that they first stayed in the Tethong house of my ancestors.

The two had fled a British prisoner-of-war camp in Dehradun, India, and had spent two punishing years trekking across the Himalayas by foot to reach Lhasa. Eight days after their arrival, they received an invitation to meet the Dalai Lama's family, but it wasn't until three years later that Harrer met the Dalai Lama himself. In the meantime, to prove their usefulness and be allowed to remain in Lhasa, they set to work. Aufschnaiter began work on an irrigation canal and on the city's first sewage system; while Harrer, who could speak English, worked as a translator, photographer, and on a fountain in the garden at Tsarong House, where they eventually took up residence. In 1949, the two were invited to a reception at the Potala Palace and were blessed by the Dalai Lama. This greatly enhanced their stature. They also found

Heinrich Harrer,
a champion skier,
frequently skated on
the frozen Kyichu River,
below the Potala Palace
and popularized the art
of ice skating—"walking
on knives"—in Lhasa.
He organized skating
parties, which included
His Holiness' brother
Lobsang Samten, after
finding several pairs of
ice skates left in the city
by British diplomats.
The young Dalai Lama,
who could not see the
rink from the Potala
Palace as his view was
obstructed by Chagpori
Hill, requested a cine-
film of the skaters and
later asked Harrer to
also build him a cinema.

Facing page: Heinrich
Harrer with Jigme
Taring, who later
became principal of
the Tibetan school in
Mussoorie, India, and
Minister for Education.

permanent employment working for the Tibetan government. Soon after, the Dalai Lama's brother, Lobsang Samten, asked Harrer if he could teach his brother about Western matters.

The Dalai Lama had inherited a film projector from his predecessor, and received a projector and generator from the British mission in Lhasa. However, none of these functioned properly. Harrer was called in by Lobsang Samten to help fix them and to build a cinema at the Norbulingka Palace. All resources were placed at his disposal, and he worked with great inventiveness to fashion a screening room with a generator shed using the motor of a jeep as a backup. Its completion coincided with His Holiness' return to the Norbulingka summer palace. Harrer was delighted to film the procession for the first time in color.

Harrer was later summoned to the cinema to meet the teenage Dalai Lama, who was very pleased and began asking Harrer many questions. As Harrer fumbled in handling the projector, His Holiness pushed him aside and skillfully loaded the reels of a documentary on Japan's defeat in World War II, much to Harrer's astonishment. Harrer then showed his own film of the Tibetan New Year Festival. The Dalai Lama himself had made films of the landscape of Lhasa, a distant caravan, and of his favorite cook, Ponpo. After the screenings, the two were left alone packing away the machines when the Dalai Lama told Harrer that he wished to learn more beyond his religious instruction. Five hours later, Harrer left in a daze, thinking it all to be a dream: "Which of my friends would have

Below: Heinrich Harrer converses on a roof at Drepung Monastery with the son of a Tibetan official.

Harrer became the young Dalai Lama's mentor on affairs beyond Tibet, and his friend. The seven years that Harrer spent in Tibet had a profound effect on him.

In 2006, when Harrer passed away, the Dalai Lama said in a condolence message, "When I first met him in 1949, he was from a world I was not familiar with. I learned many things, particularly about Europe, from him."

believed me if I had told him that I had just spent several hours alone in conversation with the Dalai Lama?" Thereafter, Harrer set out to make study materials. But to his amazement, he found that the Dalai Lama had already taught himself the alphabet, and wished to learn mathematics and geography. The Dalai Lama found his friend who he called *Gopse*, meaning "Yellow Head," to be "delightful" with a "wonderful sense of humor" and was amused with his colloquial Tibetan. In turn, Harrer found his young friend to be curious, highly intelligent, and serious minded. They met regularly over the next year and a half but dark political clouds were gathering momentum. As Harrer says, "The tone of the Peiping (Peking) radio became more and more arrogant."

The Dalai Lama greatly valued his friendship with Harrer. They remained in touch until Harrer's passing in 2006. In later years, the Dalai Lama visited him several times in Austria. In 1960, Harrer helped His Holiness' eldest brother Thubten Jigme Norbu write his autobiography. His fondness for Tibet and for its people was deep, and he often expressed feeling homesick for Tibet. Heinrich Harrer's story became known worldwide following the release of his book, and subsequently the film, *Seven Years in Tibet*. In the early years of exile, he helped set up schools for Tibetan children in India, in collaboration with SOS Kinderdorf International.

THE TRADE DELEGATIONS OF 1947

S weeping political changes across the world after World War II saw the establishment of a new world order. The Communists in China were gaining strength, and President Chiang Kai-Shek's Kuomintang government appeared to be on a poor footing, which left the Tibetan establishment insecure. While the Dalai Lama was still not actively involved in politics, his government decided in late October 1947 to send a trade delegation to India, UK, US, and China. This trade mission was to be a watershed moment in Tibetan history, as it was the first time that its government had chosen to abandon its isolationist policy and send a mission overseas. Shifting geopolitical relations and increased Chinese aggression necessitated this. The finance minister W. D. Shakabpa led the delegations, which included his younger brother Changkhyim, together with Ministers Surkhang and Pangdatshang.

Tibetan delegation photographed on the occasion of presentation to George R. Merrell, American Commissioner, New Delhi, of letters and gifts to the President.

The objectives of the mission were threefold: trade negotiations with India for wool exports' payments in dollars or pounds instead of rupees; the purchase of gold bullion to bolster the Tibetan currency; and finally, to communicate Tibet's political status to the outside world beyond China's claim. The delegation traveled mainly on Tibetan passports—the first ever issued for foreign travel. In Delhi they met Lord Mountbatten, Nehru, the newly elected first Prime Minister of India, and Mahatma Gandhi at Birla House. The delegation was "deeply moved" by the counsel from Gandhi, and shocked to receive the news of his assassination on their arrival in Nanking on 31 January 1948. In Peking the delegation met President Chiang Kai-Shek. Tensions plagued the trip as the Chinese establishment did not want to recognize the delegation as official representatives of Tibet. The former Chinese liaison officer of Lhasa tried to dissuade the delegation from visiting the UK and the US. On their insistence, he suggested that they travel on Chinese

The Tibetan Trade Delegation with British Prime Minister Clement Attlee at 10 Downing Street, London, in 1947.

passports instead, but they evaded the issue by assuring the Chinese that they would be returning to India.

In the US, the delegation met the Secretary of State, George Marshall, and General Eisenhower. However, their efforts to assert Tibet's independent status were not entirely successful. Similarly, much to the Tibetan delegation's dismay and despite their historical relations, Britain did not view the purpose of the delegation favorably, as they wished to keep cordial relations with China. The Chinese Embassy in India had weighed in, asking the British not to issue visas to the delegation. As a compromise, the British decided to issue special circumstances visas to the delegation. After weeks of diplomatic negotiations, the delegation arrived in Britain on 20 November 1948 and met with King George VI, Prime Minister Clement Attlee, Foreign Minister Ernest Bevin, and the British Board of Trade. When Shakabpa was asked by an official if the mission to Britain was a success, he replied, "The Mission has advertised to people who did not know previously the fact that Tibet is an independent country."

The Tibetan Trade Mission at Bagdogra Airport, on their way to Nanking, 1948.

THE CHINESE INVASION OF 1949–1950

The Tibetan government's concern about the political developments in China was vindicated by mid-1949; the Communist Party under Chairman Mao Tse-Tung had taken control of most of the country. On 1 October 1949, the Chinese communists announced the inauguration of the People's Republic of China (PRC), and on 1 January 1950, Radio Peking announced that the People's Liberation Army (PLA) would liberate Tibet from foreign imperialism. A shocked Tibetan government stated that Tibet did not need liberating.

W. D. Shakabpa was sent on a mission to negotiate with the new Chinese government. He met the Chinese Ambassador, Yuan Chung-Hsien, in Delhi, but there was a stalemate. As he awaited communication from Lhasa, Chinese forces attacked the western Kham region of eastern Tibet.

Soldiers of China's People's Liberation Army march into Tibet, 1950.

China already held control in eastern Kham and Amdo provinces. In January 1950, the Chinese Communists had asked the Khampas, the native people of Kham, to ally with them, but they refused to do so. However, weak Central Tibetan authority in these regions made the march of PLA troops easier. In June 1950, hostilities broke out between the Tibetans and the PLA at Dengke, where the Chinese destroyed an important radio station. This was the beginning of the events that would lead to China's annexation of Tibet.

On 7 October, Chinese troops crossed the Drichu River and soon after captured the strategic town of Chamdo, capital of Kham. They commanded that the Tibetan troops surrender. Radio Peking described this as a "peaceful liberation." The Chinese ceased hostilities, lectured the captured Tibetans on socialism, and freed them. Their objective had been met. The Tibetan governor, Ngabo Ngawang Jigme, was sent to Lhasa to instruct his government to negotiate. The fear was that Lhasa would be attacked next. On 25 October, China announced that their troops were advancing toward Tibet to free three million Tibetans from the imperialist oppression.

For Tibetans though, as Shakabpa recalled, the claim of "liberation" was "a deadly mockery."

This picture captures a show of force by Chinese troops in front of the Potala Palace.

THE DARK PLOT

Following the capture of Chamdo, the Dalai Lama's eldest brother, Thubten Jigme Norbu (Taktser Rinpoche), arrived in Lhasa with a disturbing message. He had recently been appointed the abbot of Kumbum Monastery and experienced firsthand the various ways in which the Chinese were heavily suppressing Tibetan culture and the practice of Buddhism. He had been under house arrest by the Chinese and only released on the condition that he convince his brother to support them. The continued harassment by the Chinese led Norbu to relenquish his post as abbot. In the summer of 1950, he left Kumbum for Lhasa, having tricked the local Chinese officials into thinking that he was willing to do their bidding. On his arrival in Lhasa, Taktser Rinpoche visited the Dalai Lama and revealed China's dark plot at once. "Should the Dalai Lama resist the march of progress, they indicated, ways and means would have to be found to get rid of him. At this point they even let me see quite clearly that if necessary they would regard fratricide as justifiable in the circumstances if there remained no other way of advancing the cause of communism."

Now fifteen, the Dalai Lama recalls seeing his brother, "As soon as I set eyes on him, I knew that he had suffered greatly. He was in a terrible state, extremely tense and anxious."

Taktser Rinpoche advised his brother to flee into exile immediately.

Having escaped the clutches of the Chinese in Amdo, the Dalai Lama's eldest brother, Taktser Rinpoche, (third from right) was able to travel to Yatung with his family in December 1950. Here, with junior tutor Trijang Rinpoche (second from right) and senior tutor, Ling Rinpoche (barely visible in the doorway, far right), he waits to greet his brother at Dungkhar Monastery. My friend T. T. Lingtsang is seen standing beside Taktser Rinpoche.

INVESTITURE

Amid the Chinese aggression and growing unrest, people began calling for the Dalai Lama to be given full temporal power three years earlier than the usual age of eighteen. His Holiness recalls, "A month ago I had been a carefree young man eagerly looking forward to the annual opera festival. Now I was faced with the immediate prospect of leading my country as it prepared for war." After consultations with the state oracles, the Regent resigned his post, and it was decided that His Holiness would take over his due role, ahead of time. The date set was 17 November 1950.

On the day, His Holiness recalls rising a few hours before his normal schedule, and tying an auspicious green cloth around his waist. He wrote: "…in response to the wishes and hopes of the Tibetan people… in the great reception hall called the Glories of Samsara and Nirvana, in the Potala Palace, I assumed the responsibilities of the spiritual and temporal leadership of Tibet." The fifteen-year-old Dalai Lama was ceremoniously

Lobsang Jigme, the Nechung oracle, was consulted about the Dalai Lama's investiture, along with the Gadong oracle. The consensus was that the Dalai Lama be installed at once.

Facing page: The fifteen-year-old Dalai Lama at the Norbulingka, early November 1950. Later that month he was given full temporal power. From now on he would be consulted in all matters related to the state.

handed the Golden Dharma Wheel which symbolized his assumption of power. At the end of the ceremony, His Holiness recalls, he found himself the "undisputed leader of six million people facing the threat of a full-scale war."

His first decision was to appoint two prime ministers—a layman and a monk—to maintain the traditional balance between the people and the monastics. Lobsang Tashi was the monk candidate, and Lukhangwa was His Holiness' choice of a layman.

In commemoration of his accession, His Holiness granted a general amnesty to prisoners at Shöl Prison, which was located below his rooms at the Potala Palace. He had over the years observed many of them from the window of his living quarters and considered them friends.

More than gaining temporal authority, it was an occasion for the Dalai Lama to reaffirm his bodhisattva vow to serve all sentient beings until enlightenment. These verses by Nagarjuna, who the Dalai Lama has followed most closely among the masters of the ancient Nalanda tradition, encapsulates this motivation.

With a wish to free all beings
I shall always go for refuge
to the Buddha, Dharma and Sangha
until I reach full enlightenment.

Enthused by wisdom and compassion,
today in the Buddha's presence
I generate the Mind for Full Awakening
for the benefit of all sentient beings.

As long as space endures,
as long as sentient beings remain,
until then, may I too remain
and dispel the miseries of the world.

Facing page: An elaborate mural at the Norbulingka by court painter Amdo Jampa Tseten, of the investiture in 1950, showing the Dalai Lama, his family, tutors, foreign delegations, and other dignitaries.

JOURNEY TO YATUNG AND
THE SEVENTEEN-POINT AGREEEMENT

The Chinese presence in Eastern Tibet began to grow menacing. Thubten Jigme Norbu was very insistent with his younger brother, beseeching him to leave Lhasa; under no circumstances did anyone want His Holiness to be captured by the Chinese. On 19 December 1950, the Dalai Lama, newly appointed as the temporal leader of an embattled nation, departed for Yatung (Dromo) in southern Tibet. Given the grave situation, His Holiness decided to send delegations to the US, Great Britain, and Nepal to plead for immediate support. There was no choice but to also send a team to China for negotiations.

The Dalai Lama's departure for Yatung (a day's journey away from Sikkim on the Indian border) was planned in secrecy to avoid panic among the people. Advance groups left with valuables, and the Dalai Lama's Lord Chamberlain asked him to travel in disguise at night, wearing commoners' clothes.

At a remote village named Jang, the Dalai Lama's traveling party of almost 200 people came across a number of monks who had gathered

At 2 am on 19 December 1950, the 15-year-old Dalai Lama slipped out of his palace and, along with several hundred select guards, attendants, and a few members of his family, left for Yatung. Because he developed saddlesores, he had to be carried for a part of the journey in a heavy sedan chair (inset) by alternating guards. En route, many came out to bow before him.

for their winter debate camp. The monks were overcome with emotion when they realized that the Dalai Lama had left Lhasa and was traveling south. They pleaded with Ling Rinpoche to ask him to return to Lhasa. His Holiness was deeply moved by the experience. The entire journey, although physically challenging due to the harsh winter, provided him the rare opportunity to interact with his people freely, and allowed them to share their difficulties with him.

After traveling for two weeks, the Dalai Lama reached Yatung and a few weeks later, settled at Dungkhar Monastery, where he was able to form a routine and begin his prayers, meditation, and studies once again.

Early the following year, there was news from the delegations. Much to their disappointment, Britain did not grant them a visa; the US, while sympathetic, did not want to offer open support; and Nepal was not receptive either. Britain, the US, and the United Nations looked to India to lead on the Tibet matter, and when New Delhi showed reluctance to make

His Holiness wrote, "I remember feeling great sorrow when I realized what this really meant—Tibet must expect to face the entire might of Communist China alone."

any move to jeopardize their relationship with China, the international community followed suit. India was wary of granting sanctuary to the Dalai Lama and advised him to stay in Tibet. The Tibetans had to accept the idea of negotiating with China through its ambassador in Delhi.

In 1950, the Indian leader Acharya Kripalani said in parliament, "It is on the Roof of the World that our friendship with China will flourish or flounder." On 7 November 1950, Sardar Vallabhbhai Patel, India's Home Minister, wrote to Prime Minister Nehru:

> The Chinese government has tried to delude us by professions of peaceful intentions…The tragedy of it is that the Tibetans put faith in us; they chose to be guided by us; and we have been unable to get them out of the meshes of Chinese diplomacy or Chinese influence.

Patel's health was deteriorating fast, and he died on 15 December 1950. His words proved prophetic.

Above left: The Great Mother, during the journey to Yatung.

Right: The Dalai Lama's brother-in-law, Phuntsog Tashi Taklha (looking into the camera) in Yatung.

The Dalai Lama's sisters Tsering Dolma and Jetsun Pema were in India at the time but joined the family in Yatung in time for Losar (Tibetan New Year).

After meeting the Chinese ambassador in Delhi, the Tibetan delegation was invited to talks in Peking. Spring set in with its full glory, even as the troubles for the Tibetans grew. His Holiness says he asked his tutor Ling Rinpoche for some time off, and was pleasantly surprised by the older monk's consent to grant him a holiday. His Holiness took to listening to Radio Peking's Tibetan broadcasts. One day, much to his shock, "a harsh crackling voice announced that a Seventeen-Point 'Agreement' for the Peaceful Liberation of Tibet had that day been signed by representatives for the government of the People's Republic of China and what they called the 'Local Government' of Tibet." He said he felt "physically ill as (he) listened to this unbelievable mixture of lies…"

The Chinese were completely in command. The Tibetan negotiators had been forced into a corner. As Gyalo Thondup recalled, the Chinese put Ngabo Ngawang Jigme, and the other negotiators in an impossible situation. His instructions were to reject the claim that Tibet was a part

The Dalai Lama stayed at Dungkhar Monastery while in Yatung, 1951. Here he is seen holding a golden urn containing sacred relics of Gautama Buddha, which the Maha Bodhi Society of Sri Lanka had brought for him to bless.

of China and to insist on Tibet's independence and the removal of Chinese troops from Tibet. But his efforts were to no avail. The so-called agreement had been prepared on the instructions of Mao Tse-tung himself. At first, Ngabo refused to sign, but threat of military action against Lhasa forced his hand. The Chinese even had duplicate Tibetan official seals made locally when Ngabo tried to stall them. The Dalai Lama had purposely kept the seals with him in Dromo to ensure that no one could sign without his consent. The delegation had no option but to sign the document. So on 23 May 1951 the so-called "Agreement on Measures for the Peaceful Liberation of Tibet," commonly known as the Seventeen-Point Agreement, was executed under duress.

Heinrich Harrer wrote about his experiences in Tibet and with the Dalai Lama and his family, including the journey to Yatung, in his book, *Seven Years in Tibet*. This was published in 1952 and translated into fifty-three languages.

As His Holiness observed, the clauses of the so-called agreement were "chilling." The first clause stated that the Tibetan people would return to the motherland. The second said that the PLA would enter Tibet and local governments would help the Chinese army "consolidate the national defence." Furthermore, Tibet's external affairs would be controlled directly by the Chinese central government, and the Tibetan army would be subsumed into the PLA. The Tibetans were assured that their religious freedoms would not be taken away—but as the Dalai Lama pointed out, these were all platitudes. The bottom line was this: "From now on, the Land of Snows answered to the People's Republic of China."

The situation seemed hopeless. Many people feared for the life of His Holiness, and he was advised to flee Tibet and cross over to India—a short journey away. The young Dalai Lama was now caught in the unenviable position of making a major decision while being tugged in

two equally important directions. His brother Thubten Jigme Norbu, who had witnessed Chinese aggression in Amdo, had by this time left for India with the view of leaving for the US. He wrote to His Holiness from Calcutta, urging him to move to India immediately and to foster relations with foreign allies, in particular, the US. The Americans offered to extend support if His Holiness repudiated the Seventeen-Point Agreement and "showed willingness to resist the Chinese." In the meantime, abbots of several monasteries visited the Dalai Lama and urged him to return to Lhasa. They were joined by the two Prime Ministers in this plea. Heinrich Harrer, who had traveled with the Dalai Lama to Yatung, wrote a letter from Kalimpong, in which he suggested that the Dalai Lama seek exile in India. However, Ling Rinpoche, the Dalai Lama's revered teacher and constant mentor, did not agree. Despite much pressure, the fifteen-year-old Dalai Lama made the difficult decision to return to Lhasa and to attempt to deal peacefully with the Chinese. Above all, he wanted to avoid bloodshed between the Chinese army and his people.

Signatures and seals on the Seventeen-Point Agreement that the Tibetan delegation was coerced into signing in Peking, 1951.

RETURN TO LHASA

On 16 July 1951, a Chinese delegation led by Mao's personal emissary, General Chiang Chin-wu arrived in Yatung to meet the Dalai Lama. At the frosty meeting, the General asked if His Holiness had heard of the "Seventeen-Point Agreement," to which His Holiness replied reservedly that he had. His Holiness writes that despite all the animosity and tension, "…it became clear that this man, although supposedly my enemy, was in fact just another human being, an ordinary person like myself. This realization had a lasting impact on me. It was another important lesson." General Chiang Chin-wu told the Dalai Lama that even if he was to leave Tibet, he would always be welcomed back to his country, so there was really no need to go into exile.

In the meantime, Gyalo Thondup contacted the Indian government about the possibility of his brother being granted asylum. This request was turned down, despite the Indians having condemned Chinese aggression. The political officer in charge of the Indian mission in Lhasa, S. N. Sinha,

Chinese soldiers marching in Lhasa, early 1950s, with placards of Mao and General Chu Teh.

was in regular contact with the Tibetans and reported to New Delhi that among those in the Dalai Lama's party for Yatung were the British radio operator, Reginald Fox, and Peter Aufschnaiter. The Dalai Lama's mother and two of his brothers had also traveled with him to Yatung and would later continue on to India for a pilgrimage. His sisters, Tsering Dolma and Jetsun Pema, joined the family in Yatung and were able to spend Losar together, before His Holiness left for Lhasa on 24 July 1951.

The return journey to Lhasa took three weeks, and along the way His Holiness gave teachings and enjoyed the beautiful landscape:

> …cobalt blue lakes fringed with strips of lush green pasture on which thousands of sheep grazed. The views were more wonderful than anything I had ever seen, thanks to the crisp, summer light.

No longer having to travel incognito, he stopped at almost every village and spoke to the people, informing them of what was happening in Tibet, and that they had been invaded by a foreign army.

His arrival in Lhasa after an absence of eight months was marked by celebrations, as people were overjoyed to have their leader back. Circumstances demanded that His Holiness greet General Chiang Chin-wu, who had followed him back to Lhasa. This meeting was to set the tone for the General's attitude—one of high handedness, arrogance, and ill temper. The Dalai Lama later wrote of an important lesson he had learned from this interaction, "that in some ways it was good to express anger…it is usually better than pretending to be gentle and hiding resentment." A few weeks later, an advance army of 600 Chinese soldiers marched into Lhasa. Thus began Mao's plan of Tibet's gradual integration into China. Overnight, Lhasa changed, as the population doubled, so did inflation, caused by the sudden influx of the invading army. The Dalai Lama followed the events with "increasing anxiety," as hostility and violence grew between the Tibetans and the Chinese army.

The Tenth Panchen Lama

The Tenth Panchen Lama and the Fourteenth Dalai Lama met for the first time in 1952 in Lhasa.

The Ninth Panchen Lama died in 1937. He had been instrumental in identifying the Fourteenth Dalai Lama, having given names of three potential candidates to Kewtsang Rinpoche to pursue.

As is tradition, the Dalai Lama was to be consulted about the Panchen Lama's successor, but there was a conflict between the Tashilhunpo Monastery (the seat of the Ninth Panchen Lama) and Reting Rinpoche (representing the Dalai Lama, who was only an infant at the time) as the two favored different candidates. Tashilhunpo reached out to the Chinese Nationalists for support, and with the backing of the Kuomintang government and the warlord, Ma Bufang, they announced their candidate to be the next Panchen Lama. Born on 19 January 1938 in Amdo Province, he was less than three years younger than the Fourteenth Dalai Lama and took the name Lobsang Trinley Lhündrub Chökyi Gyaltsen after his enthronement in August 1949 at Kumbum Monastery. Lhasa did not recognize him.

The Kuomintang had propped up the boy for their own strategic purpose of combating the Communists. But as the Chinese communist victory became evident, the Panchen Lama's closest advisors threw in their lot with the communists and their plan to "liberate" Tibet. The eleven-year-old Panchen Lama even sent a congratulatory message to Mao when he came to power. Mao saw him as a powerful ally against the Dalai Lama, and he later took part in major events including the signing of the Seventeen-Point Agreement. It fell on the Dalai Lama to foster better relations with the young Panchen Lama, despite China's control of him. In 1952, the Panchen Lama stopped in Lhasa on his way to resume his seat for the first time at Tashilhunpo Monastery. He arrived with a large retinue of Chinese soldiers who were clearly instructed to accompany him at all times. This was to be the first meeting between the two highest Tibetan Buddhist lamas. The Dalai Lama writes that he saw this as a "happy occasion to look forward to." The two had much in common including an interest in photography. He also recalled, "In the end I did manage to have some time alone with the Panchen Lama and my impression was of a very honest and faithful young man... It was just as well that neither of us knew what a tragic life he would lead."

THE PANCHSHEEL AGREEMENT

Tibet's relations with India were shifting. Despite China's actions in Tibet, Nehru believed it was imperative for India to foster relations with its powerful Communist neighbor in order to maintain political and military peace. Chinese Premier Chou En-lai, proposed that the former British Mission in Lhasa be made an Indian Consulate and demanded a reciprocal gesture of a diplomatic office in Bombay. Consequently, China and India began talks on 31 December 1953, seeking a "peaceful method of solving irritants directly between the two neighbors."

In April 1954, the two nations signed the bilateral Agreement on Trade and Intercourse in the Tibet Region of China which included Five Principles of Coexistence. India agreed to withdraw military stations from Gyantse and Yatung, and surrender to China free of cost, its postal, telegraph, and telephone facilities, and several guesthouses that it owned in Tibet. My friend, the French scholar and Tibetan studies expert, Claude Arpi, points out that Peking achieved exactly what it wanted as it succeeded in gaining "the Indian stamp of approval on their (Chinese) occupation of Tibet." The Dalai Lama wrote, "the world had turned its back on us...(including India)...our nearest neighbor and spiritual mentor." Nehru presented the Panchsheel Agreement to the Indian Parliament on 15 May 1954.

In October 1954, Nehru became the first non-Communist head of state to visit Peking since the creation of the People's Republic of China. Between the signing of the Panchsheel Agreement and Nehru's visit, there were several skirmishes on the India-China border. The relationship between the two countries spiraled further, culminating in the Sino-India War of 1962.

A cartoon by Kutty published in the Indian newspaper, *Hindustan Times*, depicting Jawaharlal Nehru carrying the fragile burden of befriending China.

FRAGILE
To Be Handled Carefully

FIRST VISIT TO CHINA

Having overwhelmed the Tibetans and maneuvered the Indians into an agreeable position, the Chinese establishment now wanted the Dalai Lama to attend the People's National Congress in Beijing. Many dissuaded the Dalai Lama from going, but he thought it was "an excellent idea" in that, "Not only would it enable me to meet Chairman Mao in person, but also it would give me the opportunity to see something of the outside world." On 11 July 1954, His Holiness left for China leaving behind thousands of worried Tibetans who feared that he may be detained there. There were "scenes of great sorrow and the weeping of his people" on the day he left. The visiting delegation was over 400 strong, with officials, servants, a large contingent of Tibetan elite which included his mother, brothers Lobsang Samten and Tendzin Choegyal, tutors, senior monks from different monasteries, and the Panchen Lama with his own entourage.

The Dalai Lama and the Panchen Lama arriving at the train station in Peking, September 1954. They are flanked by, *left*, Chu Teh, Commander-in-Chief of the PLA and, *right*, Chou En-lai, Prime Minister and Foreign Minister.

The visit was timed crucially, as China's new constitution was to be ratified during this time.

The Tibetan party's arduous 2,000 mile journey to Beijing was arranged by the Chinese. The Tibetans were concerned about the difficult journey, which included road, rail, horseback, and most importantly, the Dalai Lama's first flight. His Holiness recalls the journey in great detail. During the initial stretch, he traveled in his predecessor's Dodge car, avoiding landslides and flashfloods, to arrive at their first destination, Ganden Monastery. Once motorable roads ended, they set off on mules and then foot. As they approached Chamdo, the first town lost to the Chinese forces five years earlier, His Holiness saw that Chinese control was total. "In every town and village there were loudspeakers that played Chinese martial music and exhortations to the people to work and work harder 'for the glory of the Motherland.'" They met the Panchen Lama and his party at Shingang, and the two lamas traveled in the Chinese premier's private plane to Xi'an. Finally, for the last leg of the journey, the delegation set off by train. His Holiness was apprehensive and uneasy as they approached the Chinese capital. They were greeted at

The Dalai Lama presenting a traditional ceremonial scarf (*khatag*) to Chairman Mao in a gesture of goodwill at the beginning of the visit to China in 1954.

the train station by Chou En-lai, the prime minister and second-in-command after Chairman Mao, and by Chu Teh, head of the People's Liberation Army (PLA). Phuntsog Wangyal, a Tibetan, also known as Phunwang, served as a liaison officer and Chinese translator for His Holiness during this trip. A dedicated Communist, Phunwang had attended a Chinese-run school in Lhasa and believed in the values of socialism. His Holiness befriended Phunwang easily as he found him able, wise, and sincere, and his idealism appealing.

The hosts kept the Tibetan delegation very busy—"the Chinese overwhelmed us with entertainment. We were never given a moment's rest," recalls the Great Mother in her autobiography. It was not until a week after their arrival that His Holiness and Mao met—and this first of many meetings was a great success. His Holiness found the chairman to be impressive and recalls that he felt "he was in the presence of a magnetic force" when they shook hands. Mao charmed him and greeted him as he would an old friend and not a foe. He told the Dalai Lama that

the Tibetans could keep their own national flag and that reforms would be carried out according to their wishes. He also assured the Dalai Lama that the military personnel stationed in Tibet were there to assist him and that he could complain to him directly should they behave otherwise.

His Holiness began to be more positive about his visit despite many apprehensions. Preliminary meetings were conducted prior to his first private meeting with Mao, during which the Chairman suggested establishing a Preparatory Committee for the "Autonomous Region of Tibet" (PCART) in the interim. Mao also spoke positively about Tibet, its history and people, thereby reassuring His Holiness that the Chinese meant well. The more he started to learn of Marxism, the more the Dalai Lama took to it and he even applied to join the Communist Party. Although nothing came of this request, he was appointed member of the Standing Committee of the National People's Congress. He also began to learn Chinese during this period, and at the suggestion of Phunwang, started physical exercises under the supervision of a Chinese security

The Dalai Lama surrounded by his tutors, staff, lamas, ministers, and family members in Peking, New Year's Day, 1955. Front row (left to right): Phala, Lord Chamberlain, Ngawang Dhondup, Gyamtso Ling, Liusher (foreign affairs minister), Minling Chung Rinpoche, Ngabo Ngawang Jigme, Ling Rinpoche, His Holiness, Trijang Rinpoche, the sixteenth Karmapa, W. G. Surkhang, Gyalyum Chenmo, Ngari Rinpoche, Tsering Dolma, and Jigdal Phuntsog Rinpoche.

officer assigned to him.

Apart from the numerous official engagements, the hosts also introduced the Tibetans to Chinese operas and dance parties. The Great Mother writes, "As soon as (a) meal was over, a bell again rang as a sign that we're about to leave for sightseeing. I sometimes pretended to be sick…" Both the Great Mother and Ling Rinpoche fell ill during the trip.

His Holiness spent ten weeks in the Chinese capital, mostly attending meetings and functions, and even conducted some Buddhist teachings. His personal interest in science and years of tinkering with all things mechanical were piqued when he visited industrial plants and factories in China. He surprised his hosts by asking pertinent questions, and with his inquisitiveness.

The Dalai Lama's tutors, Ling Rinpoche (right) and Trijang Rinpoche (left), in China during the 1954 trip. While some members of the group were impressed with the hospitality and food that the Chinese lavished on them, Ling Rinpoche carried a bag of *tsampa* with him everywhere and was relieved when it was time to go home.

One young member of the entourage soon gained a lot of popularity and won many Chinese hearts—His Holiness' youngest brother, seven-year-old Tendzin Choegyal. The Dalai Lama recalls that he was "a constant source of delight and terror to everyone." He also picked up Mandarin quickly as he was very intelligent. This had both its advantages and disadvantages, since he was quick to aptly translate disparaging remarks made in Tibetan to the hosts. The Chinese were very vigilant in restricting the Dalai Lama's contact with ordinary people, and they ensured that he and the Panchen Lama were largely kept apart.

The Chinese had pulled out all the stops to impress the Dalai Lama, but the Great Mother recalls being "struck by the poverty in the countryside…We were never taken to see poor areas…I put some money in the peasants' hands, and quietly they appealed to me not to say a word or they would be severely punished."

The Tibetans visited the Chinese border with Mongolia and returned to Beijing at the end of January 1955. To mark the end of their yearlong visit, His Holiness hosted a banquet for Chairman Mao and members of the Big Four. It was an eventful end, for he had celebrated the Chinese New Year in Shangai and the Tibetan New Year (Losar) in Beijing. It was now time to go back home to Lhasa.

Prior to his departure, His Holiness attended a meeting of a steering committee of the PRC, following which he was summoned for a final appointment with Mao. He gave the Dalai Lama good advice on governance but left him with a parting shot, "Your attitude is good, you know. Religion is poison. Firstly, it reduces the population, because monks and nuns must stay celibate, and secondly, it neglects material progress." His Holiness was shocked and confused by how Mao had misjudged him so greatly. He writes,

> "The only possible explanation was that he had misinterpreted my great interest in scientific matters and material progress... in his ignorance of Buddhist philosophy, Mao had ignored the Buddha's instruction that anyone who practices the Dharma should test for themselves its validity."

The Dalai Lama concealed his feelings. He felt a great sense of relief when the meeting came to an end.

His Holiness and his entourage visited Kumbum Monastery on their way back from China. In the center, the Dalai Lama's sister Tsering Dolma views the vast monastic complex from above.

THE BIRTH OF THE TIBETAN RESISTANCE

The assurances "of gradual reforms" given to the Tibetan delegation did not last very long. Soon after the Dalai Lama and his party's return to Lhasa in the summer of 1955, the veneer of false security witnessed in the capital was shattered as reports of Chinese "reforms" being enforced in Kham and Amdo filtered in. New taxes, forced land redistribution, and atrocities against nuns and monks were just some of the tactics adopted by the Chinese. However, it was the Chinese demand that locals surrender their weapons that finally pushed matters over the edge.

At the end of 1955, Tibet was preparing for the opening session of the Preparatory Committee for the Autonomous Region of Tibet (PCART), "Mao's alternative to rule by military commission." A large delegation led by Marshal Chen Yi, deputy Prime Minister and Foreign Minister of China, arrived in Lhasa in April 1956. In his speech, Chen Yi spoke of "necessary reforms" that would be introduced to "rid Tibet of its backward situation." It was evident that the move toward autonomy was all a pretense on the part of the Chinese.

Resistance fighters unfurl their new flag at their headquarters in Lhoka, Central Tibet, 16 June 1958. They changed their name from *Chushi Gangdruk* to Volunteer Defenders of the Faith to include Tibetans from all regions, not just Kham and Amdo.

Soon refugees from Kham and Amdo started arriving in Lhasa, bringing with them firsthand accounts of the methods the Chinese had employed to politically re-educate the Tibetans. There were horrifying stories of public beatings and executions. In retaliation, people distributed leaflets and put up posters around Lhasa, much to the Chinese authority's dislike. For the first time, a peoples' movement started gaining momentum. In mid-1958, fundraising among Tibetans in Kham and Amdo helped the formation of a secret resistance guerrilla group called the *Chushi Gangdruk* ("Four Rivers, Six Ranges"), under the leadership of Gonpo Tashi Andrutsang, from Kham.

The resistance fighters of the *Chushi Gangdruk* had found ways to disrupt the Chinese movements, such as destroying their military roads and bridges. With instances of brave cadres of women leading attacks on the Chinese, Eastern Tibet was "ablaze with insurrection," and PLA forces retaliated with brutality. In early 1956, the Chinese ordered the 6,000 monks of Lithang monastery in Kham and the surrounding local population to give up their arms. The Tibetan response (spearheaded by armed monks) was to attack the Chinese office close by. The violence escalated, leading to the Chinese aerial bombing of Lithang Monastery. The Dalai Lama cried when he heard of the atrocities and saw pictures of the damage. The Chinese arrested the family members of those thought to be involved in the resistance movement and did not spare nuns and monks either—forcing them to kill and break their vows of celibacy. The Dalai Lama wrote to the Chinese leadership, including Mao, but his plea fell on deaf ears. Desperate, he asked his friend, Phunwang, to deliver a letter to Mao but failed to get a response.

Meanwhile the *Chushi Gangdruk* fostered relationships with two key members of the Dalai Lama's inner circle—Phala Dronyer Chenmo, the Lord Chamberlain, and Trijang Rinpoche, who became the resistance group's spiritual mentor. The Dalai Lama's two eldest brothers had by this time come in contact with the CIA to try and garner support for Tibet.

Below: Brass pin of the Volunteer Defenders of the Faith.

Following page 111: In May 1956, *The Illustrated London News* ran a cover story on Tibet: "Where insurrection and deep anti-Chinese unrest are reported. A recent photograph shows the Dalai Lama addressing a huge religious gathering at the Jokhang temple in Lhasa." This was in the Sungchora Square at the rear of the temple, where teachings were traditionally held.

The CIA's Secret War in Tibet

In 1948, Tibet's ties with the US began to develop when a trade delegation led by W. D. Shakabpa visited Washington. Soon after, Telopa Rinpoche became the first Tibetan to settle in the US when he joined Johns Hopkins University. In 1950, the Dalai Lama's eldest brother, Thubten Jigme Norbu, received an invitation via Telopa Rinpoche from the San Francisco-based American Committee for Free Asia (CFA) to visit the US. This month-old organization was a CIA front with a covert agenda to cultivate people from the East who were friendly with the US. Many hitherto unknown facts have been revealed in the book *The CIA's Secret War in Tibet* by Kenneth Conboy and James Morrison.

In 1951 he traveled to Washington, and along with CFA representative Robert Ekvall, a missionary born near Amdo who spoke Chinese and Tibetan fluently, he met with State Department and CIA officials. Not long after, the Americans would become involved with the Tibetan cause, albeit somewhat reluctantly at first. This secret association was shaped by Gyalo Thondup, who met officials in Washington in late October 1951. In mid-1955, the CIA station chief in Calcutta met a merchant from Kham, Ragpa Pandatsang, who informed him that the Khampas were seeking arms to resist the Chinese. The following year, while the Dalai Lama was in India for the Buddha Jayanti celebrations, a CIA officer in Calcutta contacted Gyalo Thondup, who by this time was living in India. He was assigned with the task of selecting suitable candidates for training by the CIA in February 1957. With approval from the US National Security Council, a series of three clandestine programs were envisaged: ST Circus, ST Barnum, and ST Bailey. The first was a training program for Tibetan fighters, the second for airlifting men and supplies to Tibet, and the third a propaganda program.

In March 1957, six volunteers made a secret nighttime crossing of the Mahanandi River into then East Pakistan, where they were met by Thubten Jigme Norbu himself and his assistant, Thondrup Gyantsen, who served as their interpreter. This first group of trainees was taken to Saipan in the Western Pacific, where they underwent guerilla training, which included radio communications, map reading, and the use of arms and explosives. In September, they were airdropped in two groups—one near Lhasa and the other in Kham. Once they established contact with the *Chushi Gangdruk*, they began to send encrypted messages to Washington, which were decoded by Geshe Wangyal, an ethnic Kalmyk monk who settled in New Jersey in 1955 and was a protégé of Dorjiev. Two of them reached Lhasa and met with the Lord Chamberlain.

This period saw the resistance strengthening, and in mid-1958, the fighters launched successful attacks on the Chinese. Following several requests, the CIA conducted two clandestine arms' drops that the Tibetans were desperate for. By late 1958, training programs were conducted at a prisoner-of-war camp for German soldiers, Camp Hale in the Colorado Rocky Mountains, and over the next five years, over 250 Tibetan fighters were trained there. While Thubten Jigme Norbu disengaged from this program at this stage and began teaching at Columbia University, Geshe Wangyal continued to decode messages received from the rebels in Tibet. By this time, the size, strength, and reach of the resistance in Tibet had grown exponentially. And while the Chinese were alarmed at these developments, they also saw it as an opportunity—to use it as grounds to unleash unforgiving retaliation against the Tibetans. A documentary film, *Shadow Circus: The CIA in Tibet,* featuring former fighters and CIA agents, brings to light important details of this secret association.

THE ILLUSTRATED LONDON NEWS

The World Copyright of all the Editorial Matter, both Illustrations and Letterpress, is Strictly Reserved in Great Britain, the British Dominions and Colonies, Europe, and the United States of America.

SATURDAY, MAY 12, 1956.

WHERE INSURRECTION AND DEEP ANTI-CHINESE UNREST ARE REPORTED : TIBET — A RECENT PHOTOGRAPH SHOWING THE DALAI LAMA ADDRESSING A HUGE RELIGIOUS GATHERING AT THE JOKHANG TEMPLE IN THE CAPITAL, LHASA.

Reliable reports recently reached Katmandu, capital of Nepal, of serious risings taking place in Eastern Tibet and of widespread unrest throughout the country. Some two months ago, it is reported, Golok tribesmen in north-east Tibet, under a leader named Ma Bofono, rose and massacred a local Chinese garrison, whose numbers are variously given as between 500 and 800 men. This was followed, it is said, by a large-scale Chinese punitive expedition and the bombing of Golok villages, during which Ma Bofono escaped from the country. These reports have all been described as " lies " by the Chinese delegation which has been visiting Katmandu for the coronation of the King of Nepal ; but the existence of a Tibetan underground national party called Memang has been known for some time, and this, together with growing Tibetan resentment, gives colour to these reports.

Postage—Inland, 2½d. ; Canada, 1½d. ; Elsewhere Abroad, 3d. (These rates apply as The Illustrated London News is registered at the G.P.O. as a newspaper.)

VISIT TO INDIA, 1956

Amid the growing violence, the Dalai Lama received some welcome news. In the spring of 1956, the Crown Prince of Sikkim visited to invite him to attend the annual Buddha Jayanti celebrations in India. It was the 2,500th birth anniversary of the Lord Buddha, making it a special occasion. Tibetans consider India to be *Aryabhumi,* the Land of the Holy, since it is the birthplace of Gautama Buddha. His Holiness also saw this as an opportunity to meet Nehru and discuss the Tibetan issue. As he recalls, "I desperately wanted to be able to make contact with the Indian Government, if only to see the way that a democracy worked."

But the Chinese were not going to make it easy. General Fan Ming, the acting head of the Chinese Communist Party in Lhasa, told His Holiness that India was "a dangerous place" and instead asked him to send a representative to India. The Dalai Lama chose his junior tutor, Trijang Rinpoche. Two weeks later His Holiness received news that the Chinese Government would allow him to travel for the celebrations, but they warned him about "reactionary elements and spies" in India and reminded him that Tibet would bear the brunt of any seditious actions.

The Sikkim Crown Prince met with senior officials at the American Consulate in Calcutta and informed them of the violence in eastern Tibet, the various insurrections across the region, and that he believed the Dalai Lama wanted to leave Lhasa. The Crown Prince also pointed out that the anti-Chinese rebels had no sophisticated weapons and suggested that arms could be brought in through East Pakistan. It appears he even suggested obliquely to them that the US could "exfiltrate" Tibetans traveling on pilgrimages via Burma and Thailand, for insurgency training.

The sudden Chinese consent for the Dalai Lama's visit appeared to be prompted by Nehru's intervention. As claimed by some historians, Nehru was "disturbed by Beijing's lack of restraint," and His Holiness' visit to India would "symbolically underscore its interest in the well-being of Tibet and its leader." When the Chinese leadership heard that

the Indian Consul in Lhasa had informed several people about this, they were forced to acquiesce to maintain the spirit of the recently signed Panchsheel Agreement.

The twenty-one-year-old Dalai Lama left Lhasa at the end of November 1956. His entourage included the Panchen Lama, his two tutors, ministers, and family members. They drove almost all the way to Sikkim and crossed over the border on horseback for the last stretch. Indian officials received the group in Sikkim, and they were taken to a small settlement where, to the Dalai Lama's pleasant surprise, his two elder brothers, Thubten Jigme Norbu and Gyalo Thondup, were waiting. Since his siblings Lobsang Samten and Tendzin Choegyal had also accompanied him, it was for the first time in His Holiness' life that "all five brothers were together." Traveling onward, the group took a flight

The Dalai Lama, followed by the Panchen Lama and his two tutors, in traveling costumes, enter India over Nathu La, the mountain pass which connected Tibet to Sikkim, 1956. Photo by Homai Vyarawalla, India's first female photojournalist.

Tseten Tashi, private secretary to the Crown Prince of Sikkim, took this unique photo of a relaxed Dalai Lama in traveling attire on a street in Yatung, 1956.

from Bagdogra to New Delhi, where they were ceremonially received by Prime Minister Nehru and Vice President Dr. S. Radhakrishnan, and were given a guard of honor. His Holiness also met the President, Dr. Rajendra Prasad, and paid a visit to Mahatma Gandhi's memorial. Recalling the experience later, he says, "As I stood praying, I experienced simultaneously great sadness at not being able to meet Gandhi in person and great joy at the magnificent example of his life."

It was at the Buddha Jayanti celebrations that I first saw His Holiness. We had traveled there especially to attend the occasion. It was a most

exciting moment for me, although I do not remember much detail.

Everywhere he went, the Dalai Lama was received by large enthusiastic crowds who sought his blessings. To them he was more than a head of state—he was an exalted avatar of the divine. While this threw up security concerns for his hosts, the Dalai Lama enjoyed his time in India and found Indians to be sincere and genuine. The Indians had planned an extensive itinerary for the visitors—a trip to the Taj Mahal, industrial centers, horse races in Calcutta, and to the military academy in Dehra Dun among others. He writes, "I felt that I had returned to my spiritual home. Everything seemed somehow familiar." His Holiness conducted teachings in which he spoke about peace among people and nations. During this period, the Dalai Lama was able to discuss with people Gandhi's ideas of *ahimsa*—the shared Hindu and Buddhist doctrine of refraining from harming any living being—and civil disobedience.

During the five-week tour of India to celebrate the 2,500th anniversary of the birth of Lord Buddha, the twenty-one-year-old Dalai Lama was met with huge crowds everywhere he went.

His Holiness used the several meetings he had with Nehru to explain to him the grave situation unfolding in Tibet. But Nehru appeared impatient and told the Dalai Lama that India could not support him. His Holiness said that he would like to seek asylum in India, to which Nehru demurred and suggested that he return to Lhasa and work things out with the Chinese on the basis of the Seventeen-Point Agreement. Nehru suggested that he meet Chou En-lai, who had organized a visit to New Delhi at the same time. The Dalai Lama agreed and met him the next day. Despite the Dalai Lama's forceful protestations, Chou En-lai smoothly assured him that everything was okay and that he should return to Lhasa without any reservations. His Holiness set off on a pilgrimage of important Buddhist destinations, including the most sacred of them all, Bodh Gaya, where Lord Buddha achieved enlightenment. Unfortunately, his visit was soon disrupted by a message from Chou En-lai to meet him in Delhi.

On learning that His Holiness intended to visit Kalimpong on his way back, Chou En-lai advised him against it. Meanwhile, Chairman

Prime Minister Jawaharlal Nehru, the Dalai Lama, President Rajendra Prasad, and the Panchen Lama at a formal lunch at the presidential estate, Rashtrapati Bhavan, Delhi, 1956.

Facing page: Nehru with Gyalyum Chenmo and His Holiness' brother Ngari Rinpoche in Calcutta, 1957. Ngari Rinpoche remembers the Prime Minister telling him repeatedly, "Go to school young boy! Go to school!"

Mao announced on 7 February 1957 that reforms in Tibet would be postponed for six years, and for another fifty, if need be. But His Holiness and the Tibetans had their doubts. Chou En-lai convinced the Dalai Lama to visit Nalanda for a function, which His Holiness readily accepted since he knew that Nehru would be there, and it would give him one last chance to request India's intervention. However, Nehru advised him to leave for Lhasa immediately and not to visit Kalimpong. Undeterred, His Holiness continued with his plans.

In Kalimpong he stayed at Bhutan House for a week, in fact in the same room as his predecessor, who had spent part of his exile there. He met his former Prime Minister, Lukhangwa, who was on a pilgrimage, who urged him not to return to Lhasa. Joining him in his plea were the Dalai Lama's two brothers, Jigme Norbu and Gyalo Thondup who also beseeched him not to go back. In fact, they had even succeeded in securing support from Indian leaders such as Jayaprakash Narayan, for the Tibetan cause. The Dalai Lama then consulted the Nechung and the Gadong oracles, who were unanimous in their advice—to return

The trip to India was the first time that the family had ever all met together and it gave them the opportunity to have their photograph taken as a family. From left to right: Ngari Rinpoche, Jetsun Pema, the Dalai Lama, Lobsang Samten, Gyalo Thondup, Thubten Jigme Norbu (Taktser Rinpoche), Tsering Dolma, and the Great Mother.

At the Mahabodhi Temple, Bodh Gaya, 1956, with junior tutor, Trijang Rinpoche (left) and senior tutor Ling Rinpoche (right). This was one of the pivotal moments in His Holiness' life. He happily recalls taking refuge in front of the Buddha statue from Ling Rinpoche, who had first taken the vows from the statue itself as a valid representation of Lord Buddha.

Facing page: Letter of appeal to Prime Minister Nehru from representatives of all three Tibetan provinces (Choklasum) who at the time were living in Kalimpong, August 1958.

to Lhasa. Gyalo Thondup became quite agitated when he learned that the Dalai Lama had decided to return and give the Chinese one more chance.

There were a number of reasons why the Dalai Lama was more assured about his decision. On Nehru's advice, he intended to become more vocal about any unacceptable behavior of the Chinese, hoped that consultations with the Tibetan People's Association (the *Mimang Tsongdu*, who were critical of the Chinese occupation) would be advantageous, and, most importantly, believed India would become more aware of what was happening in Tibet, thereby holding the Chinese to account.

After eleven months in India, with a "heavy heart," His Holiness crossed over the Nathu La in late March 1957 to return home.

Albela House, Kalimpong,
West Bengal.
5th. August, 1958.

Mr. Jawaharlal Nehru,
 Prime Minister of India,
 New Delhi.

Dear Sir,

 Tibet is essentially an independent country with
sovereign powers. Its people being religious and peace-loving,
no stocks of modern war-weapons were kept within its boundaries.
In the year 1950 the Chinese Communists invaded our land with
about five-hundred thousand of their so-called "liberation Army"
and over-powered our frontier guards. Later they settled some
four million Chinese immigrants in the eastern and north-eastern
regions. These settlers, along with their powerful armies, have
attempted to destroy our religion, culture and traditions.

 We Tibetans, both in Tibet and in India, have tried
our utmost to make the Chinese recognise their shameful injustice
to us and we have asked them several times to stop the oppre-
ssion and suppression of our people. We have also approached you,
in the past, asking you to use your influence with the Chinese
on our behalf, but all these efforts proved vain. We have
already explained the Tibetan situation to you and know that
you are well aware of the facts. In spite of this we are attach-
ing hereto a Manifesto describing the plight of our people. In
it you will read of the merciless treatment of our people by the
Chinese, and how many had to flee to the far-off deserts and
valleys. It is for these reasons that our people are now fighting
for freedom. There are hundreds being killed daily by the Chinese
in these battles.

 There is trouble also in Lhasa, the capital of Tibet.
Recently some thirty thousand people from the southern areas had
to leave their property, families and settled life to save them-
selves from the brutal treatment of the Chinese over-lords. Now
without homes, these people are also out in the deserts and it
is feared that there may be uprisings in the south and central
areas as a consequence.

 Not only have the Chinese Communists occupied our
country and set about exploiting our people, but they have also
made Tibet into a huge arsenal for their future offensive towards
her neighbouring countries and the world at large. They are
building army barracks,forts, bridges and air-fields at stratagic
places and their immense programme for constructing great roads
and railways is mainly to accelerate the movement of their armed
forces.

 It is in view of the above mentioned facts and because
of your close and cordial relations with China that we request you
to kindly make the Government of China realise the desparate
situation in our country. We request you to endeavour to make the
Chinese immediately stop their offensive which they are launching
against the patriots in Don-Kham and Amdo in the eastern regions,
and to make the situation in central Tibet easier.

India, a country which was under British domina-
tion for over 150 years, achieved her independence just
after the World War II. Similarly, a number of other
countries who were under foreign yokes for generations
have attained their independence within the past few
years. On the contrary, the independence of Tibet, an
essentially free country which, as the history proves,
was at no time under any foreign domination, was
violated by the Communist China her next door neighbour.
Shall the August World Body which stands for peace and
justice in the present world justify the atrocious
actions of the Communist China on Tibet, a peace-loving
and religious country, while the people are fighting
tooth and nail in the struggle for their very existence ?

It is in view of the above mentioned facts and
the Manifesto attached hereto that we are appealing to
you to help us by approaching China about this injustice.
China should be made to recognise the dire plight of our
country and stop their assaults on our loyal people in
Don-Kham and Amdo in the eastern regions and to relent
in central Tibet as well.

In short our appeal to you is this. Please
request the Government of China on our behalf restore
to Tibet her independence and to withdraw all their
armed forces and immigrants from the whole of Tibet.

Yours faithfully,

We the Representatives,
Tibet Chhokhasum.

The Dalai Lama debating for his Geshe Lharampa exams at Ganden monastery, 1959.

Geshe Exams

In the summer of 1958, His Holiness was concerned about the hostilities which had been ongoing in Kham and Amdo in Eastern Tibet for over a year. The Chinese had dropped bombs and fired artillery at will, making people flee the region for Lhasa. In light of these events, the Dalai Lama decided that it would be prudent to take his final monastic examinations. He departed with his entourage for Drepung Monastery for the first phase of his geshe degree. He remembers feeling deeply moved when his first debate session at Drepung began with thousands of monks chanting. Over the next few months, he would visit the other two Gelugpa seats, Sera and Ganden Monasteries, for further debates.

After the second series of debates at Ganden, some advisors suggested he move to the south, but His Holiness returned to Lhasa for the final segment of the geshe exam. The Great Prayer Festival was in full swing, and thousands of people from different parts of Tibet had gathered in Lhasa to attend it. The population of the city had almost tripled, with refugees from Eastern Tibet swelling numbers. Finally, on a day in early March 1959, His Holiness presented himself at the Jokhang Temple for debate sessions from morning until late evening before an audience of over 10,000. His Holiness had to engage in intense debates with senior scholars for hours on end and defend his thesis at each session. Monks generally spend over twenty years in rigorous philosophical study to attain this highest degree. His Holiness was twenty-three years old at the time.

His Holiness recalls that he was publicly examined in logic and epistemology before noon, and in the second session, Madhyamika (the Middle Way) and Prajnaparamita (The Perfection of Wisdom) were the subjects. In the final session, he was tested in all the five traditional major subjects. Over the course of ten hours of testing, His Holiness faced over fifty examiners, including abbots, senior monks, and student monks, in a solemn setting. At his side was senior tutor Ling Rinpoche, his "rock." By the end, an exhausted and relieved Dalai Lama had successfully earned the distinguished title, Geshe Lharampa, the highest distinction. But very soon he would be severely tested in an altogether different way.

THE PEOPLE'S UPRISING
MARCH 1959

In the six years since the Chinese arrived in Lhasa, the capital had changed immensely. An entirely new section of the city, including army barracks, a hospital, and a school, had been built to accommodate the Chinese. Violence in other parts of the country continued as the rebels became more brazen in their activities. As a result, the Chinese adopted more brutal intimidation tactics. His Holiness wrote, "Tibet was rapidly slipping not only from Chinese control, but also from my own."

Right after the Great Prayer Festival, on 9 March, Brigadier Fu, who was in charge of PLA troops in Lhasa, invited the Dalai Lama for a theatrical performance at their headquarters. He instructed Phuntsok Tashi Taklha, the Dalai Lama's brother-in-law, who was his chief of security, that His Holiness should come without protection and in secret. The young Tendzin Choegyal (Ngari Rinpoche), studying at Drepung Monastery, was also invited. This highly irregular request caused great worry. The news spread like wildfire and on 10 March, large crowds gathered outside the Norbulingka Palace to prevent the Dalai Lama from going, suspecting it was a ruse by the Chinese to hold him hostage or worse, harm him. By midday, the huge crowd of thirty thousand grew restive. A popular uprising was taking shape. Earlier that year, on 18 February, in a secret "situation report," Chairman Mao had said, "The more chaotic Tibet gets, the better. We can train troops, and toughen the masses. Furthermore, this furnishes sufficient reason for future pacification and reform." The situation at Norbulingka had become a tinderbox. To ease tensions, Tibetan officials reassured the crowds that the Dalai Lama would not attend the Chinese function.

On 10 March, General Tan Kuan-sen threatened "drastic measures." Later that day, Tibetan officials repudiated the Seventeen-Point Agreement. The General wrote to the Dalai Lama, asking him to move to their military headquarters for his safety. On 11 March,

Facing page:
10 March 1959, tens of thousands of Tibetans surround the Norbulingka Palace brimming with frustration with the Chinese occupation and desperate to protect the Dalai Lama from Chinese threat.

the Kashag requested leaders of the crowd outside the palace to withdraw. On the General's second request to move to their headquarters, the Dalai Lama tactfully agreed. He also ordered the Tibetan government to remove barricades placed on a road outside Lhasa, which were blocking the movement of Chinese troops.

The Nechung oracle advised His Holiness to remain in Lhasa and engage with the Chinese. His Holiness spent the afternoon in divination. A few tense days later, a second visit to the oracle yielded the same message—to wait and negotiate. Time was passing for His Holiness in "a dizzying, frightening blur." On 16 March, the General informed the Dalai Lama that the Chinese were preparing to attack the Norbulingka. The thought of violence and the inevitable loss of life greatly upset His Holiness. The next day he sought out the oracle again. This time, the oracle, swaying in a trance said dramatically "Go, go, go tonight," and even gave instructions on the exact escape route to take, and then fell unconscious on to the floor. Just at that moment, two shells exploded outside the palace building. On the night of 17 March, the twenty-three-year-old Dalai Lama, disguised as a soldier, left his summer palace and embarked on a long, dangerous journey to India into exile, not knowing when he would see his country or people again.

On 12 March 1959, a spontaneous gathering of 15,000 women from all regions of Tibet flocked to an area below the Potala Palace in a remarkable act of bravery. The twelfth of March is now known as Women's Uprising Day. The leaders were later either imprisoned or executed.

"In a way, it is only right that India should come to our aid. For Buddhism came to Tibet from India, along with many other important cultural influences. There is no doubt in my mind that she has a better claim on Tibet than China, whose influence was only ever slight."

HIS HOLINESS THE FOURTEENTH DALAI LAMA

Part 2:

A New Home in India

EXILE FROM TIBET AND A NEW HOME IN DHARAMSALA

(1959-1964)

"It was 17th March. We fled Norbulingka at 10 pm. We had to make it past the Chinese garrison, and when we left we didn't know if we would see the next day. It wasn't until we reached the top of the Che-la pass that we began to feel out of immediate danger. Local people had brought us horses. We mounted them and then turned to take one last look at Lhasa. Then we left."

HIS HOLINESS THE FOURTEENTH DALAI LAMA

ESCAPE FROM LHASA

Tibet's destiny would change forever on the fateful day of 17 March 1959. His Holiness had been battling confusion and distress, but the oracle's word revealed the way forward. The Dalai Lama also performed his own divination, which revealed advice from *Manjusri*, the Bodhisattva of wisdom. The oracle's advice was confirmed, and His Holiness felt the standoff could be diffused only if he left Tibet. But surely the Chinese would be carefully monitoring the situation? His Holiness informed only his immediate staff and delegated the preparations to his Lord Chamberlain, Phala Thupten Woden, and to the acting Chikyab

Escorted by members of the resistance, His Holiness the Dalai Lama (front left) and his entourage walking down a pass during his flight from Lhasa in 1959.

Khenpo, his chief of monastic staff, Gadrang Lobsang Rigzin. Three different groups set off within hours of each other. In the afternoon, His Holiness' tutors and four officials of the *Kashag* left hidden under a tarpaulin of a truck; some hours later the Great Mother, the young Tendzin Choegyal, his sister Tsering Dolma, and an uncle left in disguise, with the two women dressed as men. By this time the Lord Chamberlain had sent a message to the Indian Consul General in Lhasa on the question of exile and asylum in India. He also sent a message to the *Chushi Gangdruk* fighters in the south asking them to be ready to protect and escort His Holiness.

For one last time His Holiness visited his personal shrine dedicated to *Mahakala*, the protector deity for the Dalai Lamas. After offering a silk *khatag*, His Holiness finished his prayers and left. Shortly before ten at night, he removed his glasses, dressed as a soldier in trousers and a Tibetan *chuba* (robe), and walked out of Norbulingka. Slung across his left shoulder, was a cylindrical case which housed a very precious item—a *thangka* of the protector-goddess Palden Lhamo, which had

Accompanied by Kunga Samten Dewatshang, a leader of the Tibetan resistance *Chushi Gangdruk*, the Dalai Lama and his entourage escaping across the Yarlung Valley. The presence of the Dalai Lama—the very heart of Tibet—invigorated them.

once belonged to the Second Dalai Lama. The *thangka* was an object of great spiritual significance. Slung across his other shoulder was a rifle. Phuntsog Tashi Taklha, his chief of security and brother-in-law, was at his side. This was the third and last group to leave that day. With over tens of thousands of PLA soldiers in the area, the likelihood of being spotted and detained was a real risk. His Holiness and those accompanying him quickly crossed the Kyichu River, where the two groups were waiting on the other side. It was only then, His Holiness recalled later, that he put his glasses back on and was again able to see clearly.

The escape party rode most of the night, only stopping briefly on their way to the Che-La mountain pass, and reached the top at daybreak. His Holiness stopped to look around. It would be the last time he would get a glimpse of Lhasa. After a short prayer, they moved on toward the Yarlung Tsangpo, or the Brahmaputra River, to cross over into southern Tibet. His escape had not yet come to light, but fighting had broken out as the Tibetan forces were supporting the people of Lhasa. The Chinese launched greater attacks, and on 20 March they started shelling

The day after His Holiness escaped from Lhasa, he felt a tremendous sense of relief. He recounts, "Actually the danger was still very much alive. But despite this, we were moving freely, on our own, and we had finally come to the point of openly criticizing the Chinese."

LHASA—MUSSOORIE, 1959

▬▬▬ by horse
┼┼┼┼┼┼ by train

Lilli Mynarter

LHASA
Norbulingka
Ri Chu
CHE-LA
Kyesheng
Ra-me
Chidisho
Gyango Gyasang Shika
SABO-LA
Chongay Riudechen
Tsang-Po
(Brahmaputra R.)
Chenye
Thosam Thargayling
YARTO-TAG-LA
E-Chhudhogyang
TAG-LA
Shopanup
Lhuntse Dzong
Teulhey
LAGOE-LA
Jhora
TIBET
Tsona
KARPO-LA
Mangmang
Chhuthangmo
Gonsum Choten
Shardi
INDIA
Loonglha
Thongleh
BHUTAN
Tawang
Jang
Singl-Dzong
Derang
Rawang
Bomdi-La
Kelang
← To Mussoorie
Tezpur
Brahmaputra R.

Dharmsala
Mussoorie
Dehra
Dun
NEW
DELHI
INDIA
NEPAL
Lucknow
Benares
TIBET
LHASA
SIKKIM
BHUTAN
Siliguri
Tawang
Tezpur
CHINA
BURMA

0 300
MILES

The Dalai Lama's escape
route to India.

Norbulingka Palace. It was only the next day that the Chinese found out that His Holiness had escaped.

The Lord Chamberlain's message had been taken to two CIA-trained Tibetan radio operators, Athar and Lhotse, who were with the resistance forces holding Lhuntse Dzong, not far from the Indian border. This was where His Holiness was also headed. His intention was to temporarily set up base there, officially repudiate the Seventeen-Point Agreement, and once again set up negotiations with the Chinese from a safe place within reach of India. On 25 March, they sent a message to the Americans in

Phala Thupten Woden, the Lord Chamberlain, wearing a pale *chuba*, the Dalai Lama (center), and his teenage brother Tendzin Choegyal, with escorts from the *Chushi Gangdruk*. This was the first time the Dalai Lama conversed directly with the guerrillas.

"As the Indian people are known throughout the world for their support of humanitarian causes. In this critical situation we are entering India via Tsona. I hope that you will please make necessary arrangements for us in the Indian territory. Confident of your kindness with good wishes."

THE FOURTEENTH DALAI LAMA
Message to Prime Minister Nehru, 26 March 1959

Chushi Gangdruk fighters and local people waiting to greet the Dalai Lama at Lhuntse Dzong, a resistance stronghold in southern Tibet near the border. On 26 March 1959, the Dalai Lama sent messengers ahead to the Indian border, requesting Prime Minister Nehru to grant asylum.

Tibetan Morse code, which was developed specifically for communications between the CIA and the radio operators by Geshe Wangyal, a Buryat lama living in New Jersey. The Dalai Lama was safe. Every twenty-four hours, updates about the progress of the escape party were placed before President Eisenhower at the top of his daily intelligence briefing. News had broken out by now, and newspapers around the world were reporting

the escape journey. His Holiness received news of the Chinese attacks in Lhasa, and all hopes of a negotiated settlement were lost. A human tragedy of great proportions was unfolding. It later came to light that in the one-year period following the uprising, the PLA had eliminated over 87,000 Tibetans in central Tibet alone.

At Lhuntse Dzong His Holiness conducted a ceremony of consecration to set up a new Tibetan government. The ceremony was attended by over a thousand people. But it was clear that there was imminent danger if the Dalai Lama remained in Tibet. Consequently, messages were conveyed to the Indians and the Americans that His Holiness desired to cross over into India seeking asylum.

John Greaney, a senior CIA officer, received the message on Saturday night, 28 March. With instructions from his boss, he sent a covert message to New Delhi informing them of the Dalai Lama's request for asylum. Around this time, Gyalo Thondup writes that he visited Prime Minister Nehru in Parliament House in Delhi through B. N. Mullick, chief of India's Intelligence Bureau (IB). Nehru inquired if His Holiness was safe and when informed of his asylum request, he immediately said

The Dalai Lama formally declares Tibet an independent nation, announcing at Lhuntse Dzong the formation of a provisional Tibetan government. A huge crowd attends the ceremony. Later, this proclamation was conveyed by messengers to villages and towns all over Tibet.

yes. Both the secret escape and the asylum request seemed to be just in time.

The next day His Holiness left for the frontier, passing through the village of Jhora, and as the escape party crossed over the Karpo La mountain pass, the last one on the Tibetan side before the border, an airplane flew over them causing panic. They feared that the Chinese had spotted them. Tendzin Choegyal recounts, "…we were sure the Chinese would be on us in no time." The party decided to break into small groups and move forward for two more days. Messengers sent by Phala to the Indian border rejoined them here. They too conveyed the news that His Holiness was allowed to cross over into India. As His Holiness recalled,

An exhausted, yet jubilant Dalai Lama reaches the border checkpoint of Chutangmu on the back of a *dzomo* (female yak), as he was too weak to ride a horse.

his last night in Tibet was in rather miserable conditions at a small village called Mangmang. The escape party had endured rough weather all through their flight, and this seemed to cap it all. His Holiness fell sick with fever and dysentery. Two days later, on 31 March, he bade farewell to those who would remain in Tibet—some officials, the resistance fighters, and the two Tibetan radio operators, Athar and Lhotse, who received a special blessing. The party of approximately eighty people crossed over from the Land of Snows into the Tawang District, in the North East Frontier Agency (NEFA), now the state of Arunachal Pradesh. Waiting on the other side was the Indian Assistant Political Officer, T.S. Murthy, with greetings from Prime Minister Nehru. The exhausting, stressful two-week journey had finally come to an end.

Joy and relief on Dalai Lama's face as he arrives in India and is greeted with a *khatag*, or offering scarf. On the right, just behind him, is his Lord Chamberlain, Phala Thupten Woden. Seen on the left are the Simpon Khenpo (Master of the Robes) and the Chöpon Khenpo (Master of the Ritual).

ARRIVAL IN INDIA

By the afternoon of 31 March, His Holiness and his party reached Chutangmu, a small Assam Rifles resistance outpost near Tawang. It was decided that His Holiness' porters would be sent back, while the luggage would be ferried by the Indian porters. All weapons except those of the Dalai Lama, his immediate family, and his ministers, were to be handed over to the Indians. On 2 April, the District Commissioner of Tawang, Har Mander Singh, reported that the Dalai Lama's mother, sister, and younger brother, Tendzin Choegyal, had reached Lumla, farther south in Tawang District. Along with members of his entourage, His Holiness walked through the villages of Gorsam, Shakti, Lumla, and Thongleng, blessing hundreds of locals on the way. Netan Tashi, the IB operative escorting the party, recalled, "Every village turned out to greet him on his way to Tawang. People would stand with bowed heads, outstretched hands offering *khadag*. They would light incense and prostrate before him. Many would be crying; there was happiness as well as sorrow."

The local Mon people, or Monpas, who were devoted to His Holiness, welcomed him during his journey from Lumla to Tawang.

In Tawang, completely exhausted, the entourage temporarily settled in bungalows. The day they arrived, an Indian air force carrier dropped sacks of flour, shoes, and other essentials for the many Tibetans who accompanied him. His Holiness sought permission from the Indian authorities to meet his elder brother Gyalo Thondup, who was to come from Darjeeling. The Indians were not keen to allow this meeting immediately, and suggested that there was ample time later, to which His Holiness agreed.

On the second day in Tawang, His Holiness received an invitation to visit the Tawang Monastery. Known in Tibetan as *Gaden Namgyal Lhatse*, the monastery was built in 1680 at the instruction of the Fifth Dalai Lama by his disciple Merak Lama, Lodroe Gyatso. The region also had another significant association for His Holiness—the Sixth Dalai Lama, of Monpa ethnicity, was born here. His Holiness visited the monastery and gave teachings on the mantra of Avalokiteshvara, and was wearing a Tibetan *chuba* and not his monk's robe.

Reception for the Dalai Lama at Tawang Monastery, 5 April 1959, where he gave teachings to about 400 devotees, including monks and lamas of the monastery. Praising the Monpa people of the region, the Dalai Lama called them faithful devotees who were mentally pure and sincere.

His Holiness with his entourage on their way to Assam, escorted by the soldiers of the Assam Rifles.

The Dalai Lama recuperated for a few days in Bomdila after the exhausting journey. On reaching India, Har Mander Singh reported the Dalai Lama as saying, "Now all my anxiety and tense feeling have disappeared. Freedom is happiness...there is joy." Saying so, he remained silent for a while, deep in thought. Then he said, "The majority of our people are suffering. Since we have arrived in a free country now, we must work with dauntless courage and do everything we can, our very best, for the freedom of Tibet."

Now that he had safely left Lhasa and all the danger that had threatened him, discussions between Indian officials and His Holiness on his future plans and visions continued. On 7 April, Har Mander Singh sent a report to K. L. Mehta, adviser to the Government of Assam, stating that His Holiness had requested India to grant asylum to the Tibetan resistance fighters who were escaping the Chinese. Additionally, he wanted to maintain contact with the resistance fighters in Tibet through special messengers. The party wanted to then proceed to Bomdila to rest for a few days. The soldiers of Assam Rifles escorted His Holiness through the jungles of Arunachal Pradesh to Bomdila, 185 kilometers south of Tawang. There was a long and difficult path of pressing political matters ahead for His Holiness, as he began his life as the exiled leader of Tibet.

THE TEZPUR STATEMENT

The next day, 6 April, brought good news as Har Mander Singh shared Prime Minister Nehru's welcome message to His Holiness.

Upon his arrival in Bomdila, His Holiness was given a guard of honor and a "rousing welcome." He was met here by Nehru's special envoy, P. N. Menon, who had previously been the Consul General in Lhasa. Over the next few days, meetings took place between the Indian government officials and the escaped Tibetans, wherein the circumstances of their flight were discussed. The Tibetans requested that India should mediate with China and "espouse the cause of Tibetan Independence." Menon told the Dalai Lama and his officials that they should exercise caution and restraint at the moment in speaking to the press.

While His Holiness recuperated in Bomdila for ten days, hundreds of press reporters and camera crews from across the world were gathering in Tezpur, Assam. About their journey of almost 150 kilometers from Bomdila to Tezpur, Har Mander Singh recounts,

> I have a vivid memory of how His Holiness and we moved…on 15
> April. In the first group, there were two tutors and family members

On 18 April 1959, after recuperating in Bomdila, the Dalai Lama greeted a huge crowd in Tezpur, where the world's press was waiting. A dais had been quickly erected and the surroundings decorated in welcome. As he appeared, smiling broadly and greeting the crowd, monks blew conch shells and struck a note on brass gongs.

of His Holiness, carried by six jeeps…In the second group, His Holiness [was] accompanied by myself, Menon, and my wife. At that time there were around twenty-five jeeps in all.

After a brief halt at a small road camp called Foothills, 48 kilometers outside the city, on the afternoon of 18 April, His Holiness arrived in Tezpur. He was taken aback by the number of people present. The international press persons had rushed to Tezpur after camping in Kalimpong for days to report "the story of the century." He was overwhelmed to find hundreds of messages of good wishes from across the world waiting for him at the Circuit House he was taken to. As His Holiness recalls, "For a few moments I was lost in gratitude, but the urgent necessities of the present were almost overwhelming. The most pressing requirement, I felt, was to prepare a short statement to give the many people waiting for some word for me to send back to their newspapers."

By then China had already issued an official statement claiming that the Dalai Lama had not left of his own accord but had been coerced by the "reactionary elite." Chou En-lai said that the Seventeen-Point Agreement stood null and void, that the Chinese central government had dissolved the Tibetan national assembly, and the Panchen Lama had been appointed to head the PCART. As the Chinese asserted that His Holiness had been kidnapped by "rebels" backed by the Tibetan elite,

Both Tibetans and Indians gathered on the sports field of Darrang College, Tezpur, to welcome, and be blessed by, the Dalai Lama. Also, among the crowd to greet His Holiness was Tenzin Norgay, who along with Edmund Hillary had reached the summit of Everest in 1953. Worried about the safety of His Holiness, he had traveled from Darjeeling, almost 600 kilometers away.

the Indian government was keen that the exiled Tibetan leader did not issue any provocative statement. The Chinese had spread the canard that evidence to their claim that the Dalai Lama was forcibly taken could be found in messages that he exchanged with Tan Guansan, senior Chinese military official in Lhasa, while spontaneous protests were taking place outside Norbulingka. It appears that the Indian foreign ministry had noted the Chinese claims and, in an effort to not further provoke them, sent a carefully prepared press statement to His Holiness. Official documents reveal that on 12 April, Nehru wrote to S. Dutt, the foreign secretary:

> I agree with you that some kind of a statement should be issued by the Dalai Lama as he emerges from the NEFA. The proposed communique is not suitable for this purpose. At the same time, the statement he might issue at Tezpur should not be too bold. It should deal with the circumstances of his leaving Lhasa, but something more is needed.

Surkhang Lhawang Topgyal, left, and Yuthog Jigme Dorje, right, delivering the Tezpur statement on behalf of the Dalai Lama on 18 April 1959, Tezpur.

His Holiness saw Heinrich Harrer there, reporting for *Life* magazine, and later shared, "When I saw him suddenly, I just remembered my past life in Tibet, where I used to enjoy freedom and happiness."

In the final statement read by two Tibetan government officials on behalf of the Dalai Lama, the events leading up to His Holiness' secret departure from Lhasa were summarized succinctly. Read in English and Tibetan, it stated that Tibet had always maintained its strong desire of independence, that Tibetan people were different from the Han of China, and that the Seventeen-Point Agreement was signed under duress. Apprehending a threat to His Holiness' life amid a popular public uprising in Lhasa, it was decided that he would flee. The statement also brought up the historic ties between Tibet and India:

> The Dalai Lama is extremely grateful to the people and Government of India for their spontaneous and generous welcome, as well as the asylum granted to him and his followers. India and Tibet have religious, cultural, and trade links extending over a thousand years, and for Tibetans it has always been the land of enlightenment, having given birth to Lord Buddha. The Dalai Lama is deeply touched by the kind greeting extended to him on his safe arrival in India by the Prime Minister Shri Jawaharlal Nehru and his colleagues in the Government of India. The Dalai Lama has already sent a reply to this message of greetings.

Gyalo Thondup says that in hindsight, the Tezpur Statement was "a masterpiece of dignity and discretion." The Chinese, however, reacted angrily to India's decision to grant asylum to His Holiness. In a statement to the Indian foreign secretary issued on 16 May 1959, the Chinese denounced the Tezpur Statement (and the Mussoorie press conference that was to follow), which advocated "the independence of Tibet" as a "wanton attack on the Chinese government." India, they said, had accepted that Tibet was a province of China under the Panchsheel Agreement. In a highly charged statement, the Chinese accused India of interfering in China's internal affairs and of being two-faced.

MUSSOORIE AND
THE FIRST PRESS CONFERENCE

His Holiness left Tezpur on a special train for Mussoorie after lunch on 18 April. The decision to move His Holiness to Mussoorie had been made by Prime Minister Nehru who conveyed to Gyalo Thondup that it would be a suitable place for the Dalai Lama to stay. As Gyalo Thondup recalls, Nehru did not want too much global attention on the Dalai Lama; he wanted His Holiness "out of the limelight." There had been suggestions from the Americans to settle the Dalai Lama in Thailand or Switzerland, but India was the ideal place. Its proximity to Tibet was one thing, but there was also the matter of old historic ties.

His Holiness recalls that the train journey from Tezpur to Dehra Dun took several days. Crowds thronged railway stations, and at times tracks, wherever they passed through and shouted greetings at His Holiness. He found this very moving, recalling, "no one was unaware of my presence." They stopped at towns along the way, including Siliguri, Benares, and Lucknow, where His Holiness addressed crowds who threw flowers at him. It was most heartwarming for him and his entourage to experience such a welcome after the recent upheaval. Upon reaching Mussoorie, they were taken to Birla House, the residence of a leading industrialist and owner of the *Hindustan Times* newspaper, which was to be his temporary home for almost a year.

A few days into his arrival, His Holiness was compelled to issue another statement to counter the propaganda issued by the Chinese news agency Xinhua that the Tezpur Statement was "a crude document, lame in reasoning, full of lies and loopholes" and was not issued by the Dalai Lama.

On 24 April, Nehru came to Mussoorie to meet the Dalai Lama. In a meeting that lasted for hours and was fraught with tensions, His Holiness spoke candidly with the Indian leader. As he recalls, Nehru appeared to be irritated with him at times when the former brought up certain issues, including the establishment of his government away from Lhasa. On occasion, he even banged the table in indignation and

The Dalai Lama being received at the Siliguri railway station, in the state of West Bengal, on the morning of 19 April 1959. The special train from Tezpur had thirteen coaches and three tons of baggage. Among the many who had arrived at the station to greet the Dalai Lama were the chief secretary of the state and many senior Indian officials, King of Sikkim Palden Thondup Namgyal and his son, the queen mother of Bhutan Rani Choeying Wangmo, His Holiness' younger sister Jetsun Pema, former Tibetan government officials, and many others.

"his lower lip quivered with anger as he spoke" when the Dalai Lama said he wished for Tibetan independence without bloodshed. Nehru dismissed this as not possible. In a record of the meeting, Nehru appears characteristically blunt:

> It does not matter who started the fight and there is no good complaining. Only old women complain! Physically it is not possible to fight on behalf of Tibet. Even such a suggestion will harm them [the Tibetans] and their cause. Sympathy at present for Tibet cannot be converted into help by any country.

Cursing or quarreling with China was not a solution, Nehru went on to tell the Dalai Lama. He told him not to issue any further statements for four to six weeks. As for the question of recognizing the

new government of the Tibetans, which His Holiness intended to set up in exile, the Indian prime minister characterized that as "an act of war against China." Although the meeting ended on a cordial note, the Dalai Lama "experienced a profound feeling of disappointment."

The Dalai Lama waited for over six weeks, in strict and literal accordance of Nehru's instruction, and then held a press conference on 20 June without consulting the Indian establishment. The press interest in the story had not waned despite two months passing since his dramatic escape. Over 130 reporters from across the world attended this press conference at Birla House. At this interaction, His Holiness recounted the events that transpired leading to his secret flight. At the outset, he repudiated the Seventeen-Point Agreement. He then brought to notice the widespread Chinese atrocities across Tibet and called upon the Chinese

Nehru rides through Mussoorie, 24 April 1959. Later he met the Dalai Lama at Birla House, where they discussed Tibet's plight.

authorities to conduct a neutral investigation by an internal commission. The Chinese, he said, had gone back on their word of granting autonomy to the Tibetans and had frustrated his efforts at reform and peace in his land. He further stated that it was on Nehru's advice that he had returned to Lhasa three years earlier, although at the time he had been seeking exile. Reflecting back on this moment in his autobiography, His Holiness says that although the conference had wide press coverage, he had "underestimated the power of an efficiently conducted public relations campaign such as the Chinese government were able to carry out." Interacting with the press later, he stated again, "wherever I am, accompanied by my government, the Tibetan people recognize us as the government of Tibet," thereby indicating in principle the existence of the Tibetan government in exile. That evening, the Indian government issued a statement that it did not recognize the Dalai Lama's government in exile. The Tibetans had angered Nehru on all counts—by conducting the press conference and by issuing what he saw as provocative statements that were damaging to India's relations with China. His Holiness and his officials were hurt, but as he recalls, his "wounded feelings" gave way to gratitude.

During this time, he was also able to shed some of the old formal

The Dalai Lama held his first press conference in India at Birla House on 20 June 1959. Yuthok Jigme Dorje and Rinchen Sadutshang acted as translators. Behind His Holiness are Liusher Foreign Affairs Minister (left), and the Dalai Lama's elder brother, Gyalo Thondup (right).

His Holiness with his Mussoorie hosts, the Birla family, who offered their mansion for the use of His Holiness and members of his family and staff. Seen in the photograph are K. K. Birla and his wife Manorama Devi with their three daughters, (from left to right) Nandini, Shobhana, and Jyotsna.

practices that were expected of his position. He held weekly audiences on the grounds of Birla House and met with many Tibetans who informed him of the ongoing trouble in Tibet. One of the many Tibetans who met His Holiness at this time was a young Rinchen Khando who was studying at Wynbern Allen School. She, along with a group of Tibetan students, was granted an audience with the Dalai Lama. Years later, in 1972, she would marry his youngest brother, Tendzin Choegyal. She went on to become a formidable member of the Tibetan establishment as the education minister, was founding president of the Tibetan Women's Association, and also founded the Tibetan Nuns Project.

This year was also a turning point in our lives as my father decided to move to Mussoorie and help the Dalai Lama. He volunteered to join the Tibetan government in exile and was appointed a teacher in the first Tibetan school in Mussoorie.

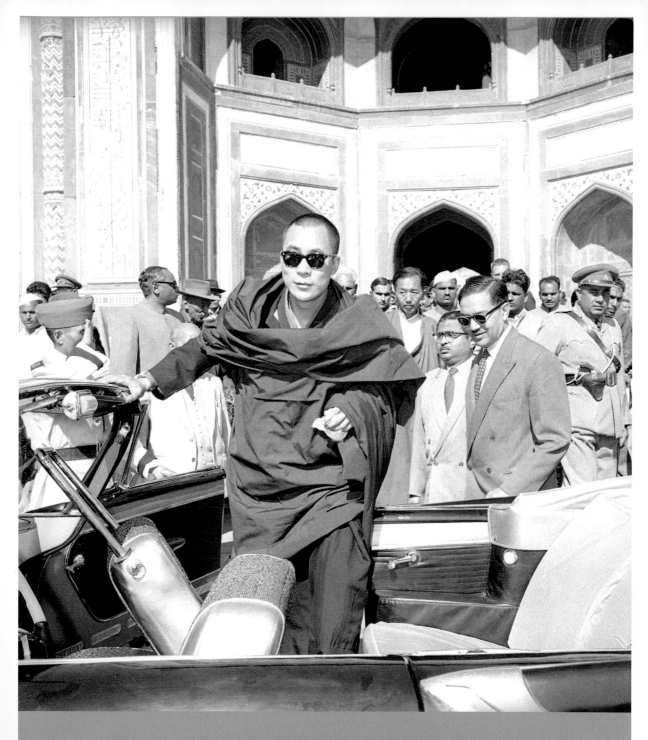

In September 1959, the Dalai Lama traveled to Delhi to meet Prime Minister Nehru and other Indian politicians. He became more familiar with India when he went on an extended trip around the country. From December 1959 to February 1960, he visited Agra, Sanchi, Ajanta, Ellora, Bombay, Madras, Madurai, Tiruchirappali, Bangalore, Mysore, Patna, Gorakhpur, Kushalnagar, Varanasi, and Bodh Gaya. This picture was taken at the Taj Mahal.

UPRISING IS CRUSHED IN TIBET

After His Holiness escaped from Lhasa, the Chinese unleashed a brutal pogrom. Rumors of the Dalai Lama's flight had spread like wildfire. On 19 March, thousands of women marched down the streets shouting anti-Chinese slogans and cries of support for His Holiness. That night, Norbulingka Palace was shelled, and His Holiness' private quarters were hit. Machine gun fire was directed at the Tibetan fighters who shot back with their rifles. Tibetan soldiers and resistance fighters were mowed down by the superior fire power of the Chinese. In parts of the city, some fighters held onto advantageous positions at higher elevations; some held Potala, the Jokhang Temple, and Chagpori Hill. The city streets were locked down in cross-fire battles between the two groups, the city exploding in street-to-street fighting. The Tibetan fighters were uncoordinated, ill-prepared for battle, and consequently many became sitting ducks for Chinese snipers. Loudspeakers continuously urged them to surrender. Many stayed until the bitter end and either died or were imprisoned. At Chagpori, volunteer fighters were told to evacuate before the final onslaught, during which every last Tibetan soldier died. The Chinese suffered losses, too, particularly at Chagpori, where a bitter battle ensued. The fifteenth-century Tibetan Medical College atop the hill was destroyed by the shelling. Later, PLA

The Tibetan "surrender" from the Potala Palace, was re-enacted several times for the purposes of Chinese propaganda.

forces surrounded the Jokhang Temple complex, which was guarded by Tibetan fighters. The Chinese had a clear view of those trying to escape. Soon Chinese armored cars were driving through the streets. The monks at Drepung and Sera monasteries were mobilized into action. The third major monastery, Gaden, is farther away from Lhasa. Many younger monks also joined the uprising, helping to retrieve guns and passing messages. Many people tried to escape, while some perished on the way.

PLA general Tan Guansan and Ngabo Ngawang Jigme urged the Tibetans to lay down arms. On 23 March, the PLA hoisted their flag at Potala Palace. The PLA forces were piling up dead bodies around the city. This was meant to intimidate the locals. By the end of 24 March, the Tibetan uprising was completely crushed. According to Chinese claims, 5,300 rebels were killed. But as His Holiness says, there is no clarity on the loss of life. A satchel of 1,500 PLA documents seized by Tibetan fighters operating from Mustang, in what came to be known as the Blue Satchel Raid during the mid-1960s, said that between March and September of 1959, 87,000 Tibetans died due to Chinese military action.

Tibetan monks, surrounded by soldiers of the PLA, lay down their arms in the vicinity of Lhasa, late April or early May 1959. This was also shot as film for propaganda purposes. Monks had taken up arms to defend themselves and their monasteries, but they were not used to using them and were quickly overcome.

UNITED NATIONS APPEALS AND THE INTERNATIONAL COMMISSION OF JURISTS

Taking note of the uprising in Tibet, the International Commission of Jurists (ICJ) instituted an inquiry to look into the legal aspects of the situation. After two months of investigation, Purshottam Trikamdas, a senior lawyer of the Supreme Court of India submitted a report in July 1959. Their report concluded that Tibet "was virtually an independent country" from 1912 to 1950, between the time of the Thirteenth Dalai Lama's Declaration of Independence to the invasion and occupation of Tibet in 1949–1950. The report estimated the loss of life during the March uprising to be around 20,000. From the violation of the Seventeen-Point Agreement, illegal confiscation of property, denial of freedom of religion, destruction of religious shrines and structures, to the systematic killing and imprisonments, it outlined China's policy of widespread oppression and "deliberate violation of fundamental human rights."

In September 1959, His Holiness met Nehru in Delhi and spoke of raising the Tibet issue at the United Nations. An irritated Nehru dismissed the suggestion. His Holiness wanted to keep the world

Below, left: The Tibetan delegation (left to right) Rinchen Sadutshang, W. D. Shakabpa, and Gyalo Thondup in front of the United Nations building in New York, 1 October 1959. Gyalo Thondup testified that their appeals were based on the International Commission of Jurists' report.

Below, right: In 1960, Indian senior lawyer Purshottam Trikamdas and his colleagues presented this report to the ICJ, whose Secretary-General submitted it to the UN and the press.

informed of Tibet. During this time Gyalo Thondup, W. D. Shakabpa, Rinchen Sadutshang, and their Indian legal counsel, D. K. Sen, traveled to New York to attend a UN General Assembly debate on Tibet. Sadutshang recalls that Secretary-General Dag Hammarskjold gave them a sympathetic ear, but most member delegates "knew next to nothing about Tibet." His Holiness had been writing to various governments for support. With little experience in international relations and diplomacy, he found it difficult but persevered.

In October, the Federation of Malaya (Malaysia) and Ireland introduced a draft resolution at the UN General Assembly which passed in Tibet's favor. Without naming China, it stated that it was "gravely concerned" at reports of the denial of fundamental human rights and freedoms of the Tibetan people and affirmed the charter of the UN for a peaceful world order. India abstained from voting. In December 1961, the UN passed another resolution, sponsored by El Salvador, Ireland, Thailand, and Malaya, which recalled the previous one, noting with "deep anxiety the severe hardships" of the Tibetan people and renewing its call to end the deprivation of their human rights. Despite the strong language, no concrete action followed to change the situation in Tibet. The Chinese appeared to be immune to world opinion.

His Holiness, at age twenty-four, gives evidence at the ICJ hearing on 14 November 1959 at Birla House, Mussoorie. Seated next to him (right) Purshottam Trikamdas, Indian chairman of the Legal Inquiry Committee on Tibet, investigating the genocide of the Tibetan people by the PLA.

SHELTER FOR REFUGEES

Soon after His Holiness escaped to India, around 80,000 refugees followed him. Many of those who crossed the border were placed in two transit camps—Missamari, near Tezpur in Assam, and Buxa Duar, a former British prisoner-of-war camp in West Bengal, close to the border with Bhutan. Most of the refugees were in poor health, destitute, and starved. His Holiness immediately dispatched officials to the camps to assess the situation. Their misery was exacerbated by the weather; the Tibetans were not used to such heat and humidity. Infectious diseases

were rife, and many succumbed. His Holiness requested Nehru to move those in Missamari to cooler climes. By that time, Tibetan officials had made plans with their Indian counterparts to employ the physically able at major road construction sites in the Himalayan region and across North India. The first group of 3,394 people was sent to Sikkim in September 1959. The Missamari camp shut in July 1960, and the refugees were sent to 95 road construction camps. Over 700 elderly lamas were accommodated in Dalhousie, while the junior lamas were sent to Buxa.

His Holiness recalls that despite Nehru's initial diffidence and India's economic difficulties, great efforts were made to rehabilitate the Tibetans.

Thousands of Tibetans followed the Dalai Lama into exile. Many were first given shelter at the Missamari transit camp in Assam, 1959.

On 25 April 1959, the very next day after first meeting Nehru in Mussoorie, His Holiness called an emergency meeting with his senior officials. Harboring false hopes of an early return to Tibet was not practical; he advised instead that

> we must concentrate on building a strong community in exile so that when the time eventually came, we would be able to resume our lives back home transformed by our experience.

The living conditions of Tibetan road builders, often working in remote areas, were difficult and many died, including children. Others earned just enough to survive the first few years of exile.

Nehru requested various state governments to donate land and the Chief Minister of the Unified State of Mysore (now the state of Karnataka) responded immediately with 3,000 acres of uninhabited jungle land amid an elevated area not too far from Mysore city at Bylakuppe. The idea was to settle an initial number of 3,000 refugees, with a budgetary outlay of Rs 40 lakh. His Holiness was at first hesitant about the area due to its hot climate, but the need for a long-term plan convinced him to accept the

Left: The Dalai Lama instructed that Buxa function as a "new college offering the curriculum of all four lineages of Tibetan Buddhism." He sent his senior tutor, Ling Rinpoche, to lecture there. Debate sessions were held outside the cramped living quarters. During a period of ten years, a rich traditional education was enjoyed by 1,500 monastics, one of whom recalled, "I've never seen such a united spirit of sharing."

land. By February 1960, the first batch of nearly 700 refugees moved in. They cleared the jungle, making it habitable, digging wells, constructing houses and kitchen gardens, and would in a few years' time transform it into an agricultural settlement. His Holiness first visited the settlements in Mysore State in March 1962. Within years, Bylakuppe became self-sustaining and a model settlement for many others.

Below: The Tibetan Refugee Self Help Center in Darjeeling was set up in October 1959 by Diki Dolkar (center), wife of the Dalai Lama's older brother Gyalo Thondup, supported by the governments of India and West Bengal and various foreign aid organizations. Diki Dolkar remained its guiding force until her passing in 1986. The center continues to be self-sustaining, producing handicrafts and supporting a large number of families to this day.

DHARAMSALA: A NEW ABODE

The limited success at the United Nations in October 1959 did little to dampen His Holiness' enthusiasm to seek international support for the Tibetan cause. However, there was another pressing matter that needed his immediate attention—the rehabilitation of the thousands of Tibetans who followed him to India. His Holiness went to Delhi again in December 1959 and called upon the prime minister. He also met the Indian President, Dr. Rajendra Prasad, whose humility moved him to tears. His Holiness recalls that the elderly Indian statesman was "a true Bodhisattva," meaning one who has great compassion. At this time, the Dalai Lama revisited places of pilgrimage he had earlier traveled to in early 1957 during his first visit to India. At Bodh Gaya, he ordained a group of *bhikshus* at the Tibetan monastery near the Mahabodhi Temple, adjacent to the Bodhi Tree where Gautama Buddha attained enlightenment. In Sarnath and the Deer Park, he conducted teachings

On the occasion of a special rite, monks carrying offerings and a small mandala house accompany the Dalai Lama holding a *thangka* painting, as yet to be unfurled, as they circumambulate Swarg Ashram.

Facing page: One of the first photographs taken of the Dalai Lama at his new home in Dharamsala, Swarg Ashram.

for over 2,000 Tibetan refugees. It was both a poignant and special occasion. The hardship and suffering of those who had fled their homes was evident, and the setting was special—the Lord Buddha had taught his disciples here more than 2,500 years before.

On his return to Mussoorie, His Holiness was taken aback to learn that the Indian government had decided to relocate him permanently to Dharamsala, in the state of Himachal Pradesh. Not knowing where it was, the Dalai Lama looked for it on the map—it was a remote hill station, much farther away from the capital, New Delhi. Thinking back to when he found out, he writes:

> I began to have some suspicion that the Indian government was now trying to hide us away somewhere without good communications in the hope that we Tibetans would disappear from the sight of the outside world.

Gyalo Thondup and other senior Tibetan officials were dismayed by this development and felt this move may prove to be an obstacle

The Dalai Lama with a television crew in the sitting room at Swarg Ashram. I had by now started working in the Private Office of the Dalai Lama, and can be seen in this photograph (in monk's robes).

Facing page: The Dalai Lama addressing a crowd gathered on an old tennis court below Swarg Ashram, where during the early years the Dalai Lama used to play badminton in the evenings.

since the town had poor connectivity, high rainfall, no hotels to speak of, and dilapidated houses. His Holiness requested that he be allowed to send a member of the *kashag* to Dharamsala on a reconnaissance trip. W. G. Kundeling visited Dharamsala and returned after a week to report, "Dharamsala water is better than Mussoorie milk." This settled matters and the decision was made to relocate. Years later, when W. G. Kundeling moved to Mussoorie, His Holiness remarked in jest that perhaps he preferred the milk in Mussoorie.

On 29 April 1960, His Holiness left Birla House and traveled by train, first to Pathankot in Punjab, and then onward by road to Dharamsala. He vividly describes the journey to his new home, which would become the seat of his government in exile, a home to many Tibetan refugees, and an inspiring destination for visitors and travelers from around the world. In a hair-raising drive in a jeep along steep, winding roads that led up to the mountain village of McLeod Ganj, His Holiness recalls the beautiful countryside that they had traversed. His new dwelling was the aptly named Swarg Ashram—the Heavenly Retreat. Previously known as Highcroft House, it had been the home of a colonial era civil servant.

I can be seen with my colleague and mentor, Kungo Tara, who had worked with my father in Tibet. Venerable Tara became one of the longest serving members of the Tibetan government and aides to His Holiness the Dalai Lama. He passed away in 2013.

Facing: In the early years in Dharamsala, the Dalai Lama had two Lhasa apso dogs, Senge (Lion) and Tashi (Good Fortune). Here Senge sits at his feet in the sitting room of Swarg Ashram.

The Dalai Lama regularly took energetic hikes during his first year or so in Dharamsala. He wore practical lay clothes during these hikes and would greet local people on the way to Triund, a ridge below the Dhauladar range above McLeod Ganj. His Holiness is seen here with a family from the Gaddi tribe of Triund.

It presently houses a mountaineering institute. Situated at a height with a panoramic view, it proved suitable for His Holiness. He shared the new home with members of his family and pets, two Lhasa apso dogs. A few other houses were also taken up for his officials. With spectacular views of the Dhauladhar range of the Himalayas, His Holiness and his entourage began a new life in their now permanent home.

Not long after they settled in, Tibetan refugees started populating the town, and within a matter of months, the once desolate, "haunted" hill station was transformed forever. It was during these early days of settling in that I first worked in the Council for Tibetan Education, which was housed at Retreat Cottage, presently occupied by Jetsun

A group of newly arrived refugees, living in tents in Dharamsala, in the 1960s.

Pema (His Holiness's older sister). This was also the time I got my first personal audience with His Holiness the Dalai Lama. The opportunity to join the Office of His Holiness, I feel, was being at the right place at the right time. It was a great blessing for me. I started as an English typist and clerk in the small office in Swarg Ashram. Working in the Private Office had its own share of privileges. I remember playing badminton in the front courtyard of the bungalow and playing table tennis in one of the bigger rooms, where His Holiness, too, joined us occasionally.

However, these were days of relentless work. His Holiness wanted radical changes. Various new Tibetan government departments were created. There was immense need to focus on education, rehabilitation, and women, who were encouraged to take part in government.

Nowrojee's

Under the British, Dharamsala had once been a popular hill station and had served as the district headquarters of Kangra. But an earthquake in 1905 had left the town almost deserted except for a few shops and some old colonial buildings. McLeod Ganj, a suburb of Dharamsala where His Holiness set up home in 1960, got its name from a British lieutenant governor of Punjab (1865–1870), Sir Donald Friell McLeod.

Our early years in Dharamsala were very modest. As one entered McLeod Ganj from Dharamsala there stood a general store called Nowrojee & Sons, which was established in 1860. It belonged to a Parsi family who initially catered to British officials, selling essential goods, food items, toiletries, tobacco, alcohol, and even guns at one time. Five generations of the Nowrojee family ran the shop until recently. Nauzer Nowrojee, who was at the helm when we first moved to Dharamsala, became a friend of His Holiness and many other Tibetans, including myself. He had properties around McLeod Ganj and one of them was requisitioned by the Indian government for the reestablishment of the Namgyal monks in 1961. Nauzer's nephew, the award-winning novelist Rohinton Mistry, based a character on him (the shopkeeper, Farokh Kohlah) in his book *A Fine Balance*. The day before Nauzer passed away in 2000, he had a chance encounter with his old friend, the Dalai Lama, who had just returned from a trip to Belfast. On his passing, I paid respects to his family on behalf of the Office of His Holiness. The shop holds many memories for us. In the early days of the Tibetan Youth Congress, members of the Central Executive Committee would often gather there to discuss matters. Ngari Rinpoche was also a part of these sessions, which often became quite loud and raucous. We were passionate in our debates, which often became all the more intense when some members had beer.

Opposite Nowrojee's were two roads: the upper one leading to Conium House, where the Drama School, later to be known as the Tibetan Institute for Performing Arts (TIPA), was housed. At the other end of McLeod Ganj was Mortimer Hall which housed the Tibetan government in exile. This included accommodation for the senior officials as well as other staff members. The Council for Tibetan Education, as it was known then, was located at Retreat Cottage. There were just three cars in town, one of them being His Holiness'. Things have changed dramatically since, and it is now a bustling town with numerous restaurants, cabs, and hotels.

REFORMING THE TIBETAN ADMINISTRATION

In the mid-1960s, His Holiness presented evidence before ICJ's Legal Inquiry Committee in Dharamsala. Once again, their investigation vindicated the Tibetan viewpoint. During his interaction with the Committee, His Holiness realized the need for administrative reform when a British member asked if the Tibetans monitored the official broadcasts of Radio Peking. He was shocked to hear that they did not. Lagging far behind, His Holiness described the situation as "a lack of sophistication" and immediately set up a monitoring committee.

Earlier in the year, during his visit to Bodh Gaya in February, His Holiness had spoken about the need for elections and democratic governance. He envisaged a legislative body of freely elected representatives from the three different provinces of Tibet and nominated members from the four main Buddhist schools. On 2 September 1960, he inaugurated the Commission of the Tibetan People's Deputies which would function as a house of parliament.

Some of the older members were resistant to the changes, but supported His Holiness nonetheless. Despite great hardships, adverse living conditions, and meager salaries, no one complained. As His Holiness recalled later, they "did all they could to rebuild the shattered lives of our people, entirely without thought of personal gain."

The next step was to draft a constitution. The Foreign Minister, Liusher, took on the job with Sadutshang as his deputy. A five-member committee was appointed to look into the matter of creating a draft constitution. The committee approached Supreme Court lawyer Purshottam Trikamdas, who had been Mahatama Gandhi's secretary in 1919, and had been of great help to the Tibetans with the ICJ. As a dual system, the draft authorized the Dalai Lama as the spiritual *and* temporal head of state. Trikamdas based his work on the Indian constitution but studied those of other Buddhist countries such as Sri Lanka, Burma, and Thailand. His draft constitution struck a balance by incorporating an independent judiciary and executive, and traditional Tibetan values.

Facing page, left: The original Nowrojee store opened on the main square of McLeod Ganj in 1860. The iconic store shut down in 2020.

Facing page, right: Mr Nauzer and Mrs Mani Nowrojee of McLeod Ganj catered to their new Tibetan customers with enthusiasm and formed lasting friendships, including with the Dalai Lama.

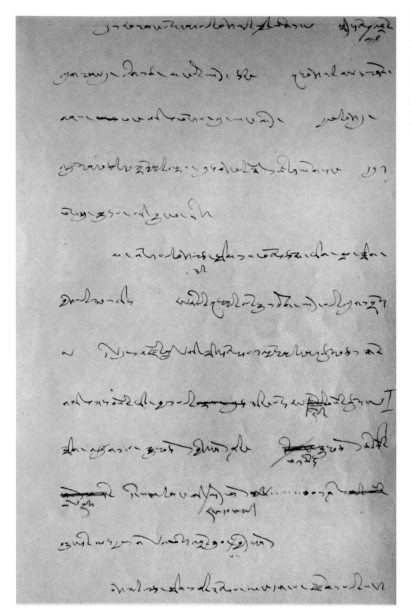

It was also mandated that a two-thirds majority of the assembly could remove the Dalai Lama as the head of state—a clause insisted upon by His Holiness despite fierce opposition. Sadutshang mentions that they also took the help of India's then law minister, G. S. Pathak. The draft was

completed in late 1963, two years after the process began. Sadutshang and Narkyi Ngawang Dhondup set out to translate it into Tibetan soon after. The Tibetan government in exile continued to function under this constitution until it was amended four decades later in June 1991, whereupon it became the Charter of Tibetans in Exile. In the early 1960s, various government departments were set up, including a home department, which facilitated refugee housing and rehabilitation; an education department, which would set up schools and train teachers; a religious department to administer the affairs of monks and set up monasteries; a health department to set up clinics; and a publicity department.

The Dalai Lama, government officials, and the Tibetan public gathered at Mortimer Hall in McLeod Ganj to celebrate the fourth anniversary of the promulgation of the draft constitution in 1967.

EDUCATION: A PRIORITY

Within weeks of his reaching Dharamsala, His Holiness opened the first nursery for refugee children arriving from Tibet, some of whom were orphans. He appointed his elder sister Tsering Dolma Taklha as the head of the Tibetan Refugee Nursery. She proved to be an outstanding leader. The Dalai Lama writes that she was never one to give into despair and always kept a positive attitude. She had acquired the fierce temper prevalent in the family, but was at heart a kind and compassionate person.

As the Dalai Lama recalls, these early days were very difficult due to the lack of resources. By year's end, scores more children arrived, and at one point, more than 120 children were living in a bungalow meant for one family, with five to six sharing a bed. His Holiness says that despite the dire conditions, it was a joyful experience each time he visited these children for "parentless as they were, these destitutes were so full of laughter and joy that they seemed to make a mockery of their hardship." Refugee children from Nepal and Bhutan also arrived,

The Tibetans helped prepare the land for the first new school buildings.

Facing page: Tsering Dolma, founder and director of the Tibetan Refugee Nursery, Dharamsala, with two pupils in their new uniforms. In 1972, the nursery was formally registered and renamed the Tibetan Children's Village (TCV).

putting more strain on the already overstretched resources. The spread of infectious diseases was an immediate danger. Over the next few years, more premises were acquired to accommodate the children. Within a few years, over 11,000 children were being taken care of. Over time, the facility grew into the Tibetan Children's Village (TCV). The Indian government was supportive of the efforts, but during the early years the conditions were such that there was never enough food, medicines, or clothes.

Tragically, Tsering Dolma passed away in 1964 at the age of forty-five due to cancer. She had devoted her life in exile to the TCV. The responsibility then passed onto His Holiness' younger sister, Jetsun Pema, who had studied in Darjeeling and Switzerland, and was preparing to enter the service of His Holiness' Office. Taking on the mantle with the utmost dedication and enthusiasm, she would successfully oversee the expansion of TCV centers across India. From its earliest stage as a facility that provided basic care to refugee children, over the next decade

The first fifty-one children brought to Dharamsala by His Holiness in May 1960, after he sorrowfully heard of many infant deaths in the harsh environment of the roadworkers' camps in Jammu. These children became the first pupils of the newly formed Tibetan Refugee Nursery, run by Tsering Dolma (third from left).

Jetsun Pema oversaw its steady development and growth. Financial support started trickling in from international organizations and private donors. This helped to construct classrooms and housing for the children, and the nursery transformed into a small, village-like enclave. In 1971, the organization started a residential school in the nearby town of Patlikhul, and the following year, it was formally registered as the Tibetan Children's Village. Known affectionately as *Ama* (mother in Tibetan), Jetsun Pema has dedicated her life to the organization, refugee children, and their rehabilitation, education, and health. As support grew over time, Jetsun Pema was able to establish a wide network, including ten residential schools, seventeen day schools, three vocational training institutes, three college hostels, and one college. Apart from several other awards, in 2018, the Indian government presented the Nari Shakti Puraskar, the highest civilian honor for women, to Jetsun Pema in recognition of her tireless efforts. Although she retired as the president of the organization in August 2006, after forty-two years of service, she

The Dalai Lama regularly met schoolchildren, inviting them to his home, Swarg Ashram. He took a personal and abiding interest in their welfare, education, and nourishment, recognizing the younger generation as "our future hope for Tibet."

continues to guide the TCV and is closely associated with The Dalai Lama Institute for Higher Studies, Bangalore.

Today only 50 percent of the students are Tibetan refugees; the other half comes from nearby Himalayan towns and villages of northern India. Earlier, 95 percent of those studying at these schools were Tibetan. There are two main reasons for the decline in their numbers. Firstly, in recent years very few children have been able to come from Tibet, and secondly as the economic situation of Tibetans in exile began to improve, families began sending their children to private schools rather than the TCV. The nurseries follow a Montessori teaching system, and the essential school curriculum is

Above: Despite crowded conditions, pupils took to their studies with enthusiasm, learning the different scripts of the Tibetan language. Very few children in Tibet would have had such an opportunity. The Dalai Lama prioritized education for the young above all else.

Left: Jetsun Pema, younger sister of the Dalai Lama, became Director of TCV schools in 1964, following the early death of Tsering Dolma. She continued in her role until her retirement, ensuring the education of more than 50,000 children.

taken from the Indian Central Board of Secondary Education. Sports are not only encouraged but emphasized by the schools, and several pupils have traveled internationally to participate in competitive sporting events. Exchange programs are implemented to broaden the cultural and intellectual horizons of the children. Truly an important achievement, this early intervention by His Holiness and his sisters has been a huge benefit to the exiled community not just in India but throughout the diaspora.

TIBETAN MUSIC, DANCE, AND DRAMA SOCIETY

His Holiness recognized very early on the need to preserve Tibetan heritage, traditions, arts, and culture. Knowing that the Chinese sought to obliterate much of it in Tibet, this became all the more important for him. In autumn 1959, he inaugurated the Tibetan Music, Dance, and Drama Society, which would be the first of several institutes established by the government in exile. A few years later, the organization came to be known as the Tibetan Institute of Performing Arts (TIPA).

However, within about ten years of its existence, the Council for Tibetan Education, which looked after TIPA, decided to close it because of irreconcilable differences between its members. I felt this would be a great mistake and intervened. I requested the Council give me at least two years to reorganize the institute and have it functioning properly again. Once I got their approval, I immediately appointed a new director and office staff, admitted new members, and above all, recruited teachers of music and folk opera from among those who had left Tibet in 1959. What finally helped to establish the institute on firm footing was the opportunity for its members to travel abroad to perform. This was possible when my young brother, Tenzin Namgyal, who was at the time the representative of His Holiness the Dalai Lama in the United States, contacted an American impresario and organized the first trip abroad in 1975. They subsequently traveled to other Western countries.

Tibetan folk opera, *Ache Lhamo,* was first performed in the fourteenth century. The main epic tales are well known to Tibetans and often performed outside informally to audiences who come and go throughout the day. Both the Thirteenth and Fourteenth Dalai Lamas enjoyed opera festivals at

Norbu Tsering, in an oracle costume, photographed in 1964. Formerly a member of the famous Kyormolung opera company in Tibet in the 1960s, he became the teacher of a newly formed troupe in Kailmpong. He became an opera master at TIPA a few years later, remaining as a highly celebrated performer for almost thirty years.

the Norbulingka. The Fourteenth Dalai Lama continues to attend TIPA's annual festival in Dharamsala.

TIPA is now a semiautonomous body that provides training for students in traditional Tibetan performing arts, with a mandate to "preserve and promote Tibetan musical heritage and associated arts." Students who train and graduate from the institute become ambassadors of our culture. TIPA has been conducting the annual Shoton Yoghurt Festival since 1972, where several troupes from across the wider Himalayan region also perform. It originally began nearly two centuries ago at the Drepung Monastery in Tibet at the end of the monks' summer retreat. Commoners would gather and offer yoghurt to the monks. The festival's name thus comes from this tradition of offering *Sho*, yoghurt, at a *ton*, which is a feast.

In the early years of TIPA in Dharamsala, the famous opera *The Two Princesses* was performed. This epic tells the story of Songtsen Gampo's Nepalese and Chinese wives, using a painted backdrop of the Potala Palace to set the scene.

Tibet Mirror and *Sheja* Journals

As far back as 1925, a publication called the *Tibet Mirror* was published from Kalimpong by Gegen Dorje Tharchin, popularly known as Babu Tharchin. He was originally from the Kinnaur/Spiti area of Himachal Pradesh. Most of the first fifty copies were sent to his friends in Lhasa, including one to the Thirteenth Dalai Lama, who became a regular and ardent reader of the paper. He encouraged Tharchin to continue with the publication, to educate him about the changing outside world as well as be a vehicle for communicating the views and wider outlook of Tibetan exiles in Kalimpong. The Fourteenth Dalai Lama inherited the subscription of the late Thirteenth and even visited Babu Tharchin, a meeting I also remember. The *Tibet Mirror* ceased to exist in 1963.

In October 1968, I began a magazine on Tibetan affairs with the help of a friend, Sonam Topgyal, and my brother Tenzin Namgyal Tethong. It began with a contribution of Rs 10,000 from His Holiness and was called *Sheja*, meaning "knowledge." Sonam Topgyal edited it for the first ten years.

Left: Cover page of *Tibet Mirror*, 1 April 1953, with its full name, *The Mirror of the News of Every Country*. With a photo of the Thirteenth Dalai Lama, it continues his biography, mentioning his travels to China and Mongolia, his Dharma teachings in China and during the return journey to Lhasa, and all the good qualities the people of Tibet had prayed for him to possess.

Below, left to right: Memorable pages from *Sheja* magazine, including special covers hand drawn by Tenzin Namgyal Tethong: Moon landing, Road to Tibet, and Gandhi. In between are pages from the "Strange, But True" section, which became quite scientific.

The intention was to provide Tibetans with a better general knowledge and understanding of the world. With news of internal politics, we also included world affairs, international politics, and interesting stories and events. We operated out of a small three-room building in McLeod Ganj and would work until late in the evening to get each edition out. Written in colloquial Tibetan, it was easily accessible and became a source of information and education, which we considered critical towards our goal of justice and freedom from Chinese oppression. The magazine was drawn by hand, then stencils were made and applied to an inked roller to make copies. It made an enormous impact at the time. We also had a popular column called "Strange, But True." We were strained for resources and consequently turned to the Tibetan Government for help in 1971. Another magazine called *Voice of Tibet,* which later became *Tibetan Review,* was started by the senior official and diplomat Lodi Gyari. That also ran into similar trouble. The administration responded with a grant and also set up a new information office to oversee the two publications. These journals finally became a part of the activities run by the Department of Information and International Affairs.

Above, left: "Vision seen in the Lake" was based on Reting Rinpoche's visit to the oracle lake in the search for the new Dalai Lama. World War II events were a big news topic.

Above, right: *Tibet Mirror* also ran advertisements, such as for the latest Baby Ford convertible—a two-door sedan.

MEN TSEE KHANG MEDICAL INSTITUTE

Seventeenth-century Tibet saw the blossoming of Tibetan medicine, with the construction of the first monastic medical college and the writing of several important texts, including Sangye Gyatso's famous *Blue Beryl*. This is a commentary on *The Four Tantras*, the ancient foundational text of Tibetan medical practice. Sangye Gyatso was the regent of the Great Fifth Dalai Lama. The indigenous Tibetan medical system was influenced by knowledge from classical India, China, Persia, and beyond. The medical college on top of Chagpori Hill in Lhasa was destroyed in 1959. However, the Men Tsee Khang school in Shöl village directly below the Potala, founded by the Thirteenth Dalai Lama, survives. Its principal, the eminent monk Khyenrab Norbu, trained

Listening to a number of subtle pulses in the wrist is an essential diagnostic tool in Tibetan medicine. Here, the Dalai Lama is having his pulse read by Dr. Namgyal Tsering.

several doctors who left Tibet to serve the Fourteenth Dalai Lama in India.

The essence of the Tibetan system lies in understanding the five physical elements of earth, water, fire, air, and space. Cosmology and the birth of the universe are also taught to demonstrate a unity of all matter. Medicine and astrology were therefore inextricably connected. Three "tempers" or "humors" of the human body exist in fine equilibrium with the physical elements of the universe, and when this balance is disturbed illness and disease occurs.

In 1960, the Fourteenth Dalai Lama established the Astrology School in Dharamsala, followed in 1961 by the Medical School, headed by doctors Dukhorwa Lodoe Gyatso and Yeshi Dhonden, respectively. Dr. Dhonden also served as the Dalai Lama's physician. Dr. Jamyang Tashi, who had studied under Khyenrab Norbu in Lhasa, headed the pharmacy from 1963 onward. Prior to this, like many educated Tibetans, he had been a roadworker. He identified many rare Tibetan herbs and plants to be used as medicines and served as physician to the Dalai Lama from 1976.

Interest in the traditional Tibetan medical system, or *Sowa Rigpa*, has grown exponentially throughout the world after Dr. Dhonden gained formidable success in curing certain cancers, even those previously thought to be terminal. In 2018, he was awarded India's civilian award, the Padma Shri.

In 1967, the schools merged to become The Tibetan Medical and Astrological Institute, or Men Tsee Khang. Lobsang Dolma, a pioneering doctor, was appointed the first woman Chief Medical Officer in 1972. She had also worked as a road construction worker and was refused entry to the institute in 1962, only to later become its director.

The welcome arrival in the early 1980s of other senior doctors trained in Tibet brought renewed vigor to the Institute; Dr. Tenzin Choedak became the Dalai Lama's senior personal physician, following almost twenty-two years of imprisonment in his homeland.

His Holiness' immediate elder brother, Lobsang Samten, became director of the Men Tsee Khang in 1980. On his death in 1985, his widow, Namgyal Lhamo Taklha, succeeded him.

Dr. Tenzin Choedak (above) and Dr. Yeshi Dhonden (below). Both were exceptional practitioners and became personal physicians to the Dalai Lama in exile.

Spiritual Friends

In the midst of many worldly concerns, His Holiness continued the most valuable studies of all with Tibetan Buddhist masters in exile in India.

His senior tutor, Ling Rinpoche, and junior tutor, Trijang Rinpoche, both accompanied him into exile and assisted him in protecting the Tibetan Buddhist tradition. Ironically, the ancient Indian Nalanda tradition, preserved by Tibetans, is now being passed back to many Indian disciples. Ling Rinpoche and Trijang Rinpoche also exchanged teachings and became good friends, sharing the responsibility of continuing to nourish the Dalai Lama's spiritual development. His Holiness has said that despite the challenges in the 1960s of the rehabilitation of thousands of refugees and unfortunate news trickling out of Tibet, he progressed in his spiritual life by gaining a deeper understanding and experience of *shunyata*, or "emptiness." This intensified as the years passed until on a mental level, he felt little desire or attachment. "These emotions related to the desire realm began to no longer arise in me."

Ling Rinpoche had immense prestige, and at His Holiness's request would undertake arduous tours of Europe and America to give teachings. His Holiness has a special veneration for him as his preceptor for the Bhiksu ordination, which he cherishes deeply. His Holiness also considered Ling Rinpoche as his spiritual bedrock and found solace in his guidance. Soon after I joined the Private Office, I discovered that Trijang Rinpoche is related to me through my maternal side. He was very warm and kind to me, and I had the opportunity to meet him several times. I discussed my desire to join a monastery to undertake Buddhist studies with him. He dissuaded me and said there is no better practice than personally serving a guru like His Holiness, and that knowledge of the dharma is no guarantee for spiritual advancement.

Serkong Tsenshap Rinpoche was the only one of His Holiness' seven debate partners in Tibet who made it to India safely. The Dalai Lama shared a close but formal relationship with the senior and junior tutors, but with Serkong Tsenshap Rinpoche he could relax and joke.

Trijang Rinpoche

Serkong Tsenshap Rinpoche

Ling Rinpoche

RESETTLEMENT AND FOREIGN AID

When His Holiness visited many of the road construction camps and the Bylakuppe settlement in 1961, he found the morale low among the frail, undernourished settlers. He made efforts to boost their flagging spirits, promising them that things would become better. Most of the settlements were set up between 1960 and 1965, including one at Bandhara, Maharashtra. Within two months of their arrival in the camp, seventy refugees had died due to the heat. This caused great alarm, and when His Holiness visited he found the settlers very distraught, with tears in their eyes pleading to be sent to cooler areas. It was His Holiness' compassion and their complete belief in him that saw them through these trying times. He also found that the settlers at Bylakuppe were

The Dalai Lama surveying land in Bylakuppe, Mysore state, in the 1960s. When the refugees first arrived, they lived in tents. The forest had to be cleared before cultivation and construction of houses could begin.

finding it difficult to reconcile the fact that the land clearing they were doing was causing the death of many small insects and other creatures. These initial years were very difficult. The fortitude of the Tibetans, as well as the support of the Indian government and foreign aid agencies helped them tackle many adversities.

Over time, small-scale industries came into being, and the Tibetan Industrial Rehabilitation Society (TIRS) was set up in 1965 to coordinate and support the efforts. Some settlements were created as Agro-Industrial ones, including the woolen mill at Bir, a tea estate at Bir and Chauntra, traditional crafts at Bejnath, a limestone quarry at Kumrao, a lime plant at Sataun, a fiberglass factory at Poanta Sahib, etc. The Himalayan Marketing Society was established to market the products made by these centers.

International governments and agencies helped during these early years. The idea of sending some of the children abroad to be adopted also became a reality. His Holiness mentions that he contacted a Swiss friend, Dr. Aeschimann, in this regard. Consequently, the Swiss Government

His Holiness visited South India in the early 1960s to liaise with those in charge of development. He appointed a head of each settlement. Behind His Holiness (far left), hardly visible, is Wangdu Dorji, Kalon for Home and Rehabilitation.

Others from left to right are: the Indian official in charge of the Tibetan settlements in Mysore state; Jampa Wangdu, an official from the Tibetan Security Office; T. C. Tara (hardly visible, wearing a hat); and Jampa Tsondru, official in charge of the settlement in Bylakuppe. His Holiness frequently consulted Nehru, Indian officials, and foreign sponsors.

agreed to take in 200 children immediately and settle them with Swiss families. Schemes for older children to receive education and for adult refugees to be resettled in Switzerland also came into being. My uncle, Rakra Rinpoche, along with his wife, Aunt Dolma la, and my other aunt, Sopal la, accompanied the first group of Tibetan children sent to the Pestalozzi Children's Village in Trogen, Switzerland in early 1960. Rakra Rinpoche acted as a Tibetan teacher and foster parent to these children.

These initial steps were greatly appreciated by His Holiness and the Tibetan administration. In the mid-1960s, contributions from international aid agencies began to come in. Individual donors from across the world were also generous with their support. Many Tibetan aid agencies opened up to help support a number of programs—from children's health and education, to resettlement efforts.

His Holiness draws particular attention to two individuals whose contribution he saw as important during the early 1960s. Maurice Frydman, a Polish man whom the Dalai Lama first met in 1956, and his friend Wanda Dynowska, known as Uma Devi, who was also Polish and lived in the Thekchen Choling premises in the 1970s, very close to the residence of His Holiness. Frydman's help in drawing up the

When he visited settlements in South India, the Dalai Lama made a point of meeting everyone who had helped.

At first, the Tibetan settlers planted crops which failed, as they were only used to high altitude farming in Tibet. Based on cooperation between Mr Luthi, a Swiss agricultural engineer, and the Indian government, well-researched programs for land use, soil tests, mechanization, and irrigation were implemented. Maize was—and is still—the dominant crop in the settlements. By the end of 1966, Bylakuppe settlement became self-supporting.

Tibetan educational policy in the 1960s and planning the settlements was very valuable. Uma Devi devoted her life to the betterment of the Tibetan people, especially in providing scholarships to deserving young Tibetans. The Dalai Lama also mentions Mr Luthi of the Swiss Red Cross who he says worked tirelessly and selflessly for Tibetan refugees.

The efforts for resettlement of the Tibetans in India were shaped and nurtured by His Holiness' own tireless passion, dedication, and vision. It is his unique position as both a political and a spiritual leader that has guided the exiled community and has also provided leadership to those who remain in Tibet, as well as the diaspora. As the scholar Franz Michael has written, the exiled Tibetans "are not ordinary refugees." They, he argues, "have taken refuge not as individuals alone, but rather as a national polity…" The story of the Tibetans in India, he adds further, is one "that demonstrates the vitality of the Tibetan culture and of the people."

In 1969, monks who had previously lived at the Buxa lama camp in West Bengal were transferred to the Mundgod settlement, the second in Karnataka (previously Mysore state). They established Ganden Shartse Norling Monastery in a small building in 1970.

THE SINO-INDIAN WAR, 1962

As early as January 1959, Chinese Premier Chou En-lai wrote a letter to Prime Minister Nehru acknowledging that there was an unresolved border dispute between the two countries. He also mentioned China's concerns about the role of the Indian government in the Dalai Lama's escape. China was unhappy with the McMahon Line demarcation of the Indo-Tibetan border. As a result, China claimed large chunks of Indian territories in Arunachal Pradesh, Ladakh, and Sikkim.

Border tensions between India and China began soon after the Panchsheel Agreement of 1954, with regular skirmishes in Ladakh and NEFA. India increased troops along the McMahon Line. They began "probing actions" against the Chinese in mid-1962, which saw a confrontation at Thag La. On 10 July, 350 PLA troops surrounded an Indian army post in Chushul in Leh. On 8 September, 600 PLA troops destroyed bridges and surrounded an outpost near Tawang in the NEFA, the very place the Dalai Lama was escorted to when he first escaped to India in 1959. The NEFA was home to around 800,000 Monpas, indigenous people culturally and ethnically closer to the Tibetans than to mainland Indians. The Indian government was keen to more firmly integrate the region into the rest of India. Tawang bore the brunt of the 1962 aggression.

Defense Minister V. K. Krishna Menon saw the Chinese aggression as an insignificant border issue. However, on 20 October 1962, the Chinese launched attacks simultaneously on two fronts, in Ladakh in the west and on the McMahon Line in the east. After four days of fighting on both fronts, Chou En-lai ordered PLA troops to stop advancing and sent a letter to Nehru on 24 October offering a negotiated settlement. Nehru responded to the Chinese premier on 27 October asking for a restoration to the boundary position prior to September 1962. Meanwhile, a national emergency was declared by the Indian Parliament. After a three-week lull, hostilities broke out once

Facing page: The Dalai Lama expressed his views about China's aggression in the 1962 war to Nehru directly. They continued to meet regularly to discuss the rehabilitation of Tibetan refugees, which the Dalai Lama deeply appreciated. On 22 May 1964, they met in New Delhi for the last time. Nehru had been weakened after suffering a stroke a few months earlier. Five days after this photo was taken, he had a second one, which was fatal.

again on the eastern front on 14 November when PLA forces attacked the Indians at Se La and Bomdila. They were able to push forward to near Tezpur. On the western front, Indian troops suffered heavy losses as the Chinese advanced on Rezang La and Gurung Hill near Chushul. The Indian forces were outnumbered and outmaneuvred, although they fought some remarkably brave battles. On 19 November, Chou En-lai declared a unilateral ceasefire to begin two days later. Nehru faced much criticism of his China policy and V. K. Menon resigned as the defense minister. The Panchsheel Agreement was in tatters. Nehru's handling of China was torn between his idealistic vision of a resurgent Asia in which India and China would be friends, and the practical consequences of a major power establishing its authority in the northern borders of India. The 1962 defeat to China was a big blow to Nehru. He died two years later at the age of seventy-four.

His Holiness felt "sadness tinged with fear" especially as the Indians, their saviors, had lost to the Chinese. Consequently, Indian officials immediately contacted Gyalo Thondup to discuss raising a secret resistance force based out of India. This would result in the setting up of the secret paramilitary force called Establishment 22.

Facing page: Although His Holiness often appeared joyful and radiant, he also poignantly displayed sorrow and deep reflection when speaking about China and Tibet.

"In my opinion the freedom of Tibet and the security of India in the north are two problems that are closely linked together. The day China completely abandons her authority in Tibet it will not only mean freedom for the people of Tibet but it will also strengthen India's freedom."

HIS HOLINESS THE FOURTEENTH DALAI LAMA in a letter to Prime Minister Nehru, 9 January 1963

"When we meet real tragedy in life, we can react in two ways—either by losing hope and falling into self-destructive habits, or by using the challenge to find our inner strength."

HIS HOLINESS THE FOURTEENTH DALAI LAMA

Part 3:
Reaching Out to the World

GLOBAL INTEREST IN TIBETAN BUDDHISM AND
WINNING THE NOBEL PEACE PRIZE
(1965–1989)

THE WEST LOOKS TOWARD THE EAST

In 1933, British author James Hilton published a novel set in Tibet called *Lost Horizon*. The book went on to become one of the first international mass-market paperback successes, selling in millions. I remember it because I received it as a prize and read it in school. This book, along with the travel accounts of Lowell Thomas Sr. and his son—two of the first few Americans to visit Tibet in 1949—sparked the initial interest in the West about our country.

His Holiness' flight from Lhasa brought more Western attention. In 1962, he published his first autobiography, *My Land and My People*, an extraordinary and poignant story in his own words. In the West after two world wars, youth had grown disillusioned, and there was bleakness and little hope. The 1960s and 1970s further intensified this disenchantment with life and young people began to explore the East in a new, determined way. This was also the time of the counterculture movement, and people traveled overland to places such as Nepal and India where they met

Tibetans. As expected, meeting His Holiness and other Tibetan lamas increased people's interest in Buddhism. There was a real desire to return to peace and kindness instead of war and destruction. His Holiness appealed greatly on this level—peaceful, loving, but also with a strong, informed, deep, and infinite wisdom. The Tibetan system offered a rich and sophisticated philosophy, a way of life, and direction.

In 1962, America's Beat writer and poet Allen Ginsberg, along with fellow poet Gary Snyder, met the Dalai Lama at Swarg Ashram. Incidentally, it was also in 1962 that Robert Thurman met the Dalai Lama for the first time. I remember meeting him in those early days when he was studying Tibetan medicine with Dr. Yeshi Dhonden. Some years later, he gave up his robes and dedicated his life to scholarship. On one occasion when His Holiness was giving a Kalachakra initiation in Bodh Gaya, he asked me to invite Bob to the early morning special prayers conducted by the Namgyal monks. I was very impressed with his familiarity with the complex rituals and his ability to navigate Buddhist prayers with the monks.

As His Holiness began to travel abroad, Tibetan centers and monasteries were established across the world. In 1997, Martin Scorsese completed his feature film on the Dalai Lama, *Kundun* ("The Presence"). In fact, many Tibetans, including me, call His Holiness by this name. For Scorsese, it was unusual to be making a film about peace and nonviolence. Featuring Tibetan amateurs and shot in the Moroccan mountains, it had a profound impact on both Scorsese and scriptwriter Melissa Mathison Ford. Scorsese writes, "I had first heard about Tibet in the 1950s. The whole movie is about loss. The boy, the man, the Dalai Lama represents a way of life we can learn a lot from." There were several drafts of the script and on two occasions His Holiness himself reviewed them. We were guests of Melissa and her husband Harrison Ford at their home in Wyoming and when the team visited Dharamsala. I witnessed Harrison breaking down because he was so moved when reading the script.

I was delighted when I heard movies were being made about the Tibetan experience, as popular culture would ensure more people would

From obscurity to celebrity: In August 1999, His Holiness gave his second talk in Central Park, New York City. No one knew how many people would come—it had been an open invitation from the city's Tibet Center and the Gere Foundation. Over 200,000 attended, filling the park's huge East Meadow. The Dalai Lama has spoken at Central Park on two other occasions, in 1991 and 2003.

Professor Robert Thurman studied Tibetan Buddhism at Harvard and became Je Tsong Khapa Professor of Indo-Tibetan Buddhist Studies at Columbia University. Together with my brother, Tenzin Namgyal Tethong, and also Richard Gere and the composer Philip Glass, in 1987 he founded Tibet House US in New York City, dedicated to the preservation and renaissance of Tibetan civilization.

Facing page, above: His Holiness studying a blueprint for the construction of the Library of Tibetan Works and Archives, presented by its first director, Gyatso Tsering.

Facing page, below: The Library of Tibetan Works and Archives. Not only did Tibetans bring the precious sacred objects they had carried with them from Tibet there, but it also became a hub of learning. The first Westerners who turned up in Dharamsala, eager to learn about Tibetan Buddhism, studied every day at "the Library."

become aware of our struggle. Despite China's interference, *Kundun* and *Seven Years in Tibet,* directed by Jean-Jacques Annaud, helped spread awareness about our plight. A film buff myself, I enjoyed my interactions with Melissa and Harrison. During their visit to Dharamsala, I invited them home for dinner. Despite being a successful Hollywood scriptwriter, I found Melissa to be gentle and unassuming. She became a true friend to the Tibetans and later joined the board of the International Campaign for Tibet, founded by my brother. I was very saddened to hear of her passing in 2015. His Holiness was not familiar with most actors, and on more than one occasion I felt awkward when an international star would greet him and he would have no idea who they were!

There is also some criticism of this Western interest. Some have argued that Tibetan Buddhism has become too exoticized in the West and this detracts from serious engagement with it. Be that as it may, the popularity of Tibetan Buddhism and His Holiness' enthusiastic engagement with people of all persuasions has brought a lot of attention to Tibetan issues. The period of exile has opened up Tibetan religion, culture, music, and art to the people of the world.

Library of Tibetan Works and Archives

In 1970, His Holiness conceived and set up the Library of Tibetan Works and Archives (LTWA). It opened in 1971. The objective was twofold: to provide people with an opportunity to learn about the richness of Tibetan culture through suitable research facilities and to also give the Tibetan people a means to preserve their heritage and way of life. The Library's mandate was to acquire precious Tibetan manuscripts, books, and works of art from different sources; provide resources for academic research; compile bibliographies, document oral histories, and publish books; and offer classes on Tibetan language, culture, and Buddhism. Tibetans who came into exile, carrying with them very little else apart from their Dharma items, donated these personal belongings to further strengthen the collection. One of the most valuable pieces here is the statue of Avalokiteshvara, which was commissioned by the Thirteenth Dalai Lama. Years later it was carefully smuggled out in sections, carried over great distances, and brought to Dharamsala.

A fusion of modern and typical Tibetan architecture, the Library became the location of the first classes for Westerners who came to study in Dharamsala in the 1960s and 1970s. During His Holiness' visits abroad, I found that those who had once studied at the Library were among the most ardent supporters of the Tibetan people and their cause. Many of them went on to become accomplished translators—some wrote books relating to Tibetan Buddhism and His Holiness, and also translated prayers and rituals from Tibetan to English.

The Library continues to offer an astonishing array of courses, and the present director, Venerable Geshe Lhakdor, has expanded and improved it, introducing numerous groundbreaking initiatives, including the Science for Monks and Nuns program. A former English translator for His Holiness, he also lectures and invites international scholars to take part in conferences at the Library, enhancing its stature.

CHINA ESTABLISHES
TIBET AUTONOMOUS REGION

n 1960 His Holiness said, "We exiled Tibetans living in free India must exert our fullest effort for the benefit of those who remained behind." Despite the immense difficulties he faced in exile, the Dalai Lama saw it as an opportunity to do things differently. He worked tirelessly to bring reform, to change the old ways of working as he declared, "We should not retain all the ancient systems of Tibet." Meanwhile the news from Tibet was not good. In 1965, China formalized the Tibet Autonomous Region (TAR) to consolidate the area they had taken over in 1951.

This completed the anticipated administrative takeover of Tibet. A military administration had now been replaced by a supposed autonomous government. This was an illusion, since the working committee of the Central People's Committee of the TAR was entirely

Facing page: The Cultural Revolution brought devastation to Tibet. Smashed statues and artifacts litter a courtyard at the Jokhang Temple, August 1966.

Below: Red Guards demonstrate their allegiance to Mao at the Sungchora, the courtyard behind the Jokhang where previously both the Thirteenth and Fourteenth Dalai Lamas had taught.

Chinese backed by around 150,000 troops. This also signaled the end of the dubious Seventeen-Point Agreement, which the Tibetans had signed under duress. The administrative takeover was a cosmetic cover for the widespread oppression of the Tibetan people. As noted by scholars, the draconian features of the Chinese Cultural Revolution that began in 1966 were already in place in Tibet.

Those who defied Chinese authority were subjected to public humiliations called *thamzing*, or public "struggle sessions" as they were known. Tibetan ways, language, dress, and customs were deemed "filthy." The creation of the TAR made way for the total subjugation of the Tibetan people.

At this time the escape of His Holiness and thousands of Tibetans into India was fresh. Anger and hatred against the Chinese was very strong among our people. News of this latest move by the Chinese toward more and complete control of Tibet and its people distressed us further. Meanwhile, the rehabilitation of Tibetans in India was in full swing. His Holiness writes in his autobiography, "The mid-1960s were a high point in the Tibetan resettlement program." Although he was equally concerned about the rehabilitation of the monk community, the first Tibetan institute established was a Tibetan school for children in Mussoorie in 1959. My father came to serve as a teacher at this school, and I traveled to Mussoorie with him. He was later appointed principal of the newly established Tibetan school in Shimla. The whole family moved to Shimla then. For a few months I taught English to the lower classes and took the physical training class as well.

Above: The Tibet Autonomous Region (TAR) was established in April 1965. TAR comprises most of the former Tibetan province of U-Tsang and western Kham. Eastern Kham, Amdo, and northwest U-Tsang were incorporated into the Qinghai, Gansu, Sichuan, and Yunnan provinces of the PRC. TAR comprises less than half of historic Tibet.

Facing page: The Dalai Lama met Prime Minister Lal Bahadur Shastri in Calcutta in October 1965. I recall Shastri often wrote long letters to His Holiness. The Dalai Lama recalls, "Despite his frail appearance, he was an outstanding leader."

Below: In January 1966, His Holiness sent a telegram of condolence to President S. Radhakrishnan following Shastri's premature death.

Lal Bahadur Shastri: A True Ally

During the creation of TAR, a third draft resolution on Tibet was submitted to the United Nations. Lal Bahadur Shastri was now the prime minister of India, and his support for the Tibetan cause was evident. India voted in favor of the resolution, marking a change from previous policy. This was clearly linked to their military debacle with China in 1962.

In 1965, when His Holiness was visiting refugee settlements in South India, war broke out between India and Pakistan. He was asked to not travel until the situation settled. While he waited, he received a message from W. D. Shakabpa, his representative in New Delhi, that the Indian government was prepared to recognize the Tibetan government in exile and that he would receive a definite answer once the prime minister returned from Tashkent. Unfortunately, Shastri died suddenly (and according to some reports, mysteriously) in Tashkent on 11 January 1966. Once again, the matter of Tibet and its independence became a casualty.

To:

> The President
> Rashtrapati Bhawan
> New Delhi.

THE NATIONAL LOSS OF YOUR PRIME MINISTER IS ALSO AN IRREPARABLE LOSS TO THE PEOPLE OF TIBET STOP THE LOSS WILL BE FELT IMMENSELY BY THE INDIAN PEOPLE AT THIS PARTICULAR JUNCTURE IN THE HISTORY OF THIS NATION STOP BUT SHRI LAL BAHADUR SHASTRI HAS CONTRIBUTED TREMENDOUSLY FOR PEACE IN THIS PART OF THE WORLD AND THIS WILL NOT BE FORGOTTEN. STOP MY PEOPLE AND I OFFER TO YOU AND THE PEOPLE OF INDIA OUR SINCEREST CONDOLENCE ON THIS SAD OCCASION.

DALAI LAMA

Swarg Ashram
Upper Dharmsala
Kangra/Punjab
January 11, 1966.

"I am a Son of India"

In 1966, when the Indian government asked His Holiness to abstain from making any statement denouncing the Cultural Revolution, he wrote to Foreign Minister Sardar Swaran Singh. His Holiness' letter of 17 September 1966 clearly shows his frustration: "We are always grateful to the Government of India for all the assistance extended to us and have at all times avoided actions which may cause embarrassment or inconvenience to the government. In view of this, is it not unreasonable to withhold the statement I had intended to release? The Tibetan people solely depend on the people and the Government of India."

This was one of the few occasions when I was deeply disappointed with the attitude of Indian leaders concerning Tibet.

In 1972, Swaran Singh made a statement that "the question of sovereignty" or "suzerainty" in Tibet was a matter for the Chinese to decide. I was shocked and deeply saddened. Clearly, India wanted to lessen tensions with China. High officials from the Ministry of External Affairs came to meet His Holiness in Dharamsala to

Above: In 1959, the Dalai Lama met Jayaprakash Narayan and his family. Top right: Prime Minister Morarji Desai's letter to His Holiness, acknowledging his respect for him and the Tibetan faith and institutions. Right: The Dalai Lama visited Dr. S. Radhakrishnan, Vice President of India in New Delhi, April 1961.

303

PRIME MINISTER

No.378-PMO/79

New Delhi
January 29, 1979

Your Holiness,

 I am touched by your letter of the 20th January and your donation of Rs.15,000 you have made for the welfare of the children of India. I am grateful for your generous acknowledgement of the assistance given by the Government of India to the Tibetans whom we have treated as guests in the traditional manner of our country. But I would like to say that whatever little we have done is primarily a token of our respect to Your Holiness, the Tibetan faith and its institutions and the community of culture and good neighbourliness. It is for you and the Tibetans who have chosen to come to India of their own free will and faith in our hospitality to exercise judgement as to how long you wish to be with us. As long as you are in India, we shall be happy to continue to assist the Tibetan community, preserving our ancient sense of hospitality.

 With the assurances of my highest esteem and consideration.

Yours sincerely,

(Morarji Desai)

His Holiness The Dalai Lama,
Thekchen Choling,
Dharmsala Cantt,
Kangra District

Left: Old friends, former Indian President Dr. APJ Abdul Kalam and the Dalai Lama, Dharamsala, 2009.

Below: His Holiness with former Indian Defense Minister George Fernandes. He called Fernandes a great humanitarian, a voice for millions of poor and needy people, with a firm conviction in justice and freedom.

dissuade him from making his annual statement on 10 March. He explained that not issuing a statement, which he had been doing since 1959, would be seen as caving in to Chinese pressure.

As time went by, Indian leaders became increasingly disinterested in the Tibetan issue to avoid confrontation with China. We now faced restrictions that never existed before. Students of our Tibetan schools in India were banned from singing the Tibetan national anthem. Our travel within India was closely monitored as we were instructed to report to the Foreigners Registration Offices about our movements, also making it mandatory to carry our Registration Certificates with us at all times. Any form of agitation against China was strongly discouraged. Some officials rationalized these actions as part of the agreement that had been in place since 1959. This was not true. These new restrictions were imposed under the watch of Prime Minister Indira Gandhi.

However, things changed when the Janata Party government came into power in 1977. They were not as deferential to China as the previous government and several leaders were openly sympathetic to the Tibetan cause. His Holiness' meeting with Prime Minister Morarji Desai in July 1977 was very cordial. Desai spoke about the cultures of India and Tibet, and shared that they were like two branches of the same tree. The Dalai Lama has often quoted this phrase.

His Holiness used to regularly call on Indian leaders and our early years at the Private Office were spent drafting letters and tracking correspondence with them. The popular Indian socialist leader, Jayaprakash

Narayan, was a staunch supporter of Tibet, as were George Fernandes, Raj Narain, and Atal Bihari Vajpayee, who even spoke about Tibetan independence when he was a member of parliament. Unfortunately, Vajpayee later changed his position when he became foreign minister and later prime minister. George Fernandes was unwavering in his support for the Tibetan cause. He was openly supportive of the Tibetans, even as the defense minister in the Vajpayee government. In a letter to Fernandes in October 1987, His Holiness wrote, "India has as much at stake in the future of Tibet as we Tibetans have."

Rajiv Gandhi became India's youngest prime minister after the assassination of his mother, Indira Gandhi, in 1984. He was a breath of fresh air — sensitive, gentle, and decent. My impression of him was confirmed because of the way he treated His Holiness. His tragic death in 1991 ended all hopes of the Indian government adopting a favorable Tibet policy.

Unfortunately, subsequent prime ministers such as P. V. Narasimha Rao and Manmohan Singh were aloof and did not show much interest in our cause. It is of great sadness that we no longer had the staunch support of the Indian leaders at that time.

A NEW RESIDENCE, REESTABLISHING NAMGYAL MONASTERY, AND A NEW TEMPLE

A few years into my employment, there was talk about moving from Swarg Ashram, as we had outgrown the location. The relocation would include His Holiness, his Private Office, and his monastery. The Dalai Lama had spent eight years at Swarg Ashram, and although we had settled in well, the facilities were barely adequate. Several staff members shared tiny residential quarters. I shared a small quarter with Venerable Lobsang Gawa, the senior attendant to His Holiness. He was also a mentor to me in those early days. I have fond memories of going for jogs in the morning with him. Those were tough times, but despite the difficulties, the damp climate, and the ramshackle accommodation, we all kept a positive attitude in our duties.

In 1968, Byrne Estate was chosen as the location for His Holiness'

His Holiness' new temple, the Tsuglakhang, was not lavish, but small and simple. He took great joy in commissioning a new statue of 1,000-armed Avalokiteshvara. Made in Dharamsala, Tibetans donated their silver and jewels to be placed inside this statue.

Facing page: The Dalai Lama is a keen gardener. He took part in planting his new garden and regularly discussed gardening with others.

"My main concern is the preservation of Tibetan culture...to keep alive the Tibetan spirit, the Tibetan cultural heritage, that's my main concern. This not only benefits the six million Tibetan people, but also is of interest for the larger community...."

HIS HOLINESS THE FOURTEENTH DALAI LAMA

new residence. Though the building itself was not much bigger than his previous home, the estate had a newly constructed compound that could accommodate more staff and other facilities. While His Holiness moved to his private quarters at the new location, the Great Mother, who had been living with him, moved to Kashmir Cottage (where His Holiness' youngest brother Tendzin Choegyal and his wife Rinchen Khando now live). The new complex, renamed Thekchen Choling (meaning Great Mahayana Place of Dharma), also housed the Private Office, the Indian Security Office, a room for public audiences, his personal office, and quarters for the staff and Tibetan security personnel of His Holiness.

His Holiness was now able to relocate Namgyal Monastery to a new structure next to his residence at Byrne Estate. Until then, the monks had lived in Nowrojee Villa above Swarg Ashram. Named after the deity of longevity Namgyalma, or Usnisavijaya in Sanskrit, Namgyal is the personal monastery of the Dalai Lama and was founded by the Third Dalai Lama, Sonam Gyatso. Fifty-two Namgyal monks had managed to flee Tibet and resettle in Dharamsala. With the setting up of the monastery, several young and new monks from the various refugee settlements were able to join it. This ensured the continuation of an important nonsectarian institution even in exile. The various ancient and specialized rituals, traditions, and arts which had been part of the original monastery in Tibet found a new home.

Within the Thekchen Choling complex is also Tsuglakhang Temple, set up in 1969. The violence of the Cultural Revolution that began in 1966 resulted in extensive damage to the Jokhang Temple in Lhasa. The presiding deity of Avalokiteshvara located within it was

dismantled and disfigured. A portion of this disfigured image was smuggled out of Tibet and brought to Dharamsala to be kept in the new shrine. The main image in the temple is a statue of the Buddha Shakyamuni. On the left side of this are the images of one-thousand armed Avalokiteshvara and Padmasambhava, or Guru Rinpoche, as he is commonly known. These two images are placed in the direction of

The Dalai Lama's new residence, named Thekchen Choling, provided more space and was more peaceful.

"We must each lead a way of life with self-awareness and compassion, to do as much as we can. Then, whatever happens, we will have no regrets."

HIS HOLINESS THE FOURTEENTH DALAI LAMA

Tibet for auspicious reasons and because of their special connection to Tibet and its people. The temple became a focal point for everyone to gather, pray, and listen to His Holiness give teachings on important days. As His Holiness said, the establishment of the temple made it easier for large numbers of the people to participate in the various religious events of the Tibetan calendar. Institute of Buddhist Dialectics, a nonsectarian institute open to both men and women is housed adjacent to the Tsuglakhang. This area is always teeming with monks, nuns, and visitors; truly a picture of activity and spiritual energy graced by His Holiness' presence. In this manner, His Holiness put into place a practical long-term vision for life in exile that included all aspects of Tibetan spiritual life.

His Holiness presiding over a New Year ceremony with Namgyal Monastery monks on the roof of the Tsuglakhang, Dharamsala.

Monks of the Namgyal Monastery

The Namgyal Monastery holds a special status since it is the personal monastery of His Holiness and has the privilege of conducting special spiritual rites for the Tibetan government and people by performing public ceremonies and offering prayers for the welfare of Tibet. It was a wonderful coincidence that the *Garpon* (dance master), *Umdze* (chant master), and several others escaped Tibet in 1959. By 1961, they had regrouped and were living in Dalhousie, working on oil construction sites, when His Holiness called them to Dharamsala. Facing difficult circumstances, some of them made the journey with no shoes. A senior monk, Venerable Ngawang Tashi, who passed away in 2019, contributed, with others, to reestablishing the unique traditions of the monastery. As the monks were able to take out very few valuable texts and prayer rituals when they left Tibet suddenly in 1959, His Holiness requested them to urgently write down not only hundreds of pages of prayers and rituals, but also special musical notation to convey the unique sounds of the Tibetan overtone that the *umdzes* chanted so that new students could learn. Handwritten, illustrated books became the basis for preserving ancient knowledge and educating young monks up to the present day.

In 1963, His Holiness appointed Venerable Samten Chopel as the first abbot of the Namgyal Monastery in exile. The Namgyal Tantric College now has four other branches in India, and one in Ithaca, New York. In the early 1960s, His Holiness sent Ngari Rinpoche and me for *Dharma* studies to the Khen Rinpoche, the abbot. Ngari Rinpoche would set an alarm to ensure our lessons did not exceed the designated time! Our studies did not last more than a few months.

During the 1960s, fifty-two monks served at the monastery, and today there are over 200. Only three remain of the original fifty-two, including two who live in His Holiness' residence—Lobsang Gawa, senior attendant, and Paljor, assistant attendant. I had the privilege of knowing well one of the Namgyal monks who came to India in the 1980s. Venerable Thubten Chokten was in a Chinese prison for eighteen years in Tibet before he escaped into exile, where he rejoined Namgyal Monastery. His Holiness appointed him *Lopon* (Disciplinarian) of the monastery. He

Top and middle: Original hand-drawn prayer book, signed by His Holiness, made in the 1960s by senior Namgyal monk, Ngawang Tashi.

Bottom: His hand-drawn book of musical notation for chant masters in the Tibetan tradition. He later became a chant master himself.

Facing page, left: 97-year-old monk and senior teacher, Ngawang Tashi, in his room at Namgyal Monastery, Dharamsala, 2019. He passed away a few months later.

Facing page, right: 97-year-old monk, Thubten Choephel, former *Lopon* (Disciplinarian) and *Umdze* (chant master), in his room at Namgyal Monastery, Dharamsala, 2019. He escaped from the Potala Palace in 1959 as the Chinese began to open fire on the building.

and I used to sit side by side during the teachings of His Holiness. His Holiness often recounts an anecdote about my monk friend. Soon after he arrived in Dharamsala, His Holiness asked him, "What did you find the most difficult in the Chinese prison?" His Holiness expected him to say something about the terrible conditions or treatment he received. Instead, he said, "What I found most difficult was trying not to lose my compassion toward the jail warden." I was moved when I heard this—such a deep teaching about the practice of compassion.

INTERFAITH ENCOUNTERS:
A LIFELONG DEVOTION

In November 1968, His Holiness had a fateful encounter with Thomas Merton, a thinker, scholar, and Catholic monk from a rural Kentucky monastery. Merton's formative years were peripatetic. After enrolling in Cambridge University in 1933, he lived a life of excess. In 1938, Merton had a transformative experience when he met Mahanambrata Brahmachari, a Hindu yogi, who was at the time a research scholar at the University of Chicago. On his advice, Merton turned to Catholicism. In May 1939, Merton received Confirmation, and in 1941 entered a monastery. His life thereafter was dominated by scholarship and he was to become one of the most influential Christian writers of his time.

I was asked to look for a suitable place for Thomas Merton to stay while he was in Dharamsala. Helped by Harold Talbott, an American student and practitioner of Buddhism who was a private student of His Holiness in the 1960s, I found a place at Lower Dharmsala. I would send

The American Trappist monk, Thomas Merton, visited Dharamsala in 1968 to meet the Dalai Lama, who was greatly impressed by his inner Christian practice. After Merton's passing, His Holiness visited his grave at the Lady of Gethsemani Abbey in Kentucky.

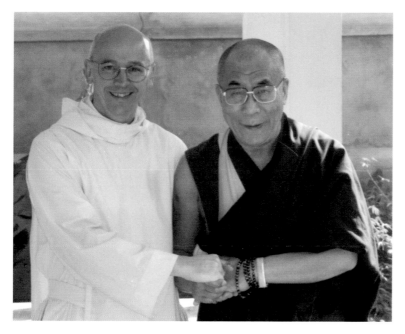

His Holiness with Father Lawrence Freeman, a Benedictine monk and director of the World Community for Christian Meditation, during a visit to England. On his invitation, at the 1994 John Main seminar, His Holiness shared a Buddhist perspective on the four Gospels of the Christian Bible.

an office car to fetch him for his meetings with His Holiness. They met over three days for sessions that lasted about two hours each time.

His Holiness greatly enjoyed his meetings with Merton. The monk had a striking personal appearance, but His Holiness says more striking was his "inner life." He said Merton introduced him to the real meaning of the word "Christian" and called him a Catholic *geshe*. Perhaps what drew the two to each other was that they were both men of dialogue, especially between religions. They discussed several topics including monastic vows and practices, meditation techniques, the Bodhisattva ideal, and Tantra. Merton, who was deeply interested in Buddhism, found the Dalai Lama to be "a very solid, energetic, generous, and warm person."

After his encounter with Merton, His Holiness visited many Christian monasteries and became drawn to the admirable "practical work of Christians"—charitable work, especially in health and education. He encouraged Tibetans to also set up similar charitable organizations for public good. On 10 December 1968, shortly after his visit to Dharamsala, Merton was found dead in his room at a monastic

retreat near Bangkok, Thailand. He appeared to have died due to an electric shock.

His Holiness was especially keen to meet leaders of other faiths. Apa Pant, the Oxford-educated prince turned freedom fighter and diplomat, describes the meeting between the philosopher, speaker, and writer J. Krishnamurti and the Dalai Lama in 1956: "It was breathtaking to feel the elect affection that instantly flashed between them." These instances of interfaith dialogues were to increase in number as he traveled widely. In 1980, Pope John Paul II and the Dalai Lama met at the Vatican for the first of their eight official meetings. They had a profound friendship, despite their religious and cultural differences. The Pope had experienced both Nazi aggression and Soviet Communism in his native country Poland and could therefore empathize with His Holiness' own experience. We were saddened to hear that recently the Vatican would not agree to meetings with the Dalai Lama for fear of antagonizing China, where there are more Catholics than members of the Communist party.

The Dalai Lama met the Muslim community in Bodh Gaya in 2003.

Facing page: The Dalai Lama prayed at the National Cathedral, Washington DC, 2003, during a commemorative service marking the second anniversary of the 9/11 terrorist attacks in New York.

"This is my simple religion. No need for temples. No need for complicated philosophy. Your own mind, your own heart is the temple. Your philosophy is simple kindness."

HIS HOLINESS THE FOURTEENTH DALAI LAMA

In 1980, His Holiness also met Father Lawrence Freeman, Director of the World Community for Christian Meditation, in Montreal at an interfaith meeting. In his book *Towards the True Kinship of Faiths,* he describes how moved he was by this meeting. Some years later Father Freeman asked His Holiness to speak on the Gospel from Buddhist tradition. This was the beginning of The Good Heart Seminar of 1994. The book of the same title has become a classic on interreligious dialogue, and the Dalai Lama often says it is one of his favorite books. He has received many letters from Christians around the world saying that his commentaries on the Gospel have helped them to reconnect with their own tradition.

His Holiness strives to build bridges between the various religions of the world through the message of love, compassion, tolerance, and peaceful coexistence. Since retiring from his political role, he continues to meet and pray with religious leaders. Setting aside his vows of abstaining from intoxicants, he received Holy Communion from Archbishop Desmond Tutu, visited Israel several times despite criticism, and has visited several Islamic countries.

His Holiness' continued advocacy of universal values of peace and brotherhood have made him one of the greatest teachers in the world. He advises, "Keep your own tradition. But, if some Buddhist methods come from my lecture which you find useful, then use them. If they are not useful, then leave them."

Below: His Holiness and Tibetan monks reciting the Heart Sutra during an interfaith service for world peace, Shizuoka, Japan, 2013.

Facing page, above (left): At the Golden Temple, Amritsar, 2019, where the Dalai Lama was invited to participate in an interfaith conclave to celebrate the 550th anniversary of the birth of the first Sikh Guru.

Facing page, above (right): The Dalai Lama in an interfaith prayer meeting for world peace at Mahatma Gandhi's memorial, Raj Ghat, New Delhi, 2008.

Facing page, below: Interfaith Conference, London, 2008. Beside the Dalai Lama sit (left) his long-term English translator, Dr. Thupten Jinpa Langri, and (right) the Archbishop of Canterbury, Dr. Rowan Williams.

TIBETAN YOUTH CONGRESS

After a decade in India, we had successfully established a community with functioning institutions. It was now time for action. The Tibetan Youth Congress (TYC) emerged out of a need to politically activate the younger generation of Tibetans in exile and to set objectives and goals. Ngari Rinpoche, Lodi Gyari, Sonam Topgyal, my brother, Tenzin Namgyal Tethong, cousin, Jamyang Norbu, and I came together to found the TYC. I was elected the founding President. His Holiness supported the initiative and inaugurated the first session on 7 October 1970 in Dharamsala. Both his tutors were also in attendance. Even though I was not politically astute, it was an extremely exciting moment for me.

The TYC campaigned for full independence of Tibet from China. During the early years, we held protests against Chinese occupation, often outside the Chinese Embassy in New Delhi. As young Tibetans educated in exile, we wanted to take our message beyond the confines of Dharamsala. We worked as a pressure group. Due to this, the Chinese administration characterized us as a "terrorist organization," despite

At one of the Tibetan Youth Congress' meetings in the early 1970s. I can be seen sitting in the center between Ngari Rinpoche, Lodi Gyari, and other members. Over the years, TYC has grown substantially, with over 30,000 members worldwide, making it the largest pro-independence organization of Tibetan exiles. The TYC publishes a quarterly journal, *Rangzen*, and conducts various activities like marking important days in Tibet's history.

the fact that we never advocated violence. We would also periodically conduct cultural events, blood-donation camps, adult education classes, and other activities to improve the lives of Tibetans in exile. At one point, this meant helping to build a new road from Lower Dharamsala to McLeod Ganj. At another, we were responsible for building new toilets. I was happy to be working with my friend Ngari Rinpoche at the TYC. Both he and his wife, Rinchen Khando, were active members of the organization. Those were simple days. We were young, passionate, and idealistic. What we lacked in terms of resources, was made up for by our zeal and determination. As we did not have an office space, we would meet in small restaurants or at Mr. Nowrojee's shop.

Our charter emphasized dedication to His Holiness, promoting Tibetan national unity, preservation of our religion and culture, and the struggle for Tibet. In 1988, His Holiness announced the "Middle-Way" approach of advanced autonomy for Tibet. After much discussion among various sections of the Tibetan society, the vast majority opted to follow the Middle-Way Approach. When the Central Tibetan Administration subsequently adopted it as its policy, TYC faced difficulties because of its mandate of complete independence for Tibet from China. But over time, there was reconciliation. The TYC advocating for independence did not mean the organization was against His Holiness or the administration.

As the former president, I look back with amazement at how the organization has grown from a small group of impassioned young friends to a Tibetan national body with a strong voice.

Tibetan Youth Congress members help to smooth over the new road from Lower Dharamsala to McLeod Ganj.

They contributed to the improvement of living conditions in the early days.

THE MUSTANG RESISTANCE FORCE TRAGEDY

A decade into my work at the Private Office, a most troubling episode occurred. It caused a great deal of sadness for His Holiness and the Tibetans. As American foreign policy toward China changed, President Nixon and Mao met. The latter made it clear that any rapprochement was conditional on America dropping support of the Tibetans. In 1974, under pressure from the Chinese, the Nepalese government instructed all the CIA-trained Tibetan resistance fighters based in Mustang to give up their arms and surrender peacefully. Mustang, a secluded northern region of Nepal, was historically an ancient Tibetan kingdom named Lo, a part of the powerful ruler Songtsen Gampo's empire. Bordering Tibet on three sides, flanked by some of the highest Himalayan mountain ranges, it was a Tibetan province until an eighteenth-century land treaty between royals changed its status. Twelve villages and a walled city called Lo Monthang remained mostly autonomous.

For Gompo Tashi Andrugtsang, founder of *Chushi Gangdruk* and leader of the resistance movement, and his associate Lhamo Tsering, Chief of Operations of the Mustang Resistance Force and mastermind of intelligence gathering missions inside Tibet, Mustang was the ideal place to raise a guerrilla force from where attacks on PLA forces could be conducted. Gompo Tashi was familiar with the

Lhamo Tsering, left, and Gyato Wangdu, second from left, respectively Chief of Operations and Commander of the Mustang Resistance Force, in northern Nepal. Lhamo Tsering later worked at the Department of Security in Dharamsala and was appointed a minister in the Kashag.

territory, and the local populace supported them. After CIA support suddenly ended in 1969, the Mustang Resistance Force continued until 1974. Resistance leaders Lhamo Tsering and Gyato Wangdu felt betrayed by the Americans.

In November 1974, King Birendra of Nepal issued orders declaring the country's borders as "restricted areas." Troops were deployed close to the guerrilla headquarters. His Holiness feared that there would be unnecessary bloodshed and confrontation with the Nepalese authorities, which could only harm their cause. He sent a recorded voice message which was played at the camps. It said: "For many years you have risked your lives and struggled for our cause. I know the present situation will cause you much disappointment. However, we must try and achieve our objectives through peaceful means…" Some of the men cried upon hearing the message. They had no choice but to surrender. One of the leaders slit his throat in despondency, not wanting to defy His Holiness. Some others threw themselves in the river and ended their lives. The dedicated and brave fighters were demoralized and broken. They were resettled in two refugee camps in Nepal. Barely able to make ends meet, they took up carpet weaving and wool spinning for livelihood.

Tibetan resistance fighters in Mustang. Lhamo Tsering in an interview said: "I don t see our armed struggle as something that was helpful only at a certain point in our history, something that is finished. We should look at it as one chapter in our continuing struggle for freedom, one that still has some meaning."

THE WORLD OPENS UP: FIRST TRIP TO EUROPE

Michael van Walt van Praag had been an enthusiastic Tibet supporter since he was twelve years old. He would write impassioned letters to His Holiness about his outrage against the Chinese occupation of Tibet. His boyish conviction remained strong and he became one of our most valued and effective supporters in the West. By age twenty-one, he had met the Dalai Lama and when the spiritual leader expressed a desire to visit Europe, Michael did the groundwork, organizing the trip. He went on to become a legal counsel to the Dalai Lama and Tibetan government in exile.

The year 1973 marked a new phase in His Holiness' life as he traveled to Europe for the first time. This was his first visit to the West; the first trips abroad were to Japan and Thailand in 1967. The Indian government expressly asked him not to make any political statements during this trip and to strictly stick to religious matters. This did not dampen our excitement.

The Dalai Lama and his entourage arrived at Kloten Airport, Zurich, on a Swissair flight. From right: Former Lord Chamberlain, Phala; His Holiness' representative in Geneva; Kunga, His Holiness' bodyguard; His Holiness; me holding the flowers; L.T. Negi, the Indian Intelligence Bureau officer; Venerable Paljor, His Holiness' attendant; Lodi Gyari and Michael van Walt on his left.

The eleven-country tour began with a visit to the Vatican, where His Holiness found similarities between St. Peter's Basilica and the Potala Palace in their size and antiquity. His desire for interreligious dialogue began to take root during this landmark trip. He had a short meeting with Pope Paul VI and expressed his belief in the universal nature of the spiritual values of humanity.

We stayed at a monastery in Rome. The living quarters were spartan, but the kitchens were modern, unlike in our monasteries. I was taken aback when wine (often brewed by the monks themselves) was served at meals, as Tibetan monks are not allowed alcoholic beverages. Another contrast was the size of the monasteries. While our monks often had to sleep on verandas owing to lack of space, in Europe many of the monasteries had fifty to sixty monk residents living in spacious buildings.

Our next stop was Switzerland, where the first Bureau of Tibet in Europe had been set up. Kungo Phala and Lobsang Samten, His Holiness' older brother, had been representatives here. Since 1961, the country had taken in thousands of Tibetan refugees, including children

The Dalai Lama in Switzerland, 1973. Lodi Gyari Rinpoche and Michael van Walt stand in front of the car. One highlight was a violin recital by two young girls, which His Holiness enjoyed very much.

who were adopted by Swiss families. His Holiness met with 200 or so of these children. It was unfortunate that, for most, years away from their country meant that they had lost their mother tongue and were not familiar with Tibetan culture. We needed a translator to communicate with them, which I found uncomfortable. His Holiness asked the monks at the Rikon Monastery, founded in 1968, to set up language classes for them. I was impressed with the cleanliness and discipline of people in Europe, particularly in Switzerland. I could hardly believe the punctual timings of trains, not just to the minute but to the second!

Traveling on, we went to the Netherlands and then to Belgium, Ireland, Norway, Sweden, Denmark, United Kingdom, West Germany, and Austria. His Holiness prioritized meeting all those who had provided aid and helped the Tibetan cause. He met with the Johnsons of Norwegian Tibetan Aid and on his return to India wrote to them, "There is a great and urgent need for a sense of universal responsibility in the world today, and in order to build that we must all create a genuine atmosphere of brotherhood, love, and respect of all mankind." In Sweden, His Holiness met friends who had helped in establishing schools and relief in India. In Denmark, he met the Fennebergs of

A 1965 letter from Rinchen Wangmo, one of the Tibetan children adopted by a Swiss family.

```
                                    Rinchen Wangmo
                                    c/o Mr.Klemm
                                    Juraweg 11
                                    4310 Rheinfelden

                                    Switzerland

Dear Dalai Lama,

J am well. J cannot write you in Tibetan, but we learn it at scool
with Lama Wangyal.
J have got here in Switzerland a new amala and a pala and a dear
sister and two big older brothers. One of the brothers makes
allways fun with me. We have two dogs, three ducks. Last year we
had a lot of young ducks. We have five turtles, two dwarf parrots
and one canary too.
Every evening, when J said my prayer, J wish you a good night.

            Many greetings from
            Rinchen Wangmo and amala Klemm
```

The Dalai Lama with Hermann Gmeiner (to his left in an overcoat) at SOS Children's Village, Hinterbruhl, Austria.

the Danish Committee for Tibetan Assistance who had visited him at Swarg Ashram in the early years. In Austria, he visited one of the SOS Children's Villages and met with the founder, Hermann Gmeiner, who had offered us so much help and funded TCV schools in India. Heinrich Harrer had originally introduced us to him.

During our ten-day visit to the UK, His Holiness was delighted to meet some of the British civil servants who had served in Tibet. Among them was Hugh Richardson, British political officer and Tibetologist, who had lived in Tibet from 1936–1940 and 1947–1950. At the invitation of Lady Egremont we attended a house party at her estate, Petworth House, which included many distinguished guests. His Holiness planted a Himalayan cedar during our two-day visit. Known to be an adventurous traveler, supporter of charities, and a generous hostess, Lady Egremont requested His Holiness for a consecrated prayer scroll for her Tibetan prayer wheel. His Holiness did not forget her generosity, and on his return to India, sent her the scroll along with a letter of gratitude for her

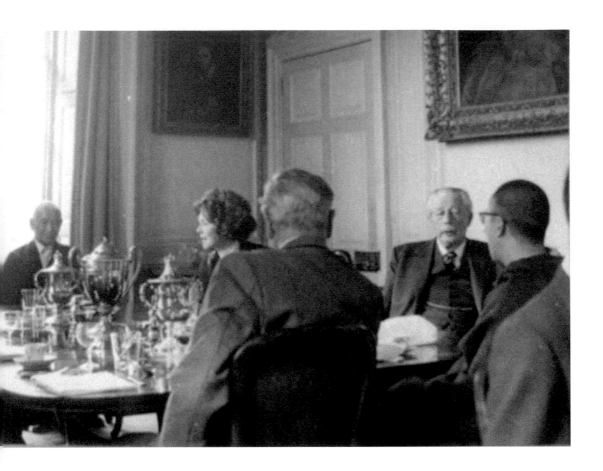

hospitality. Thanking His Holiness, Lady Egremont wrote in March 1974, "During all the hundreds of years of this house's history, it could have had no guest more honored or more welcome than Your Holiness…"

During this milestone trip, His Holiness met with many leaders, as well as ordinary practitioners of Christianity. This was a precursor to the close association he developed with the Christian world. He met with the Archbishop of Canterbury and was "encouraged by his liberal thoughts." He also met the Aga Khan, setting the tone for his future trips during which he would seek out leaders of other faiths. He viewed this trip as "a beginning in establishing a personal contact with the people of the West."

His Holiness' enthusiasm and inquisitiveness was inspiring. He took a keen interest in all that we saw and experienced. He gave his complete

The Dalai Lama at Lady Egremont's estate, Petworth House. Her son, Max Egremont, later wrote, "My mother assembled a fine array of guests… Lord Mountbatten, last British Viceroy of India; Harold Macmillan, our former prime minister; the political philosopher Sir Karl Popper; the violinist Sir Yehudi Menuhin, who played for us in the evening; and Sir Olaf Caroe, who was co-organizer of the UK trip."

attention to those he met, asked questions, and joked. He has always had a way with people and this helps break barriers, making everyone comfortable in his presence. Over the many trips that I had the fortune to accompany him on, I was most impressed with his dedication to his studies, prayer, and meditation, despite keeping a punishing schedule. Our trips in the early years were more leisurely. In those days, the Dalai Lama was not one of the most recognized faces in the world and would often take a stroll in the open or walk into a shop (although he seldom bought anything!). We would stop for meals at roadside restaurants, and the entire entourage would eat together. By the time I retired from service, the trips were very tightly scheduled, and the list of engagements was endless. It amazes me how much energy His Holiness had.

Left: His Holiness crosses the Prime Meridian line passing through the Royal Greenwich Observatory, London. As the reference point for Greenwich Mean Time (GMT), each location on Earth is measured in terms of its angle east or west from this line.

Right: His Holiness with the Archbishop of Canterbury, Michael Ramsey, at Lambeth Palace.

WINNING HEARTS IN AMERICA

Six years after the success of his maiden visit to Europe, His Holiness made two historic trips in 1979—a combined visit to Mongolia and the USSR, and a tour of the United States. Early in 1979, the US formally recognized the PRC. Soon after, His Holiness received an invitation to visit Buddhist communities in the USSR and Mongolia. Indian Diplomat Bakula Rinpoche helped organize this trip. His Holiness left for Moscow on 12 June. Despite widespread state control, he received great affection from the people. In the Buryat Republic, he visited the monastery that had been built during Stalin's time and was an outcome of the efforts of the Thirteenth Dalai Lama's friend, Dorjiev. His Holiness felt a great kinship with the congregation and the monks in attendance, despite the language difficulties. The next stop was Ulan Bator, where he visited the house where his predecessor had stayed. He was received by a group of monks in an emotional welcome.

On 2 October 1979, a crowd of 3,500 filled the East Field of the University of California, Santa Cruz, to hear the Dalai Lama speak on "The Bodhisattva Motivation: Giving and Taking." A student sums up the atmosphere: "We were insatiably curious, and at least some of us were oriented toward growth in every aspect of our lives. So when we saw the flyers announcing that a Tibetan holy man was coming to speak on the East Field, we flocked to see him."

For several years the Dalai Lama's representatives in the US were in touch with key political figures in Washington about a possible visit of His Holiness. My brother, Tenzin Namgyal, who led the Office of Tibet in the US, worked with senior staff in the US government, notably Joel McLeary and Tom Beard, to secure this first visit of the Dalai Lama. The impetus had come from Geshe Wangyal, who had emigrated to the US in 1955 and set up the Tibetan Buddhist Learning Center in New Jersey in 1958. Relations between the US and China had entered a period of rapprochement, and consequently their foreign policy objectives changed. President Jimmy Carter, while not willing to engage officially with the Dalai Lama, was sympathetic to the human rights angle of the Tibet issue.

His Holiness spoke at seventeen universities and colleges, including Amherst College and Harvard University, where students "fell in love" with him, some becoming lifelong supporters of Tibet.

The Dalai Lama tours the grounds of the University of Virginia with Professor Jeffery Hopkins, front left, his official English translator at the time. To the right, my brother, Tenzin Namgyal, who helped organize the visit to the US, talks to Dutch lawyer Michael van Walt van Praag, who has enjoyed an enduring relationship with the Dalai Lama since the early 1970s and advised the Tibetan government on international peace processes for many decades.

This seven-week tour began in New York on 3 September 1979. On his arrival, His Holiness spoke of his visit being a nonpolitical one and of his desire to learn about new systems, culture, and in particular about the latest scientific discoveries. He had been invited by religions groups, universities, and cultural societies, and his engagements during the trip reflect his own diverse interests—a parapsychological laboratory, a cancer institute, an atomic research station, and an arboretum. He impressed scientists with his pertinent questions. In a press conference in Massachusetts, he said:

> I have learned some explanations and heard about scientific research about consciousness and mind, the nature of the brain and about molecules and the small atoms...As a Buddhist trying to find a fact, we would attempt meditation. Then we may discover the explanations. They may also exist in our scriptures. But if research

finds another answer, then we have to accept the facts. Therefore, I am very interested in scientific findings."

Bob Thurman, who had last seen His Holiness in 1971, was amazed at his increased self-assurance. The forty-four-year-old Dalai Lama had grown in confidence and authority, and he charmed his delighted audience in the twenty-five cities he visited. The press praised him for spreading ideas of love and compassion. The Dalai Lama found Americans to be "open and straightforward." He was conferred an honorary doctorate by three universities, of which two were Christian institutions.

Two significant events during this visit were the interfaith service held at St. Patrick's Cathedral in New York and the reception on Capitol Hill in Washington, DC. The service at the Cathedral was hosted by Cardinal Cooke and New York's Mayor Koch and attended by leaders of many faiths, including Jewish, Baptist, and Episcopalian. "Without

His Holiness visited Capitol Hill for the first time on 11 September 1979. He first visited the Library of Congress and met the Senate Foreign Relations Committee. Later, more than 180 Congressmen attended a reception at the US House of Representatives, hosted by Charles— "Charlie"—Rose, greeting His Holiness in the photograph. The event launched the Dalai Lama and the issue of Tibet in the US government.

inner peace, it is impossible to have world peace," the Dalai Lama told his 5,000 strong audience, apologizing for his "broken English." He received a standing ovation. The reception at Capitol Hill on 11 September was organized by Congressman Charlie Rose. In stark contrast to the White House, which did not meet or acknowledge the Dalai Lama for fear of offending the Chinese, the legislative branch of the US government met him with great warmth and understanding.

For Buddhists, even those who did not follow the Tibetan tradition, it must have been encouraging to see the attention and respect America gave the Dalai Lama. He met with Buddhists of different traditions—including visiting Japanese Zen centers and Vietnamese pagodas.

This first trip was nothing like our later trips would be. We relied on the support of well-wishers, traveled economy, and were not always well organized. What we lacked in official machinery and resources, His Holiness made up for more than adequately with his natural charm, genuine ease, and passionate interest in the world. The Americans were impressed that the exiled leader did not speak about injustices toward him or his own sufferings, but of his people. He didn't mourn the past, but looked to the future with curiosity and vigor.

Right to left: His Holiness, Geshe Wangyal, one of his students, and Aku Gendun Thargay, a volunteer at the Office of Tibet. Geshe Wangyal, who had played a vital role in the escape of the Dalai Lama in 1959, leads him on his first visit to the Tibetan Buddhist Learning Center of America in New Jersey, 1979. The overall visit was so successful that one commentator wrote: "It demolished the unspoken ban on US visits; instead it marked the start of America's love affair with the Dalai Lama."

Childlike Enthusiasm

Years later, in 1991 on another trip to the US, a small community of Tibetans who had settled in Sante Fe, New Mexico, convinced His Holiness to visit them through their community leader Paljor Thondup. I was a part of the entourage.

A local resident, Douglas Preston, was appointed press secretary to His Holiness during the weeklong visit and wrote an endearing account of this trip. The press converged from several states to cover this big story. A packed schedule of meetings with politicians, film stars, billionaires, and Native American leaders and late-night dinner receptions in his honor left little time for leisure. Despite these appointments, the Dalai Lama kept his daily schedule of waking up at 3:30 am to meditate for hours. From the day we arrived in Santa Fe, His Holiness expressed his desire to see the mountains up close, and when he heard there was a ski resort nearby he was excited, as he had never seen skiing before. On the penultimate day of our trip, we drove to the ski basin. The owner of the lodge made arrangements for us to ride a ski lift. Preston sat between His Holiness and Thondup, and recounts that His Holiness could not contain his childlike excitement. Thondup wanted to hold him back, fearing that he might fall out of the ski lift. On witnessing an expert skier make a fast pass, His Holiness exclaimed in wonderment that he found skiing to be a wonderful sport. In the picturesque setting, with snowy mountain ranges and fir trees, His Holiness made a poignant remark—"This looks like Tibet."

Preston recalls that in their excitement to take in the views, His Holiness and other monks accidentally stepped into the line of an oncoming ski lift. Just then a group of teenage girl skiers came off the quad chair and skied straight down toward the Dalai Lama and his group, knocking them down. Preston rushed over, terrified that the Dalai Lama was injured. But His Holiness emerged from the crash pile laughing. His spontaneous sense of humor and ability to laugh in difficult circumstances is an incredible trait. A young waitress attending to the entourage asked His Holiness, "What is the meaning of life?" His Holiness replied, "The meaning of life is happiness." He added that hers was the easy question. The more difficult one is, "What makes people happy? Money, big house? Or compassion and a good heart?"

UNCOVERING DEVASTATING TRUTHS

After nearly twenty years, the Chinese government made indirect contact with His Holiness when they approached his brother Gyalo Thondup, who was by now living in Hong Kong. Deng Xiaoping was in power in China and had repudiated the Cultural Revolution and in 1977 launched the "Beijing Spring," which allowed open criticism of the excesses committed during this time. With his brother's permission, Gyalo Thondup traveled to Beijing in March 1979, where senior Chinese leaders told him that the Dalai Lama should send a group to Tibet "to see with one's own eyes" the improved conditions and development. The Chinese were confident that once the exiled community's delegation reported the improved conditions in Tibet, the Dalai Lama would be persuaded to return. As we were preparing for our first trip to America, His Holiness gave his blessings for a five-member delegation from the Tibetan government in exile to travel to Beijing and Tibet. We were eager to get news from inside Tibet, as many of us had given up hope of ever hearing about loved ones we had left behind. The delegation

Lobsang Samten, elder brother of the Dalai Lama, visited their birthplace, Taktser, during his trip as a member of the first delegation to Tibet. The area had been powerfully affected by the Chinese occupation and incorporated into the Qinghai province of China.

included His Holiness' elder brother, Lobsang Samten, and was headed by Juchen Thupten Namgyal, senior minister of the cabinet.

Starting in August 1979, the delegation traveled across eastern China and Tibet for five months. After spending two weeks in Beijing where they met with PRC officials, they traveled to Amdo, where locals thronged to meet them to seek news of His Holiness. In scenes from an archival film, one can witness the desperation on people's faces as they crowd the delegates and are overcome with emotion at having come into contact with the Dalai Lama's representatives. The delegates shared the news that His Holiness was well and expressed concern about their well-being. People gave them handwritten messages surreptitiously, which carried information of family members killed, tortured, or imprisoned. Some aired their grievances in front of the delegation and the Chinese minders. Many were later arrested. Perhaps the only silver lining of this trip was meeting the Panchen Lama in Beijing, who had been released from a long jail sentence and was living in reasonable health.

Lobsang Samten was greeted by an eager crowd when he visited Kumbum Monastery, where he and his younger brother had lived together for one and a half years before their journey to Lhasa in 1939. Most Tibetans here were wearing "Mao suits."

An unexpected crowd of thousands thronged to meet the first delegation to Tibet when they visited the Jokhang Temple in Lhasa. Soon after the photo was taken, the Tibetans pushed through the barriers and fell upon the delegates, in a desperate wish to see them and share their news. One member of the delegation remembered, "The Tibetans tried even to tear our *chubas* to have them as relics."

Deng Xiaoping's government was shocked at how the Tibetans had responded to the delegation's visit. The Communists had fallen for their own propaganda and had been convinced that they had won over the Tibetans. In the two decades since his departure, His Holiness continued to be deeply loved by the Tibetan people. His Holiness met the delegation on their return to Dharamsala and received the first comprehensive review of the situation in Tibet. Aside from 7,000 letters, they carried back hundreds of rolls of film, recorded conversations, and other information. It was evident that Tibetans had become second-class citizens in their own country. Tragically, their religion and way of life were seriously threatened. Tibetan students were not allowed to learn their own language, land resources were severely exploited, and any improvements in health care, education, and infrastructure in Tibet were for the sole benefit of the Chinese settlers. The Dalai Lama was deeply disturbed but decided to send another team to Tibet to investigate further.

Tenzin Namgyal Tethong surrounded by Tibetans in Barkham, Amdo Province.

My younger brother Tenzin Namgyal Tethong headed the second delegation that left for China in May 1980. Being of a younger generation, he was more forthright, which resulted in some tensions with the Chinese. This group was also received very warmly by crowds of people in Tibet. Unfortunately, their trip was cut short as authorities accused them of inciting the Tibetan people to rise up against the Chinese government. In July 1980, a third delegation of teachers and administrators, led by His Holiness' sister Jetsun Pema, left for China. Her experience was not that different from the first two delegations, and she was dismayed at seeing Tibetan culture being systematically destroyed. On her return to Dharamsala, she offered to send teachers to Tibet to give the children classes in Tibetan language. A fourth delegation went to Tibet in 1985, but their visit was limited to Amdo.

At first, these fact-finding delegations opened up a dialogue towards bilateral negotiations with China and the Dalai Lama.

Tibetan children learning Chinese at school. Jetsun Pema was appalled by what she experienced in Tibet. Although there were schools, they were completely oriented toward a Chinese education. She wrote a powerful, outspoken account of her trip and commented, "I can never forgive the Chinese for all the pain and agony, the misery and suffering, which they have brought on the children in Tibet."

A PERSONAL LOSS

Gyalyum Chenmo was an exceptional woman. Being the mother of three Rinpoches, she was regarded very highly. However, the beauty of her character was that she had no pretensions. She knew the sweepers who worked at Swarg Ashram by name and was equally at ease engaging with high-ranking Indian officials. She would tell her children, "Remember that your roots are from a peasant family."

Born in 1901 in Churka village in Amdo, in northeastern Tibet, Gyalyum Chenmo was named Sonam Tsomo by her parents. She would stitch clothes for her family and even made their boots, cooked meals, and tended to the farm. "By what she told us, it seems she only slept three hours every night!" says Rinchen Khando, her daughter-in-law. Following His Holiness' discovery and installation in Lhasa, she became Gyalyum Chenmo, or the "Great Mother." Over time though, she was simply known by her married name, Diki Tsering, which she preferred.

"I used to go to my mother and cry when my lessons with my junior tutor didn't go very well. She would shower me with love. She didn't care about tradition—she was concerned about her child's desire," said the Dalai Lama in *Women of Tibet: Gyalyum Chemo—The Great Mother* (2006), a movie based on her life. He said, "The quality of leadership—my mother had more than me. When we were still in Lhasa, she came to the Potala every month with homemade bread for me." Her cooking skills were legendary! She took pleasure in cooking and would bake different kinds of breads and traditional dishes. Years later, she passed on these recipes (many of which she developed herself) to Rinchen Khando, who continues to serve this delicious fare.

After His Holiness moved to the new residence at Thekchen Choling, Gyalyum Chenmo went to live with Ngari Rinpoche and Rinchen Khando at Kashmir Cottage, a charming home perched between Dharamsala and McLeod Ganj. Our meetings became less frequent, but I was often invited to their new home.

Gyalyum Chenmo embodied the mother figure for all us Tibetans.

The Great Mother, Gyalyum Chenmo with her son, Lobsang Samten. Ngari Rinpoche once asked their mother who was her favorite among her children. She said it was Lobsang Samten. He was the only one of her children to be with her when she passed. Closest elder brother to His Holiness, Lobsang Samten was a sensitive person, quick to offer his help to causes that would benefit others. He also served at the Bureau of Tibet in Geneva and assisted the first group of refugees there. He was later the director of Men Tsee Khang Institute.

I shared a warm relationship with her. She was quite fond of me. At times she would tease me, but her affection was evident. The Great Mother passed away on 12 January 1981, after a brief illness. Hours before she passed, she sat up, thanked all the staff for having been so kind and good to her. She then recited her mantras and passed away peacefully.

His Holiness was at Bodh Gaya pilgrimage site and was deeply saddened to hear this news. Although the time he spent with her had reduced over the years, they remained spiritually connected. He had confirmed her to continue with her prayers and have no fear of death. "She remained a very warmhearted person—she was always more concerned about other's suffering and well-being than her own…For her next life, I have no worry." On hearing the news of her passing, the monks of the monasteries in Dharamsala turned up voluntarily to say prayers and the

"Mother, I consider, our first teacher. She teaches compassion.
Soon after birth a child experiences mother's compassion and
affection. That is the most important part of building a healthy
family, and that means healthy humanity."

HIS HOLINESS THE FOURTEENTH DALAI LAMA

general public lined up for hours to pay their respects. It was a personal tragedy for us all. Her strength, simplicity, and immense kindness is still remembered.

Another particularly difficult time for His Holiness was when his beloved brother and childhood playmate, Lobsang Samten, passed away prematurely at the age of fifty-three in September 1985, after contracting pneumonia and hepatitis. His Holiness felt a great sense of regret that he could not be at his brother's side during his illness. Although His Holiness had been upset when Lobsang Samten discarded his robes to become a layman, they remained very close. He served as the director of the Men Tsee Khang Institute, and in 1979, was appointed a member of the first fact-finding delegation to travel to Tibet. I believe he never recovered from the emotional trauma caused by what he witnessed there. Once he returned from that trip, he fell into depression. His Holiness wrote, "I do not think it an exaggeration to say that he died of a broken heart."

I respected Lobsang Samten deeply because of his humility. He had kept his identity a secret during his time in the US in the mid-1970s. He initially worked at a Tibetan crafts store in Manhattan and then as a janitor at a school in New Jersey, until his identity was revealed in newspapers. When asked in an interview if he was satisfied with his job of a janitor, he said, "I have never been to school, except in the monastery where I studied Buddhism until I was 17. I have no truly modern skills. I am better off if I don't plan too much ahead. No disappointments then." I had the good fortune to spend time with him and his wife, Namlha, who is related to me. She took over as director of the Men Tsee Khang after her husband's passing and was general secretary of the Health Department (then later director of Songtsen Library). I have known their children Tenzin Namdak and Chuki since they were little. Tenzin Namdak, while studying in the US, undertook special security training. On his return I requested for him to be inducted into the Private Office. He is now one of the secretaries of the Office of His Holiness. Despite our generational gap, we worked extremely well together at the Private Office.

Facing page: The Great Mother, Gyalyum Chenmo. She gave birth to sixteen children, seven of whom survived. Three of her sons were discovered to be reincarnate *tulkus*, who choose to be reborn in order to help others. Her son the Dalai Lama very often speaks of her unconditional kindness and also her humility, never taking advantage of her status. "I first learned compassion from my mother," he has said. "Also, she never, ever, became angry. That I find really wonderful."

THE DALAI LAMA'S FAMILY TREE

1. DOMA YANGZOM
Maternal Grandmother
married to **TASHI DHONDUP**

2. CHOEKYONG TSERING
Gyalyab Chenmo,
the "Great Father"
1899–1947

3. DIKI TSERING
Gyalyum Chenmo,
the "Great Mother"
1901–1981

Born Lhamo Thondup on 6 July 1935, His Holiness the Fourteenth Dalai Lama came from a small village in northeast Tibet, called Taktser. A family of farmers and herders in a region close to China, his mother, Sonam Tsomo, was married at the age of sixteen to his father, Choekyong Tsering, in December 1917. Lhamo's eldest sister, Tsering Dolma (literally "wish-fulfilling goddess"), was born eighteen years before him. She was followed by three sons, before the "Precious Protector" was born. In the end, there were seven children in the family, five boys and two girls. When the four-year-old Dalai Lama took his seat in Lhasa, the family was elevated to the rank of highest nobility. Spiritually close to his mother and other members of the family, His Holiness, along with his siblings, their spouses, and their children, have always been committed to the Tibetan cause and played prominent roles through these years in exile. Each of them has provided their expertise and services to fellow Tibetans in the fields of refugee settlements, education, health, and conservation of Tibetan heritage and culture.

1. **TSERING DOLMA**
Eldest Sister, 1919–1964

2. **THUBTEN JIGME NORBU**
Taktser Rinpoche
Eldest Brother, 1922–2008

3. **GYALO THONDUP**
Brother, 1928–

4. **LOBSANG SAMTEN**
Closest Elder Brother, 1932–1985

5. **LHAMO THONDUP**
HIS HOLINESS THE DALAI LAMA
Tenzin Gyatso

1935–

6. **JETSUN PEMA**
Youngest Sister, 1940–

7. **TENDZIN CHOEGYAL**
Ngari Rinpoche
Youngest Brother, 1946–

In Service of the People

His Holiness in an interview said, "My youngest sister [Jetsun Pema] and brother [Tendzin Choegyal] and I, we are very close. As soon as we get together, it's just all sorts of nonsense and jokes and teasing and pranks. We're very, very close; when we're together, it's like we're at the top of the world. I think we're quite similar, too. Straightforward, openhearted."

Each member of His Holiness' family has conducted their lives with a deep sense of purpose. I am fortunate to call some of them my friends. I came to know Jetsun Pema and Ngari Rinpoche when I joined the Private Office because we lived in the same compound in Swarg Ashram. As the three of us had attended schools in Darjeeling, we had much in common. Both Ngari Rinpoche and I were monks at the time and would often escape and go on hikes. We would fly paper planes, read poems, and quote lines from plays and books we admired. I am sure Gyalyum Chenmo took a liking to me not only because of her natural kindness but also because I was friends with her two youngest children.

Ngari Rinpoche taught at TCV for some time and later joined the Private Office where we

1. Jetsun Pema, Gyalo Thondup with children Tenzin Khedroob and Yangzom Dolma, and Khandro Tsering, daughter of Tsering Dolma. **2.** In 1978–79, many of His Holiness' family gathered at Kashmir Cottage. Standing, left to right: Tenzin Choedon (daughter of Jetsun Pema), Gyalo Thondup, Lobsang Samten, Jetsun Pema, Rinchen Khando (wife of Ngari Rinpoche), Namgyal Lhamo (wife of Lobsang Samten). Front row: Tenzin Namdak (son of Lobsang Samten), Gyalyum Chenmo, Tenzin Choezom (daughter of Ngari Rinpoche) with Chuki (daughter of Lobsang Samten), Kalsang Yangzom (daughter of Jetsun Pema), covering her eyes, Tenzin Choedak (son of Jetsun Pema), on a tricycle. **3.** Tendzin Choegyal and Rinchen Khando. **4.** Thubten Jigme Norbu and wife Kunchok Yangkyi with children Lhundrup, Kunga, and Jigme. **5.** Tenzin (left) and Chuki (right), children of Lobsang Samten and Namgyal Lhamo.

worked together. Rinchen Khando is director of the Tibetan Nuns Project, has been president of the Tibetan Women's Association, and both she and Jetsun served in the Tibetan government as elected ministers. Namgyal Lhamo worked in the Department of Health, directed the Men Tsee Khang. Her son, Tenzin, became Secretary to His Holiness in 1996. Gyalo Thondup's wife, Diki Dolkar, did great service at the Self-Help Centre in Darjeeling. Her son, Khedroob, took over after his mother's death; he had also been a member of Parliament. His sister, Yangzom, worked at the LTWA. Tsering Dolma's daughter Khandro became Head of the Tibetan Homes Foundation and worked in the Department of Information and International Relations. Her brother, Ngawang, was earlier at the Council for Tibetan Education and later edited the *Tibetan Review*.

A PEACE PLAN FOR THE FUTURE
AND STRASBOURG PROPOSAL

While Tibet still did not have official support in Europe and America, by the mid-1980s, small groups of influential supporters had emerged. In 1987, His Holiness was invited to speak before the US Congressional Human Rights Caucus, giving him a valuable opportunity to put forth our ideas. He hoped that China would feel some pressure due to these developments.

In a powerful speech on 21 September, the Dalai Lama referred to the holocaust of the Tibetan people and said, "Though Tibetans lost their freedom, under international law Tibet today is still an independent state under illegal occupation." He then put forward a proposal called the Five-Point Peace Plan for the Future of Tibet.

Five-Point Peace Plan

• The transformation of the whole of Tibet into a zone of peace.

• Abandonment of China's population transfer policy which threatens the very existence of the Tibetan people.

• Respect for the Tibetan people's fundamental human rights and democratic freedoms.

• Restoration and protection of Tibet's natural environment and the abandonment of China's use of Tibet for the production of nuclear weapons and dumping of nuclear waste.

• Commencement of earnest negotiations on the future status of Tibet and of relations between the Tibetan and Chinese people.

His presentation was very well received at Capitol Hill. A month later the Senate passed its bill, and on 22 December 1987, President Ronald Reagan signed the Foreign Relations Authorization Act. Containing amendments specific to Tibet, this law called upon China to respect international law and end the violation of the human rights of the Tibetan people, reciprocate His Holiness' peaceful gestures, and release all Tibetan political prisoners.

This historic proposal by His Holiness was an exciting and inspiring moment for us. However, the Chinese immediately rejected His Holiness' proposal. Soon, widespread protests erupted in Lhasa against the dismissive Chinese response to the peace plan. On 27 September, monks of Drepung monastery took to streets in protest. Two American mountaineers, John Ackerly and Blake Kerr, who were arrested, threatened, and released after a few days, witnessed the next protest by the monks of Sera Monastery and the Jokhang Temple on 1 October, joined later by lay people. Both shared their eyewitness accounts of the events, and Ackerly's photographs of the protests were eventually published. Robert Barnett, who later founded the Tibet Information Network, also wrote about the brutal violence unleashed by Chinese forces that he had witnessed. Numerous monks and lay people were arrested. Chinese sources claimed that protestors had run amok attacking the police, and the *People's Daily* described the events of 1 October as "a serious political incident instigated and engineered by the Dalai clique."

On 6 October, 250 armed police attacked a peaceful protest of 50 unarmed monks. Chinese authorities expelled foreigners and journalists from Lhasa immediately. Police violence had resulted in the death of 12 people, although some reports say 20 died. The police conducted

I translated for His Holiness at Capitol Hill, Washington DC, on a few occasions, such as this one. On 21 September 1987, His Holiness announced his Five-Point Peace Plan for Tibet. Congressmen Charlie Rose and Tom Lantos—who was also co-chair of the Caucus—supported his presentation. I had the honor to translate on this occasion, too.

widespread arrests in the aftermath, and over time almost 2,000 people were arrested. Many were beaten and tortured in custody, and nearly 40 people were executed. This cycle of violence was to continue over the next year.

Early in 1988, in an effort to give an impression of normalcy, the Chinese authorities ordered monasteries to conduct the *Monlam* Prayer Festival. The festival had been reinstated in 1986 after a ban of twenty years. The monks were forced to go ahead with preparations. On March 5, trouble broke out again. A group of monks demanded the release of a *tulku* named Yulu Dawa Tsering, who had been arrested by the Chinese the previous October. Some of the monks gathered for the festival began shouting anti-Chinese slogans and throwing stones at the police. The police chased the protesters, beating and killing several of them. They entered the Jokhang Temple at noon killing twelve monks and beating up several others. As His Holiness writes, "Tibet's holiest shrine became like a butcher's shop." Widespread riots broke out later as Tibetans retaliated in anger, which led to more vicious Chinese reprisals.

Several world leaders called upon China to open a dialogue with His Holiness. This pressure forced China to accept an independent fact-finding mission to Tibet in 1987, led by Lord David Ennals, who later became a tireless campaigner and a close friend to His Holiness.

Amid this, His Holiness received an invitation to address the European Parliament, in Strasbourg, on 15 June 1988. Emphasizing universal responsibility and the world's interconnectedness, His Holiness elaborated on the fifth point of the Five-Point Peace Plan and offered an olive branch to the Chinese—autonomy for Tibet:

> The Government of the People's Republic of China would remain responsible for Tibet's foreign policy. The Government of Tibet should, however, develop and maintain relations, through its own foreign affairs bureau, in the field of commerce, education, culture, religion, tourism, science, sports, and other nonpolitical activities.

His Holiness also said that he was aware of the disappointment in store for Tibetans about his proposal but felt it was "an essential and invaluable

part of any process of change."

China immediately denounced His Holiness' speech, but within months they expressed willingness to engage with the Dalai Lama at a venue, date, and with a delegation of his choice. His Holiness suggested January 1989, in Geneva. Once again there was an impasse as the Chinese put forward impossible conditions: they preferred Beijing as the venue; no foreigners were permitted in our delegation; and no member of the Tibetan government-in-exile was welcome, since they did not recognize it.

Many Tibetans were disappointed when His Holiness spoke of autonomy instead of complete independence. I was, too. For the first time, Tibetans in exile were divided in their opinion. But I realized it was the only practical approach His Holiness could adopt. Later, when the Chinese agreed to hold talks with our representatives, I was hopeful. But after a few meetings, I was once again convinced that the Chinese were not sincere. Despite our best efforts for peaceful dialogue with China, things were to take a turn for the worse when, in December 1988, two people were shot and killed at a peaceful demonstration in Lhasa. Tibet had become a tinderbox.

Jokhang monk, Jampa Tenzin, and protestors, in Lhasa, 1987. After emerging from a burning police station, having led the rescue of fellow monk prisoners, Jampa Tenzin was hailed by the crowd. Though the monks were rescued, Jampa Tenzin suffered bad burns and was arrested and tortured. He later died.

CHINA EXPOSED: MARTIAL LAW IN LHASA, TIANANMEN SQUARE INCIDENT

The year 1989 brought great turmoil and change. The *Monlam Prayer Festival*, scheduled to start on 7 February 1989, was canceled due to continued unrest. On 5 March, tens of thousands took to the streets of Lhasa. In a change of tactics, the Chinese stood by, filmed the demonstrations, and aired the images on television that night. However, the next day the police did not hold back. The *Washington Post* reported that police fired on a pro-independence protest march of monks and nuns, killing many. The death toll was estimated to be around thirty by eyewitnesses, the report said. There were even reports of Chinese forces shooting at people's homes, killing entire families.

Widespread condemnation of the violence followed, with France, the US, and the European Parliament issuing statements denouncing China. On 7 March, Chinese authorities asked all foreigners to leave

Monks from the Jokhang Temple were beaten, arrested, and detained by the PLA during unrest in Lhasa, 1989.

Lhasa. Armed reinforcements entered the city, and by 3 pm a shoot-on-sight order came into effect. On the follwing day martial law was declared. Detentions began, as Chinese officials went door-to-door asking people to produce proof that they had not taken part in the recent demonstrations. Soon, detention and "reeducation" centers were filled beyond capacity and additional ones had to be opened. His Holiness was aghast by the brutality but also saddened that Tibetans had resorted to violence and had attacked security forces. On 10 March, the anniversary of the 1959 People's Uprising, the Dalai Lama wrote to Deng Xiaoping to ask him to stop the Chinese violence and killing, to no avail.

While Lhasa was still reeling from the brutal crackdown, China received a shock that would draw the world's attention. The progressive Chinese leader Hu Yaobang died suddenly of a heart attack during a Politburo meeting in Beijing on 15 April. This provided a pretext for the nascent pro-democracy student movement. Thousands of students gathered to mourn his death and to show support for his policies at

Arrest of a Tibetan in 1989.

Tiananmen Square. On 17 April 1989, about 3,000 students of Peking and Tsinghua universities marched to Tiananmen Square, where they drew up a list of demands for the reforms. Hu's funeral was scheduled for 22 April, and the authorities closed the square as a precaution. But on the eve of his funeral, defying orders, over 100,000 students gathered.

On 13 May, the students began a hunger strike. Deng Xiaoping tried to persuade the students to leave, but by now the movement had grown exponentially, and over a million people took to the streets. On 20 May, the government declared martial law and ordered a massive troop deployment in the capital. The students remained steadfast and blocked the entry of the forces into the city. On the evening of 3 June, the crackdown began. On 4 June, as helicopters hovered over Tiananmen Square, the Chinese authorities sent in armored tanks and ruthlessly crushed the demonstrations. We were shocked and could hardly believe this brutal action taken against their own people.

The international press, already in Beijing to cover Soviet leader Mikhail Gorbachev's historic visit from the 15th to the 19th of May, stayed on as the Tiananmen story developed. On 5 June, the brutal attack became headline news through the now-iconic image of a lone man defying a military tank by standing in its way. Chinese authorities claimed the death toll to be 300, but declassified documents released later show the figure to be closer to 3,400. The Tiananmen Square incident remains one of the worst examples of state violence against its own people.

The implementation of martial law in Tibet and the Tiananmen Square crackdown brought increased global attention to Beijing's repressive methods and to the Tibetan cause. This resulted in the founding of many Tibet support groups around the world.

"Tiananmen Square proved that a regime that would have no hesitation to shoot their own people, such a regime... There should be no doubt about their attitude towards other nationalities."

HIS HOLINESS THE FOURTEENTH DALAI LAMA

THE POISONED ARROW

Following the Dalai Lama's escape to India in 1959, the Panchen Lama was named the vice-chairman of the Tibetan National People's Congress so that he could become the spokesperson for Chinese policy in Tibet. In this capacity, the Panchen Lama traveled extensively across many regions of China and Tibet. Following the tour in 1962, the Panchen Lama wrote the "70,000 Character Petition," the most detailed and informed attack on China's policies in Tibet that would ever be written, It revealed the systematic abuse of the Tibetan people. This proved to be his undoing. Mao described it as "...a poisoned arrow shot at the Party by reactionary feudal overlords." In 1964, after the Panchen Lama openly called for Tibetan independence, he was removed from office, humiliated by the Politburo, declared an "enemy of the Tibetan people," and imprisoned. He spent the next eleven years in prison and four more under house arrest. He later gave up monkhood, and in 1979 married a Chinese woman. Following his release, the Communist Party of China fully rehabilitated him. He then made great efforts to restore Tibetan culture and way of life by establishing educational and cultural institutions.

At the time of his death at the age of just fifty-one on 28 January 1989, the Panchen Lama was at the Tashilhunpo Monastery in Shigatse while on a rare trip to Tibet from Beijing. Many felt that his death at his traditional seat was indeed symbolic—"the deliberate gesture of a true spiritual master." His Holiness considered the Panchen Lama to be a "true freedom fighter" of Tibet.

The Panchen Lama. His Holiness was invited by the Buddhist Association of China to attend the Panchen Lama's funeral in Beijing. This could have only come at the instruction of the highest authorities in China. The Dalai Lama turned down the invitation despite "personally" wanting to go. He writes, "Had the Geneva talks taken place as planned, this might have been opportune."

The Middle Way

For a long time, His Holiness had been considering a solution that would be mutually acceptable to both China and Tibet. In 1979, after Deng Xiaoping conveyed to His Holiness that "except independence, all other issues can be resolved through negotiations," the idea of a Middle Way took more immediate form. On 6 June 1988, a four-day conference was organized in Dharamsala, bringing together members of the Tibetan Assembly, the government, civil servants, Tibetan NGOs, and legal advisors such as Michael van Walt. After due consultations, His Holiness announced the Middle-Way Approach, marking a shift away from the government-in-exile's demand for complete independence, put forth in Strasbourg in 1988. He saw it as a vision for Tibet as an autonomous region much like the other ethnic regions within China.

The Middle-Way Approach proposed that an autonomous region of the three traditional provinces of Tibet be created with meaningful, genuine autonomy. The Dalai Lama assured the Chinese that they would not seek independence from PRC and would accept the central Chinese government's control in international relations and defense, but Tibetans would become autonomous in matters of religion, culture, education, economy, health, and environment. Further, the proposal called for China to stop human rights violations against Tibetans. His Holiness considered this middle path to be a method leading to peaceful reconciliation and coexistence of Tibetan and Chinese people, which he believed would be mutually beneficial to both, and stated that he would sincerely pursue this agenda with the Chinese government.

While China did not respond positively, Tibetan opinion too, was divided. Though His Holiness' pragmatic approach was lauded by international leaders, and even mentioned in the 1989 Nobel Prize citation, certain sections of the Tibetan community were not in favor of a demand that did not include full independence.

His Holiness reiterated the proposal in 1996, which remains in effect even today. In 1997, an opinion poll was conducted among the Tibetan people, and the results showed that a large number were supportive of His Holiness' plan. As a result, on 18 September 1997, the Assembly of Tibetan People's Deputies passed a resolution in favor of the proposal. In his annual 10 March statement in 1998, His Holiness said,

> I wish to thank the people of Tibet for the tremendous trust, confidence, and hope they place in me. I continue to believe that my "Middle-Way Approach" is the most realistic and pragmatic course to resolve the issue of Tibet peacefully. This approach meets the vital needs of the Tibetan people while ensuring the unity and stability of the People's Republic of China. I will, therefore, continue to pursue this course of approach with full commitment and make earnest efforts to reach out to the Chinese leadership.

Unfortunately, China has not allowed for any progress, and we are still as distant from a peaceful solution as we were sixty years ago.

Facing page: Mural of Nagarjuna at the Norbulingka Institute, Dharamsala. The Nalanda Monastic University scholar and master, Nagarjuna (c. 150–250 AD) expounded the philosophical doctrine of the Middle Way, influencing debate for a thousand years after his death. The Middle Way continues to be the pinnacle of philosophical sophistication in the Mahayana tradition of Buddhism to the present day.

NOBEL PEACE PRIZE

In early October 1989, while Tibet was still under martial law, I traveled with His Holiness to Newport, California, to attend a conference with prominent American neuroscientists. While there, we received the news that he had won the Nobel Peace Prize in recognition of his sustained nonviolent campaign to end China's domination of his homeland. The Norwegian Nobel Committee said the Dalai Lama was being recognized because he "consistently has opposed the use of violence" in his campaign:

> We immediately held a press conference, where His Holiness said,
>
> I very much appreciate that kind of recognition about my beliefs. In fact, I always believed in love, compassion, and a sense of universal respect. Every human being has that potential. My case is nothing special. I am a simple Buddhist monk—no more, no less.

This tremendous accolade followed the violent suppression of the Chinese democracy movement, as well as the crushing of pro-independence demonstrations and the imposition of martial law in Lhasa. Egil Aarvik, chairman of the Norwegian Nobel Committee, said that events in the East had contributed to the decision to honor the

His Holiness received the Nobel Peace Prize in Oslo, December 1989, from Egil Aarvik, chairman of the Nobel Committee.

Facing page: His Holiness traveled to Oslo to receive the Nobel Peace Prize. Acommmpanying him are (left to right) Lodi Gyari and Kelsang Gyaltsen, both of whom were subsequently appointed special envoys of the Dalai Lama, entrusted with conducting dialogues with the Chinese leadership.

Dalai Lama and that the selection could be interpreted as a signal of encouragement for the democracy movement.

For His Holiness it was "a cruel counterpoint" to the martial law in Lhasa but it meant "a great deal to the people of Tibet, for it was they who were the real 'winners' of the prize." It was an acknowledgement of the values he espoused— of compassion, forgiveness, and love.

The Tibetan community was ecstatic, and there were many celebrations among Tibetans in exile. As we readied to attend the ceremony, His Holiness prepared his acceptance speech. He provided the main points, and Michael van Walt and Lodi Gyari worked on the speech. It was then looked at by me and my colleague at the Private Office, Kelsang Gyaltsen, before it was finalized by His Holiness. On -10 December, we attended the ceremony in Oslo. He accepted the Prize on behalf of "the six million Tibetan people...(my) brave countrymen and women inside Tibet, who have suffered and continue to suffer so much."

The prize was a turning point in many ways. From here on, the Dalai Lama became one of the most recognized global leaders, bringing much-needed attention to the Tibetan cause. It also brought a new direction in his life. He had begun his speech with the message of unity of all people, despite their differences.

Inset: The Nobel medal, featuring Swedish inventor and industrialist Alfred Nobel, whose will set aside a fund for the awarding of five annual prizes "to those who, during the preceding year, shall have conferred the greatest benefit on mankind."

His Holiness the Dalai Lama, delivering his Nobel Peace Prize lecture in Oslo, 1989.

"We are all basically the same human beings. We all seek happiness. We have the same basic needs and concerns." This is the essence of his concept of "universal responsibility" or human values, secular ethics. Over the next few years, this idea developed and formed the core of his political thought, as well. Since then, his talks have centered on ethics as the only way to save the world from self-destruction.

Many of His Holiness' international friends came to Oslo to celebrate with us. The ceremony was followed by a grand official dinner. A crowd spontaneously came out onto the streets of Oslo. Many were holding the Tibetan national flag. His Holiness greeted them from the balcony of his hotel. Robert Thurman shouted out, asking His Holiness to join them. True to his character, His Holiness agreed. Tashi Wangdi, our representative in Delhi, gave the Tibetan flag he was holding to His Holiness to wave. This was one of the most thrilling moments of my life.

Rapid changes had been taking place around the world. A month earlier, the Berlin Wall had fallen. His Holiness went to the Wall during his visit to Germany before traveling to Oslo. As he recalls:

> As I stood there, in full view of a still-manned security post, an old lady silently handed me a candle. With some emotion, I lit it and held it up. For a moment, the tiny dancing flame threatened to go out, but it held and, while a crowd pressed round me, touching my hands, I prayed that the light of compassion and awareness would fill the world and dispel the darkness of fear and oppression.

The Dalai Lama traveled to Karasjok, northern Norway, after receiving the Nobel Peace Prize, at the invitation of Ole Henrik Magga, first president of the Sami Parliament. The Sami are an indigenous people who, like the Tibetans, are intent on keeping their culture and language intact. Their discussions were followed by a reindeer-led sleigh ride, to the delight of His Holiness who had not seen a reindeer before.

"I believe that to meet the challenges of our times, human beings will have to develop a greater sense of universal responsibility. Each of us must learn to work not just for oneself, one's own family, or one's nation, but for the benefit of all humankind. Universal responsibility is the key to human survival. It is the best foundation for world peace."

HIS HOLINESS THE FOURTEENTH DALAI LAMA

Part 4:
Universal Compassion and Healing the World

DEMOCRACY AND THE ART OF HAPPINESS
1989 ONWARD

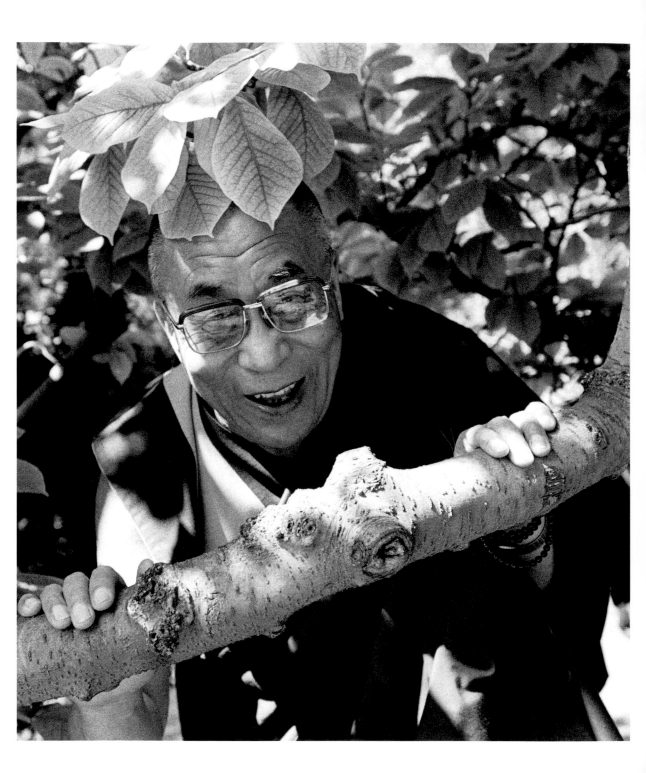

A GLOBAL ICON

It would be an understatement to say that after being awarded the Nobel Peace Prize, His Holiness was catapulted into prominence and is today one of the most recognized faces in the world. This is particularly moving for me because I am reminded of our early years as new refugees in India, when he would tirelessly appeal to world leaders to garner support for the Tibetan people. We did not always receive a favorable response. Two years after the Nobel Prize award, His Holiness was received for the first time by a serving American president, George H. W. Bush, during his visit to Washington. This endorsement, despite China's response, paved the way for him to be welcomed by other world leaders—from Prince Charles to the Pope and from the president of Estonia to the prime minister of Australia. Today, His Holiness fills stadiums across the world, has admirers everywhere, including those of other faiths, is a bestselling author of more than 200 books, has received several honorary degrees and keys to cities, and has been voted several times as one of the most acclaimed public figures in the world.

As we entered the 1990s, His Holiness' travels increased as he was invited by influential political and religious leaders, scientists, and cultural figures to their countries. With increased media coverage of his visits and His Holiness' popularity, the world's focus on the Tibetan cause rapidly ascended.

Shortly after the Berlin Wall fell on 9 November 1989, the Velvet Revolution ousted the Czech Communist Party. On December 29, playwright and human rights activist Vaclev Havel became president. In his first New Year's speech on 1 January 1990, Havel said, "I would be happy if Pope John Paul II and the Tibetan Dalai Lama visited our country even if for a single day." In 1990, President Havel invited His Holiness to Czechoslovakia. We (his entourage) were hosted at Lany Castle on the outskirts of Prague. During the two-day stay, they held discussions about freedom, peace, and ethics. The president invited His Holiness to visit the Wenceslas Square for martyrs and also fulfilled a long-held desire—

Facing: His Holiness peeks over tree branches in the garden of Lany Castle, near Prague, during a visit with Czech President Vaclav Havel in 2002.

In 1990, President Havel became the first head of state to invite His Holiness for an official visit.

to meditate with him. When the two met, it became a tradition that His Holiness would insist on pouring tea for the president. His reception in Prague rivaled the Peace Prize ceremony in Oslo.

His Holiness pouring tea for President Havel during his visit in 2002.

His Holiness visted Warsaw in 1993 to meet with Lech Walesa, president of Poland, who won the Nobel Peace Prize later that year. Their meeting was a symbolic endorsement of the shared values of peace, justice, and democracy. In April 1994, during a visit to the US, His Holiness met President Bill Clinton and Vice President Al Gore. The White House issued a statement characterizing the violations of human rights in Tibet as a matter of concern and linking it to the most-favored-nation status that China enjoyed with the US. This angered the Chinese government, which criticized the US administration, adding that their meeting with the Dalai Lama was a "serious interference in China's

1. His Holiness with Lech Walesa. **2.** The Dalai Lama met with Nelson Mandela in South Africa in 1996. **3.** Soviet Union leader Mikhail Gorbachev had contributed to a change that had global impact, said His Holiness. **4.** Barack Obama first met the Dalai Lama while he was a senator in 2005. This meeting at the White House took place in 2016 when he was president. **5.** In 2014, fellow Nobel Laureates Shirin Ebadi (Iran) and Jody Williams (US) joined celebrations in Dharamsala to mark twenty-five years since His Holiness received the Nobel Peace Prize. **6.** The Dalai Lama with then Taiwanese President Lee Teng-hui in Taiwan, in March 1997.

internal affairs," reiterating that Tibet was a part of China. Unfortunately, Washington buckled under this pressure and reversed its policy in mid-1994. The mood in Dharamsala became despondent.

In August 1996, His Holiness met Nelson Mandela, another fellow Nobel Laureate, in South Africa. It had been just two years since apartheid had been dismantled, and a new era had begun. Clasping Nelson Mandela's hand in his, the Dalai Lama said that his had been a freedom struggle of nonviolence. The enemy, he said, was the best teacher from whom to learn patience, tolerance, and develop genuine compassion.

In 1997, for the first time, the Dalai Lama met the first popularly elected president of Taiwan, Lee Teng-hui. On his passing in July 2020, His Holiness wrote, "His contribution to Taiwan's democratic developement was an exceptional achievement. I regard him as a personal friend." In 1998, he met Mikhail Gorbachev. Thanks to his *glasnost* policies, religious freedom was again allowed by law after seventy years of restrictions. This was welcomed by the many Buddhists in the Soviet Union.

In the same year he also met former US President Jimmy Carter, French President Jacques Chirac, and the UN Secretary General Kofi Annan. His Holiness had on several occasions met Danielle Mitterand, the wife of the French president, who was a prominent supporter of the Tibetan cause. His Holiness also met with Willy Brandt, the former chancellor of West Germany.

Over the years, the Dalai Lama has enjoyed meeting people from all strata of society. Some of his fellow Nobel Laureates have been consistent friends, such as Betty Williams, Elie Wiesel, Archbishop Desmond Tutu, Jody Williams, Shirin Ebadi, and recently, Kailash Satyarthi, a champion of children's rights in India. During his travels, he goes out of his way to meet the staff of places he visits, such as homeless shelters, women's empowerment centers, and high-security prisons, to engage with all people as "a simple Buddhist monk."

Facing page: Tibetans keep their photos of His Holiness hidden. In Nepal (bottom left), a framed photo is worn on a topknot on the head.

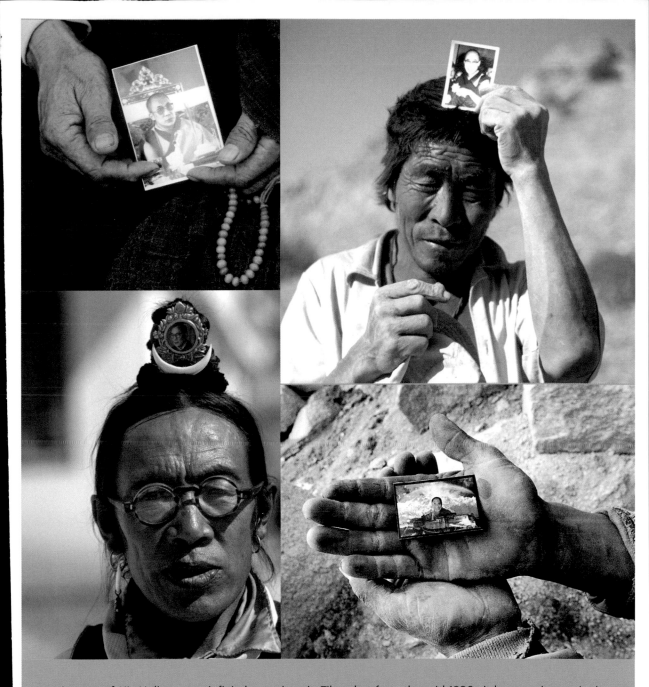

Images of His Holiness are infinitely precious in Tibet, but from the mid-1990s it became increasingly dangerous to display them. After sweeping policy changes in Beijing, new restrictions were placed on the practice of Buddhism, and this led to bans on Tibetans keeping any images of the Dalai Lama. Tibetans responded to the ban with imagination and ingenuity, displaying empty picture frames as a symbol of their devotion, or images of Avalokiteshvara, the Buddha of compassion, whose manifestation is recognized in the Dalai Lama. In areas subject to intense crackdown, raids on people's homes in search of Dalai Lama images still take place, and now the Communist Party authorities require Tibetans to display images of Xi Jinping instead, and even to prostrate to those pictures. Nevertheless, images of the Dalai Lama are still treasured, often hidden on secret shrines in homes and monasteries today.

Human rights groups around the world continue to campaign for the release of Gendun Choekyi Nyima, or at the very least, for observers to be allowed to visit him. His Holiness holds his photo during a private audience and interview in 1997.

World's Youngest Political Prisoner

Two years after the sudden death of the tenth Panchen Lama in 1989, His Holiness sent a message to the Chinese authorities offering to assist in the search for his successor. This was in accordance with tradition, as both the Dalai Lama and the Panchen Lama generally help oversee the selection process of each other's reincarnations.

The Chinese authorities allowed Chadrel Rinpoche, the abbot of Tashilhunpo Monastery and head of the search party committee, to contact the Dalai Lama. At the end of 1994, he sent a list of twenty-five names to His Holiness, indicating that one of them, Gendun Choekyi Nyima, seemed to be the right candidate. His Holiness' divination confirmed this choice, and on 14 May 1995, he announced the young boy as the eleventh Panchen Lama. The Chinese government immediately disqualified the appointment, saying His Holiness had not consulted them before making the announcement. They later installed Gyaltsen Norbu instead. The six-year-old Gendun Choekyi Nyima, together with his entire family, was forcibly detained three days after His Holiness's announcement, becoming the world's youngest political prisoner. He has not been seen in public since. His Holiness issued a statement in 2018 saying that "a reliable source" had confirmed that Gendun Choekyi Nyima was alive.

"NO END TO OUR PAIN"
SELF-IMMOLATION BY TIBETANS

Since 2011, more than 150 Tibetans have self-immolated in Tibet and China, and ten in exile, the youngest being just fifteen years old. This desperate action of Tibetans, including monks, nuns, teachers, students, and herdsmen, is to bring the world's attention to their plight. Many protestors have called for the protection of Tibetan culture and religion, the Panchen Lama to be freed, for human rights and freedom in Tibet, and most of all, for the Dalai Lama's return to Tibet.

The first Tibetan to self-immolate for the cause of Tibet, Thupten Ngodup, did so in Delhi during a 1998 hunger strike. This was the precursor to an unprecedented series of self-immolations that began in Tibet in 2009. In March 2012, nearly 3,000 Tibetans gathered to protest against the Chinese occupation of Tibet and the upcoming visit of Chinese President Hu Jintao to Delhi. Twenty-six-year-old Jampal Yeshi was one of the protestors. Originally from Kham, he had escaped Tibet in 2006, trekking for over a month across Nepal and then into India. Upon reaching Dharamsala, he fulfilled his dream of meeting His Holiness. He settled in Delhi, where he lived in Majnu ka Tilla, a colony of Tibetan refugees set up in 1963. During the protest, "Jashi" (to his friends) set himself on fire, on 26 March 2012. His friends, with the help of the police, put out the flames, but it was too late—he had suffered fatal burns.

Above: Tapey, a monk in his twenties, self-immolated near his monastery, Kirti, in eastern Tibet, in 2009, after the cancellation of prayer ceremonies by Chinese authorities and ongoing persecution of the monks.

Below: Jampal Yeshi set himself on fire during protests in New Delhi in 2012.

Images of Jashi engulfed in flames made the news the next day, and there was an immense outpouring of grief. His Holiness has described the burnings as acts of desperation he is powerless to stop. We were all shocked and deeply saddened by the incident. His Holiness was very disturbed. A memorial service was held in the main temple in Dharamsala, where his body was laid, wrapped in the Tibetan flag. Thousands came to pay their respects, including several members of government. Jampal Yeshi's act was a reminder to us all that Tibetans (especially the youth) were frustrated with the lack of progress in negotiations with the Chinese.

"THE WORLD BELONGS TO HUMANITY"
ESTABLISHING DEMOCRACY

As a small boy in Tibet, His Holiness was attracted to democracy. He recognized that in the existing Tibetan system of government too much power rested in a few hands. He describes witnessing the regent bullying a supplicant and deciding then that things had to change. After taking responsibility for Tibet in 1951, he set up a reform committee to bring about that change. However, the committee's work was hampered by the Chinese authorities. They saw Tibetan-driven reforms as antithetical to their own designs. On his 1954 visit to China, the Dalai Lama witnessed the long-winded, ponderous meetings of the Chinese communist government in Beijing. But he was enthralled in 1956 by the vibrant energy of the Indian Parliament, where he saw democracy in action.

Within his first year in exile, he encouraged the establishment of a body of elected representatives within the Tibetan refugee community. When members of the Commission of Tibetan People's Deputies took

Professor Samdhong Rinpoche became chairman of the *kashag*, or Tibetan cabinet, in August 2001, after being elected by popular vote among Tibetans in exile. His Holiness then stepped back from involvement in the day-to-day affairs of the Central Tibetan Administration.

their oaths of office in September 1960, it was the first time in our history that representatives of the three provinces of Tibet and of Tibet's four major Buddhist traditions had assembled together.

On 10 March 1963, the second anniversary of Tibetan Uprising Day, His Holiness presented a draft constitution for discussion. These were his first steps in a long process of encouraging and educating Tibetans to exercise power through their elected representatives. This culminated in 2001 with the election of the chairman of the Kashag, which enabled His Holiness to feel he could retire from his political responsibilities.

In 2011, the Dalai Lama renounced his political role entirely. The current *sikyong* (president) serving his second term of five years, is Dr. Lobsang Sangay, a Harvard law graduate. They are pictured at his swearing-in ceremony on 27 May 2016.

In his travels around the world, His Holiness has frequently been the guest of parliamentarians and democratic representatives. He is a keen advocate of democratic values of freedom, equality, and justice. He frequently mentions what an honor it is for him to speak to elected representatives of the people. When he compares India and China, he notes that India is a democracy with a functioning judiciary, where there is freedom of speech and a free press. China is economically and militarily powerful, but, he remarks, if it is to exercise a positive influence in the world, it would need to earn the world's trust. The values of democracy, freedom, and the rule of law are globally cherished. Even China faces internal democratic movements, so it must find a more realistic approach.

His Holiness has often affirmed his support for democratic values:

> The world belongs to humanity, and each country belongs to its people, not to their rulers. Democracy is the best way to govern a country, as it's a system in which the leadership is accountable to the public. A free media is essential. But the media must be honest.

He points out that democracy is rooted in having a sense of concern for others and respecting their views. Since human beings need to live together, the only way to settle conflicts is to engage in dialogue and avoid violence and the use of force.

US CONGRESSIONAL GOLD MEDAL

In a historic move, on 27 September 2006, US President George W. Bush signed "The Fourteenth Dalai Lama Congressional Medal Act," bestowing America's highest civilian award on His Holiness. The legislation was a result of two resolutions: one sponsored by Diane Feinstein and Craig Thomas in the Senate; and the other by Ileana Ros-Lehtinen and Tom Lantos in the House of Representatives. It was passed under Nancy Pelosi's tenure as speaker of the House. She continues to be a strong supporter of the Tibetan cause.

They outlined that His Holiness is widely recognized the world over as a "leading figure of moral and religious authority" and has led the Tibetan people as its spiritual and cultural leader, advocating through peaceful means a negotiated settlement of the Tibetan issue with China.

On 17 October 2007, in a ceremony in the Rotunda of the US Capitol in Washington, His Holiness was formally awarded the medal by President Bush, in the presence of House and Senate leadership.

Facing page: His Holiness celebrates the Gold Medal award with supporters who had gathered on the west lawn of the Capitol building.

Below: Receiving the Congressional Gold Medal. Left to right: Representative Ileana Ros-Lehtinen, First Lady Laura Bush, the Dalai Lama, behind him Speaker Nancy Pelosi, Senator Robert Byrd, and President George W. Bush.

Inset: Obverse of the medal.

"I am deeply touched that this great honor
has been given to me, for this monk, born of a
simple family from a remote mountain region
of Tibet."

THE FOURTEENTH DALAI LAMA

Many involved in the Tibetan cause, from Richard Gere, chairman of the Board of the Washington-based International Campaign for Tibet (ICT), to representatives of global Tibet support groups, attended the ceremony. ICT had been actively involved in this Congressional initiative. The award was in part due to the diplomatic efforts of Lodi Gyari, special envoy of His Holiness in Washington, DC. My brother, Tenzin Namgyal, who had helped found ICT, accompanied him. Samdhong Rinpoche, then a political leader, was also present.

In his acceptance speech His Holiness said the award was not only a source of encouragement for the beleaguered Tibetan people, whose welfare is his motivation, but also a powerful message to those who strive for peace and harmony in the world. He reiterated his stance that he was not demanding total independence but "meaningful autonomy" for Tibet. Despite the conciliatory language, China objected to the award and issued a warning to the US that an official award ceremony would have "an extremely serious impact" on China-US bilateral relations.

The awarding of the Gold Medal further solidified His Holiness' standing in America. For thousands of Tibetans living in the US at the time, it was an honor they could hardly have dreamt of. I retired the same year and was sad not to have witnessed this proud moment.

WHO WILL LEAD US NEXT?
GUIDELINES FOR THE NEXT DALAI LAMA

As early as 1969, His Holiness announced that the discovery and installation of the Fifteenth Dalai Lama would be up to the Tibetan people to decide. He no longer wanted it to be taken for granted. He was motivated, on the one hand, by the wish to see the Dalai Lama's role in a democratic context. On the other, he was provoked by the Chinese government's suggestion that the struggle for freedom in Tibet amounted to nothing more than satisfying the personal interests of the Dalai Lama and restoring the Tibetan society of old.

For him, the aim of the Tibetans' struggle for truth and justice is to secure the welfare of the Tibetan people, not to restore Tibetan society as it was, nor to promote the personal interests of the Dalai Lama. As far as he is concerned, there is no need to insist that the institution of the Dalai Lama continue. He denies that the survival of either the Tibetan nation or the Buddha's teachings depend on this.

The reason for finding a reincarnation is so that he or she can fulfill the previous incarnation's life's work. Thus, his or her discovery is very

Depiction of the Dalai Lama's succession dilemma by exiled Chinese political cartoonist Rebel Pepper. First published by Radio Free Asia on 5 January 2018.

important for Tibetans. Within the Tibetan system of recognizing *tulkus,* reincarnates, there are those who belong to the same mind-stream as the predecessor, those who are connected to others through the power of karma and prayers, and emanations who come as a result of blessings and appointment. Reincarnation takes place through the voluntary choice of the person concerned, or at least on the strength of his or her karma and prayers. Therefore, it is up to the person who reincarnates where and how he or she takes rebirth and how their reincarnation is to be recognized. Since the institution of the Dalai Lama arose in an entirely Buddhist context, the question of finding a future reincarnation is the sole concern of Buddhists. His Holiness has declared that people with no belief in religion or spirituality have no business involving themselves in matters related to reincarnation.

His Holiness has regularly faced questions about who will succeed him and how a successor will be chosen. He often tells the story of his encounter with a particularly persistent journalist in Newark, New Jersey, who doggedly sought an answer. His Holiness took off his glasses, looked him in the eye, and said, "Look at my face. Do you think there's any rush?"

In a detailed statement published in 2011, he explored several options. A future Dalai Lama could be appointed from among learned lamas. A similarly accomplished candidate could be elected from among existing scholars. He also discussed an emanation before death, which involves a lama identifying a living person as his reincarnation before he dies.

In the event that it is decided that the reincarnation of the Dalai Lama should continue, and there is a need for the Fifteenth Dalai Lama to be recognized, responsibility for doing so will primarily rest with the concerned officers of the Dalai Lama's personal Gaden Phodrang Trust. They will seek advice and carry out the procedures of search and recognition in accordance with past tradition. His Holiness has stated that since he has lived the majority of his life outside Tibet, it will be logical for his reincarnation to be found outside, too.

SEEKING COMMON GROUND WITH
THE CHINESE PEOPLE

His Holiness constantly stresses dialogue as a tool of conflict resolution. It is for this reason he has always expressed affection and friendship toward the Chinese from mainland China. Setting politics aside, he has interacted and developed friendships with many from the mainland, to listen and seek greater understanding among them. He has held many meetings, some private and some publicized, where significant issues have been discussed openly and with a great wish to understand conflicting "truths" on behalf of both parties.

In March 2008, protests in Lhasa led to violence. His Holiness issued an open appeal assuring the Chinese people of the historic bonds between them and the Tibetans, and that he does not seek separation

Below: On 10 December 2010, in Oslo, Nobel Committee chairman Thorbjorn Jagland sat next to the chair where Liu Xiaobo's Nobel Peace Prize medal and diploma had been placed in absence of either the recipient or a representative.

Liu Xiaobo was awarded the Nobel Peace Prize for "his long and nonviolent

from China. In it he sought to "dispel the misunderstandings between the two communities […] and help us find a peaceful lasting solution…"

Some Tibetans in Tibet and also in China (those who live in Beijing significantly) are expressing their views openly, which His Holiness appreciates very much as it gives him hope for the future. Many Tibetans have been brought up as subjects of an entirely Chinese education system, yet their Tibetan identities remain intact and strong. Following the great unrest in Tibet throughout 2008, a contemporary movement of creative expression increased hugely. His Holiness was deeply moved by the prolific writings of so many Tibetans in Tibet, who wrote about him in their poetry, literature, plays, music, and blogs, expressing their appreciation and love for him. At the Kalachakra teachings in Amaravati in 2006, His Holiness read out a letter from a Tibetan in Tibet who had written to thank him for spreading awareness of Tibetan Buddhism and the path of nonviolence throughout the world.

His Holiness has interacted with many Chinese dissidents (many of whom came to the West after the Tiananmen Square incident), writers, lawyers, journalists, and activists, who speak out against the one-party Communist regime of China, advocating reform and liberal policies.

I witnessed some very moving exchanges between His Holiness and Chinese students abroad. On two occasions (in Australia and the US) when His Holiness met with students, Chinese students stood up and apologized on behalf of the Chinese people for the suffering caused to the Tibetans. They said it was only on leaving China that they became aware of the truth of what happened in Tibet. One incident is particularly vivid. We were in Norway with His Holiness. Once again he sought out young people and met with a Chinese student who wanted His Holiness to sign the *khata* (scarf) that was given to him. He told us about his plans to participate in an upcoming pro-Tibet demonstration in Oslo. His Holiness inquired whether he was on a Chinese government scholarship. He answered in the affirmative. His Holiness warned him against taking part in the demonstration for the Tibetans, as he may lose his scholarship. He agreed and promised to be careful.

struggle for fundamental human rights in China."

The first Chinese citizen to have been awarded the honor, Liu Xiaobo had fought for an open China, coauthoring *Charter 08*, the 2008 pro-democracy manifesto signed by Chinese intellectuals, academics, and activists. This resulted in the subsequent imprisonment, illness, and finally his passing in 2017.

Together with writer Wang Lixiong and ten other Chinese intellectuals, he had also authored an open letter to urge Beijing to open direct dialogue with the Dalai Lama and support his appeal for understanding between Chinese and Tibetans, in the wake of protests throughout Tibet in 2008.

Prominent others who have written openly on Tibet include US-based Jianglin Li, Yang Jianli, Yan Jiaqi, Fang Lizhi, "barefoot lawyer" Chen Gyangchen, Canada-based Zhu Rui, and Beijing-based Tibetan blogger Woeser.

THE THIRD POLE:
ENVIRONMENTAL CONCERNS FOR TIBET

His Holiness began to seriously consider environmental concerns soon after his exile in India. While he lived in Tibet, the human population was small, and the environment was pure and beautiful. There was no mining, no deforestation, no damming of rivers, and no burning of fossil fuels. In Tibet, all the sources of water were clean, and he was shocked to learn when he came to India that in many places water was too polluted to drink.

However, once he became aware of such issues, he understood quickly that addressing them was a matter of human survival. He saw this planet as our only home and recognized that it was our collective responsibility to take care of it. He observed that people had treated our natural resources as inexhaustible. Destruction in the past resulted from ignorance. Today, we must act more responsibly.

His Holiness is said to have been the first Nobel Peace Laureate to mention in his Nobel Peace Prize lecture the need to protect the natural environment. In it he outlined strict proposals for environmental protection in Tibet and took courage from young people repeatedly calling for an end to the dangerous destruction of the environment in the name of economic development.

In the early twenty-first century, His Holiness began to talk about his main commitments. One involves both the preservation of Tibet's rich and peaceful culture and speaking up for the protection of its natural environment. He was very taken with the scientific evaluation that at an average altitude of 4,000 meters above sea level, Tibet's glaciers are the Earth's largest ice mass beyond the North and South poles. The Tibetan plateau, aptly described as the Third Pole, needs to be protected, not just for Tibetans but for the environmental health and sustainability of the entire world.

Moreover, the Indus, Ganges, Brahmaputra, Irrawaddy, Salween, Mekong, and Yellow rivers ultimately have their sources in Tibet, and

Facing: His Holiness delivered an impassioned speech at a groundbreaking global conference on human survival, held in Oxford, England, in 1988. It was attended by 200 spiritual leaders, lawmakers, and scientists from sixty nations who discussed solutions to worldwide environmental problems.

more than 1 billion people across Asia depend on their waters. Human activities that affect the environment in Tibet, such as mining, damming, diversion of rivers, and felling of forests have a direct impact on the lives of people in the Indian subcontinent and beyond. Consequently, His Holiness has persistently urged that those who recklessly exploit such resources in Tibet should be educated to change.

He has appealed to supporters across the world to assemble a group of experts to visit Tibet, examine the conditions there, assess the environmental damage, and advise on what can be done to prevent things from worsening. He is keen that whatever information is gathered in this way should be shared with the Chinese authorities who are often not properly informed. Although policy may change tomorrow, damage to the environment can take decades to recover.

Kalachakra: The Cycle of Life

In January 2006, His Holiness conducted a Kalachakra initiation at Amaravati, an ancient town in southeastern India, located on the banks of the Krishna River. This thirtieth Kalachakra ceremony by His Holiness was historically significant for Buddhists, since it was at the location where Gautama Buddha had taught the first Kalachakra Root Tantra at the request of the King Dawa Sangpo, or Suchandra. Remnants of an important stupa dated to the fifth century BCE are located there, many fragments of which are on display in the Amaravati Gallery at the British Museum in London. It was auspicious also for the fact that the date was coincidentally the 2,550th anniversary of Buddha's Mahaparinirvana. Beginning on 3 January, the events took place over thirteen days.

It was in March 1970 that His Holiness performed the first Kalachakra initiation in exile, in Dharamsala. Though I do not remember many details since we were immersed in official duties, over 30,000 people attended the ceremony. Open to the general public, this initiation was to promote peace and prepare practitioners for tantric meditations. Basic Buddhist teachings are given first. Dharamsala was abuzz with the sense of something special in the air during that time. His Holiness had performed the Kalachakra ritual only twice before in the mid-1950s in Norbulingka Palace, Tibet. This event was also a sign that the Tibetan exiles had made their new home a little more permanent. His Holiness has said that, prior to performing it in Dharamsala, he had a dream, and upon waking up he realized that he would be performing it many times more in the years ahead. "I think in my previous lifetimes, I had a connection with the Kalachakra teaching. It's a karmic force."

Primarily based on the cosmological concepts of time and the cycles of both planetary movements and human life, the elementary meaning of Kalachakra is drawn from its two Sanskrit roots—*kala* for time, and *chakra* for cycle. In combining the two, a composite sense of all existence and omniscience is derived.

The practice belongs to the Vajrayana tradition of Buddhism and is performed before an audience. It combines tantra, philosophy, astrology, meditation, chanting, and other mystical practices. The Kalachakra Tantra is a complex system of teaching and encompasses three aspects: the first is the outer or external environment, the universe, and its cycles; the second is the inner world of sentient beings, the cycles of death and birth, and the flow of breath and energy; and the third is the practice of purification undertaken by an individual so that death, birth, and manifestation, on both an individual and universal level, become purified into the fully enlightened state of complete Buddhahood.

The first Kalachakra ceremony to take place in the West was in July 1981 near the town of Madison, Wisconsin, at the Deer Park Buddhist Center. Professor Jeffrey Hopkins was His Holiness' translator. It stirred considerable curiosity and excitement in the local community, given in particular the large student population of Madison. Questions of how it would be received by Americans, how the ceremonial practice would be translated into English, and what would be lost in translation came up in the discussion prior to the event. For the ceremony, monks from Namgyal Monastery created a sand mandala and performed prayers, meditation,

In May 1954, at the age of 18, the Dalai Lama gave his first Kalachakra initiation at the age of 19. An exquisite costume of elaborate brocade, adorned with interlinking bone and pearl beads in auspicious patterns, was made over several months by the Dalai Lama's tailors at the Potala Palace. It was worn just once over his monk's robe for this unique occasion attended by 100,000 devotees.

Above: His Holiness has often performed Kalachakra ceremonies in very poor, remote regions in the Himalayan regions of India, necessitating hardiness on the part of participants! Here, Ladakhi women wear exquisite cobra-shaped ceremonial headdresses called *perak* to attend the Dalai Lama's Kalachakra teachings in Zanskar, 1988. Situated at high altitude in the Indian state of Jammu and Kashmir, Zanskar is snowbound and cut off for most of each year.

and tantric dances. The thousand people in attendance watched on and participated in the sacred atmosphere, as the painstaking rituals unfolded before them. The ceremony was intended to promote peace, happiness, and blessings in people's minds, and also bring favorable circumstances to all. It saw the participation of a new generation of Americans who had trained under Tibetans who had settled in the US. In many ways, it heralded a new era for

Above: The Dalai Lama on his throne, bestowing the first initiation in Bodh Gaya in 1974. Further initiations were given here in 1985, 2003, 2012, and 2017. Below: His Holiness places the first grains of colored sand to begin the skillful construction of the intricate sand mandala during the 32nd empowerment in Bodh Gaya, on 1 January 2012. A mandala symbolizes an entire sacred universe of spiritual energy.

Tibetan Buddhism. At the conclusion of the initiation, the mandala was dismantled, and His Holiness released the sand into the nearby Lake Mendota in a final ritual, thereby diffusing the spirit of Kalachakra Tantra "into the spiritual lives of millions of Americans." His Holiness has often said that his intention was to demystify an important part of our spiritual tradition by giving public initiations as well as to benefit mankind by performing the Kalachakra.

DIALOGUE WITH SCIENTISTS

The Dalai Lama's interest in science and technology was first sparked when he was a small boy looking at pictures of the world beyond Tibet in *Life* magazine. His curiosity got the better of him when, wanting to know how they worked, he carefully dismantled mechanical toys, clocks, watches, and the Thirteenth Dalai Lama's cars. The real test, he says, was being able to put them back together. Regularly having to repair a movie projector taught him the basic principles of electricity.

A key event in his growing interest in science occurred while he was still in Lhasa when he decided to look at the full moon through a telescope he had inherited from the Thirteenth Dalai Lama. Observing shadows cast by mountains on the moon's surface, he deduced that the heavenly body was not self-illuminating, as he had been led to believe, but like the earth, was lit by the sun. The implications of this simple observation undermined the traditional description of the universe presented in Buddhist scriptures.

His Holiness wanted to open discussions with scientists. He mentioned this to an American woman married to a Tibetan. She advised against it, warning that, "Science is the killer of religion." But he was not so easily deflected. He often recalls that in his consideration of this issue, he concluded that Tibetan Buddhist traditions, with their strong foundation in reason and logic, could hold their own.

In 1979, on his second trip to Europe, His Holiness met physicist David Bohm and established an immediate rapport with him. They had several meetings over the years, and His Holiness credits Bohm with having explained subtle scientific ideas to him. He has expressed his admiration for Bohm's scientific mind, characterized by a great openness. It was Bohm who introduced His Holiness to the idea of "thought experiments."

Another renowned scientist His Holiness developed a close friendship with was Carl Friedrich von Weizsäcker, who he also met several times in Europe. Weizsäcker gave His Holiness tutorials on

quantum physics and discussed the importance of empiricism and inference. His Holiness has observed that Buddhist understanding of empiricism is broader than that of modern science because it includes meditative states, as well as the evidence of the senses.

The Dalai Lama has said that, "Buddhism is not so much a religion as a science of the mind…an inner science." In 1987, His Holiness met Francisco Varela, a philosopher and neuroscientist, and businessman Adam Engle, who had together convened a weeklong discussion between His Holiness and scientists in Dharamsala. The idea was to bring together science and the transformative power of contemplative wisdom. From this first meeting grew the Mind & Life Institute. Over the course of more than thirty years, thirty-three dialogues have taken place. His Holiness has remarked:

> One of the purposes of this kind of meeting is to expand our knowledge. Modern science has detailed knowledge of the material world, but much less understanding of mind and our inner world. The second purpose, in the context of highly developed knowledge

Astrophysicist Carl Sagan and the Dalai Lama enjoyed a deep connection during their dialogues. After their first meeting at Cornell University in 1991, Sagan and his wife traveled to India the following year to meet with His Holiness. They discussed science, religion, and consciousness.

and complex economies, is to ask whether people are happy. We face a lot of problems, many of them of our own making...we have a responsibility to reduce if not eliminate problems. We need to find ways to educate people about the importance of combining the potential of our marvelous brains with warmheartedness.

At the beginning, there were scientists who were convinced that consciousness was but a function of the brain, and it was the brain and its workings that should be the focus of investigation. His Holiness would contend that if the mind were completely dependent on the brain, it ought to be possible to achieve peace of mind by means of surgery or medication—for which there is no evidence. As imaging techniques have become increasingly sophisticated, it has become possible for neuroscientists like Richard Davidson, Mind & Life chief scientific advisor and founder and director of the Center for Healthy Minds at the University of Wisconsin-Madison, to see that mental experience can bring about changes in the brain. Meditation on compassion, for example, has been shown to result in such changes.

The Science for Monks and Nuns program has led to new initiatives, such as this 2016 seminar with an audience of schoolchildren at Sherab Ling Monastery in Himachal Pradesh, on "Regulating and transforming emotions."

Two landmark Mind & Life dialogues were held—in Mundgod in 2013, and in Bylakuppe in 2015. Opening the Mundgod meeting, His Holiness explained:

> I started this dialogue with scientists out of my own curiosity. But when it became clear how helpful it could be for Buddhists already familiar with the inner world to learn more about physical reality, I wanted to open it up to them, too. Our monks have heard about this dialogue and I thought it would be really meaningful for them to have a taste of it…

A parallel development has been the Emory-Tibet Partnership, founded in 1998 with Emory University in the US, which has resulted in several projects fostering the convergence of science and spirituality. The Emory-Tibet Science Initiative (ETSI) has successfully implemented comprehensive, modern science education into the core curriculum of Tibetan monastic institutions. As a result, science textbooks have been written in Tibetan, and Tibetan monks and nuns have been trained to teach the subject. His Holiness has been pleased to see the number of monastic scholars able to engage in deep dialogue with scientists on topics of mutual interest.

In 2009, the Dalai Lama's largest donation to date to a scientific enterprise led to the launch of the Center for Compassion and Altruism Research (CCARE) at Stanford University School of Medicine. The prime aim of CCARE is to study the neurology of altruism and compassion. The Altas of Emotions by Paul and Eve Ekman is another initiative conceived of by His Holiness. It represents what researchers have learned from the psychological study of emotion.

Cognitively-Based Compassion Training (CBCT), a compassion meditation program appropriate for both scientific research and for use by individuals of any background or faith tradition, is another such initiative. His Holiness has been encouraged by research on CBCT that shows compassion promotes resilience, social connectivity, and emotional well-being.

In 2012, the Dalai Lama won the prestigious Templeton Prize in London, awarded to celebrate those who "harness the power of the sciences to explore the deepest questions of the universe and humankind's place and purpose within it."

"Everybody knows that science gives us an important method for exploring reality," His Holiness has remarked. "And coming to an understanding of reality is important if your approach to what you are doing is to be realistic. If it isn't, it's not likely to succeed."

In 2018, at the Nieuwe Kerk church in Amsterdam during a panel discussion on "Robotics and Telepresence," His Holiness met twelve-year-old Tilly Lockey from the UK who, after contracting meningitis at fifteen months old, had lost her hands and been fitted with bionic arms.

THE TURNING POINT:
END OF A 369-YEAR-OLD TRADITION

In 2001, when the Tibetan people in exile elected the *kalon tripa*, or political leader, directly for the first time, the Dalai Lama announced his semi-retirement. He said he would no longer involve himself in the day-to-day affairs of the administration, but looked forward to being able to dedicate more time to wider issues concerning the whole of humanity. Ten years later, in 2011, a new kalon tripa and people's representatives were elected by the people within the framework of the Charter for Tibetans in Exile. From the early 1960s, His Holiness had repeatedly stressed that Tibetans need a leader, elected by the Tibetan people, to whom he could devolve power. He declared:

> Now, we have reached the time to put this into effect…One-man rule is both anachronistic and undesirable…In order for our process of democratization to be complete, the time has come for me to devolve my formal authority…This is necessary, in order that the Tibetan administration in exile can become self-reliant rather than being dependent on the Dalai Lama.

Elected representatives, Tibetan elders, even people from Tibet, appealed to His Holiness to reconsider. They requested him to at least remain their titular head. But he was adamant, insisting that he wished to bring an end to the 369-year-old rule of the dalai lama as both the spiritual and temporal authority. However, he would continue to give a lead in spiritual affairs, as the first four dalai lamas had done.

This marked a turning point in His Holiness' life. Since then he has spoken frequently of having taken on three commitments. Firstly, as a human being, to encouraging people to be happy—helping them to understand the importance of incorporating human values into their lives and securing peace of mind. Secondly, as a Buddhist monk, he is dedicated to encouraging harmony among various religious traditions. Thirdly, as a Tibetan, he is committed to preserving Tibetan language and culture, while also speaking up for the protection of Tibet's natural environment. Lately, he has added a fourth: a determination to try to revive ancient Indian knowledge in India.

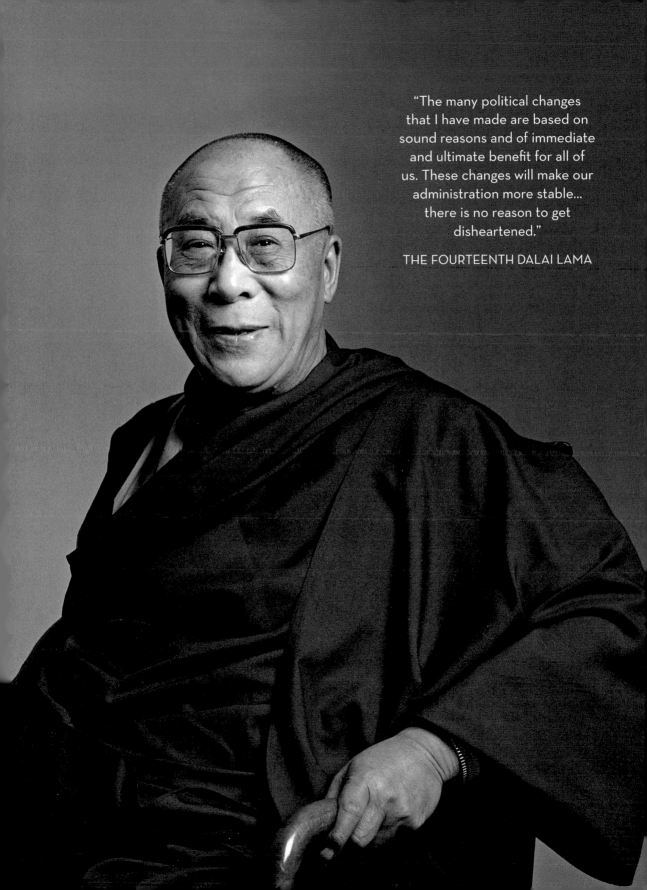

"The many political changes that I have made are based on sound reasons and of immediate and ultimate benefit for all of us. These changes will make our administration more stable... there is no reason to get disheartened."

THE FOURTEENTH DALAI LAMA

The Monk who Fixes Watches

His Holiness likes to work with his hands and has said he would have been an engineer if he was not a monk. His interest in science and technology began at an early age when he had a fascination with World War II warships, planes, tanks, and submarines. A famous story dates back to when the Dalai Lama was a teenager and Austrian mountaneer Heinrich Harrer was summoned to the Norbulingka to fix a film projector. As Harrer fumbled with the projector, His Holiness stepped in and skillfully loaded the reels of a documentary on Japan's defeat in the war. Harrer was astonished by the mechanical skills of the young Dalai Lama.

In later years, his love for nature manifested in his keen interest in gardening. In both his residences in Dharamsala, he has had a greenhouse built to house a variety of flowers, including rare orchids that His Holiness has found difficult to nurture in the damp weather of Dharamsala. He would bring cuttings from his many travels in India and abroad, and many were even gifted to him. During our early visits abroad, His Holiness would relish his visits to botanical gardens such as the one in Kew, London, and the Brindavan Gardens of Mysore. He would often feed birds and keep ailing ones he had rescued in his garden.

His love of watches is well known. The story began when he inherited a collection of clocks and watches from the Thirteenth Dalai Lama. He set up a small space with the appropriate tools to repair watches, clocks, and even tape recorders. He said, "As a child, I had always wondered what moved the hands of clocks, the same hands that make the world go round.

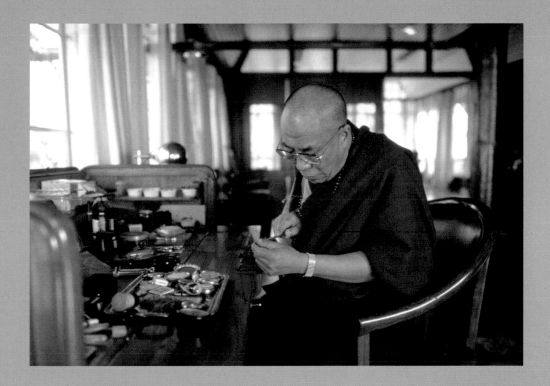

Above: His Holiness immersed in his hobby of repairing watches at his residence in Dharamsala, 1996.

Facing page: One day I had gone to meet His Holiness at his residence. There he was, sitting on the floor in front of a dismantled kerosene heater. All the parts had been carefully laid out. I am sure it took a long time just to put it all back together again!

Right: The young Dalai Lama is pictured here with a Rolleiflex camera. While living at the Potala, he took many photographs from the roof, where he also made use of his predecessor's telescope to view life in Lhasa. In India, in 1956, he relished the chance to use a cine camera.

So I got cracking on these tiny devices and experimented to the hilt with them." He jokes that when he was given watches to repair, more often than not they were returned in worse condition than when given to him. I have often seen His Holiness working with a watch.

CELEBRATING ALL SCHOOLS OF TIBETAN BUDDHISM

Reflecting his nonsectarian values and openness, His Holiness has received teachings from lamas of different traditions, as well as from his own Gelugpa tradition. Prominent among them was Khunu Rinpoche. Khunu Lama Tenzin Gyaltsen was born in 1894, in the Himachal Pradesh district of northern India, which is host to the Dalai Lama. Although he was a lay person, neither a Buddhist monk nor a reincarnate *tulku*, Khunu Rinpoche was a highly respected teacher of the nonsectarian Rimé tradition of Tibetan Buddhism, which embraces and draws upon multiple schools of Buddhist thought. His Holiness used to seek his views to clarify philosophical concepts.

Khunu Rinpoche gave teachings to His Holiness on *The Guide to the Bodhisattava's Way of Life*. Believed to be the single most important text for training the mind, it was written in the eighth century by the renowned Buddhist monk, Shantideva. The Dalai Lama received precious instruction on Bodhicitta from Khunu Rinpoche, whose life embodied the spiritual practice of compassion. He passed away in 1977 at the Shashur Monastery in Himachal Pradesh.

His Holiness received teachings from Geshe Rigzin Tenpa. This illustrious monk had met Mahatma Ghandi in 1947, when he served as interpreter for the Tibetan delegation. On Mahatma Ghandi's request, he explained the "Three Principal Aspects of the Path"—freedom, altruism, and emptiness.

Another teacher the Dalai Lama often mentions is Shakur Khen Rinpoche Nyima Gyaltsen, for whom he had much respect because of his knowledge on the subject of emptiness, or *sunyata*. Others from whom His Holiness has received instructions and oral lineage transmissions include masters of the different Buddhist traditions. His Holiness has recognized the ancient Bonpo, reinstated the Jonang, and revived the Bodong traditions, celebrating all schools of Tibetan Buddhism.

The Dalai Lama receiving an empowerment from one of his spiritual teachers, Trukshik Rinpoche. Tulku Pema Wangyal (right) and Venerable Tashi (center), His Holiness' long serving ritual master, are helping with the steps of the ritual.

Clockwise from top left: **1.** Venerable Paljor, personal attendant to His Holiness, has served him for over sixty years. **2.** Khunu Lama Rinpoche. **3.** Nyingma master and highly revered guru to the Dalai Lama, Dilgo Khyentse Rinpoche. **4.** Chogye Trichen Rinpoche, Sakya lama and a primary teacher of His Holiness. **5.** Khenpo Jigme Phuntsok, head of Larung Gar Buddhist Academy in Serthar, eastern Tibet. His Holiness held him in utmost regard. **6.** When His Holiness' principal teacher, Ling Rinpoche, passed away in 1983, he was deeply struck by the loss of his mentor and confidant. In 1987, he was overjoyed to recognize a young boy, who had been living nearby at the Tibetan Children's Village in Dharamsala, as his reincarnation. Photographed here at Ling Labrang, Dharamsala, in 1988, Ling Rinpoche has since passed his geshe exams, completed several meditation retreats, and taught internationally.

From left: His Holiness' bodyguard Kunga, Paljor la, His Holiness, author Doboom Tulku, Alan Wallace, Indian security officer Mr. Thapa, and Lobsang Gawa la in Greece, 1979.

A Dedicated Team

Since coming into exile, two monks, Venerable Lobsang Gawa and Venerable Paljor, have been His Holiness' closest personal attendants. We Tibetans believe that such people have a special bond with His Holiness, due to their spiritual association during many lifetimes. Together, they hold important responsibilities that are directly connected to His Holiness, making their positions unique. There are a host of other important members of His Holiness' staff who work tirelessly behind the scenes. Venerable Tashi and Venerable Bhuchung were members of the Namgyal Monastery. They began working with His Holiness in the late 1970s and early 1980s as assistant to the ritual master. Tashi continues to work as the ritual master, and Bhuchung works as an accountant in the Private Office.

Several bodyguards of His Holiness were formerly members of the Tibetan armed forces who had come to India post-1959. Dresang accompanied His Holiness during the escape to India. Following his retirement in the early 1970s, he moved to Bylakuppe, and later passed away there. Kunga, who joined service shortly after I did, traveled with us on many trips abroad. After retirement, he was put in charge of the Branch Office of the Security Department at McLeod Ganj. Senior bodyguard Choegyal was previously a monk of the Dzongkha Chode Monastery. He and I joined the judo class conducted by Gyurme Wangdak, a Tibetan who had trained in Japan. After retirement, he was in charge of the reception center for recent arrivals from Tibet.

Phuntsok Tsering and Namgyal served as His Holiness' cooks for over forty years, before retiring. I have known them ever since I joined the Private Office. His Holiness' *namsa chenmo*, or master tailor, who is now eighty-two years old, lives at Namgyal Monastery. He began to work as a young boy in Potala Palace and has served His Holiness all his life.

GENDER EQUALITY AND GESHEMA DEGREE

His Holiness has always encouraged and supported gender equality. In his own family, women have played prominent roles in the refugee resettlements. Although girls were not restricted from enrolling in schools in Tibet, women never participated in political affairs. However, the popular Women's Uprising in Lhasa, on 12 March 1959, demonstrated their collective strength.

His Holiness the Dalai Lama speaking to nuns who had just concluded their annual winter debate session at the Tsuglakhang in Dharamsala, 2013.

Participation of women at the highest levels of government has been a long-standing wish of His Holiness. Women were given the right to vote almost immediately after coming into exile. The Tibetan Women's Association (TWA) was reestablished in 1984, with the blessing of His Holiness. Rinchen Khando Choegyal, his sister-in-law, was its first president. In 1963, Tibetan women first entered the Tibetan parliament as representatives. Since then there has been a good representation of women in prominent positions. Dolma Gyari was elected the first woman deputy speaker of the parliament in 2002, while in July 2020,

Delek Wangmo, a Geshema, became the first woman to be elected as additional election commissioner.

Before the Chinese occupation of 1950, there were over 600 nunneries and over 12,000 nuns in Tibet. After 1959, many nuns had to flee Tibet due to persecution. As their numbers in exile gradually increased, nunneries were set up in many settlements. The first was in Dalhousie, run by Freda Bedi, a British woman who later became a nun herself. His Holiness was keen that formal study of Buddhist philosophy be introduced in these nunneries. In 1987, TWA launched the Tibetan Nuns Project, which now contributes to the support and education of hundreds of nuns throughout India and is an independent body.

Two other causes close to His Holiness' heart were to allow nuns to study for the geshema degree in Buddhist studies and for them to be able to take full ordination, which has not been a part of Tibetan Buddhist tradition. In 2007, His Holiness said:

> I am sure if Buddha were here today, he would certainly give us permission for *bhikshuni* vows. Given that women are fully capable of achieving the ultimate goal of the Buddha's teachings, the means and opportunity to achieve this should be completely accessible to them.

The first cause was realized in April 2011 when the German-born nun Kelsang Wangmo received a geshe degree from the Institute of Buddhist Dialectics, after devoting twenty-one years to Buddhist studies. Soon after this, His Holiness presided over nuns' debate sessions during the New Year Prayer Festival celebrations in March 2012. He was impressed and felt that the nuns' debating had reached the highest level of their studies. In May 2012, the CTA took a historic decision, announcing that all nuns were to be allowed to become geshemas. In May 2016, the first group of twenty nuns sat for the examinations, and since then, forty-four nuns have received their degrees at graduation ceremonies presided over by His Holiness.

Nuns from Spiti, in Himachal Pradesh, practice their debating skills. Debate in Tibetan Buddhism is structured and stylized; it includes the ritual of stepping the left foot forward and clapping the hands when challenging a defender.

A NEW STYLE OF EDUCATION:
SOCIAL, EMOTIONAL, AND ETHICAL LEARNING

For more than thirty years, in public talks all over the world, the Dalai Lama has shared his observation that material development alone will not make human beings happier. He sometimes wonders if animals, when they are not living under threat or danger, are not more content and peaceful than human beings. On the other hand, he says, because of our wonderful human brain, we are intelligent. And the key to opening up our intelligence is education. His Holiness declares:

> Although none of us wants to encounter problems, we face a host of them, many of our own creation. Our existing modern education is incapable of ensuring that as individuals, families, and communities we will be happy. This is something we need to think seriously about. One reason is that it tends to have materialistic goals, whereas for humanity to be happy depends on peace of mind. Therefore, we have to carefully consider how to incorporate inner values into our education on a secular basis.

His Holiness has remarked that as children we do not care very much about differences of faith, family, or nationality; we just play with our companions. But as we grow up, we function less on that basic human level and learn to pay more attention to secondary differences, like faith, race, social background, and level of education. By seeing each other in terms of "us" and "them," we lay the ground for conflict. We seek ways for "us" to win and "them" to lose. This is the basis for bullying, cheating, and exploitation that gives rise to violence, corruption, and the gap between rich and poor.

His favored solution is to teach children how to tackle their destructive emotions, such as anger, fear, jealousy, and suspicion. Just as they are brought up with an appreciation of physical hygiene, we need to introduce them to an equivalent emotional hygiene that entails discovering how to temper anger and fear, and cultivate warmheartedness towards others.

> "My hope and wish is that one day, formal education will pay attention to what I call education of the heart. I look forward to a day when children and students will be more aware of their emotions and feel a greater sense of responsibility both towards themselves and towards the wider world. Wouldn't that be wonderful?"
>
> **HIS HOLINESS THE FOURTEENTH DALAI LAMA**

His Holiness has spoken for years of the need to take concrete steps to bring about a real transformation in the ways we educate our future generations. It involves combining education of the mind and heart so that children grow up to be responsible, caring citizens, equipped to meet the challenges of today's increasingly globalized world.

His Holiness invited Emory University, in Atlanta, Georgia to create such a program that would be grounded in common sense, common experience, and scientific evidence—and be equally acceptable to those of any religious faith, and those without. The result is Social, Emotional, and Ethical (SEE) Learning, an innovative kindergarten to graduation program that provides educators with the tools they need to foster the development of emotional, social, and ethical intelligence among students and themselves. It also enables students to learn about attention training, compassion, and ethical discernment, systems thinking, and resilience. SEE Learning is a fulfillment of His Holiness' vision for the education of heart and mind.

The program, which is available in twelve languages including English has been implemented in a number of schools in India, the US, and European countries. Expressing satisfaction at the launch of the program in New Delhi in April 2019, His Holiness put what has been achieved into a broader perspective:

> The results of this program will not be seen next week, but in the course of the next generation when we may hope to see emerge from it more compassionate human beings, who will be happier individuals, belonging to happier families.

COMPASSION AND SECULAR ETHICS

When His Holiness began to speak in public about compassion during his first visits to Europe in the 1970s, it was a word with limited currency. Now, more than forty years later, appreciation of its value is so widespread that even politicians seek to be associated with it. He explains that there are three reasons for developing compassion. It is based on our common experience—everyone responds positively to kindness. It is common sense, because it's obvious that people who are warmhearted are happier. And finally, scientific findings show that negative emotions like anger, hatred, and fear undermine our immune system, whereas there is evidence that warmheartedness and compassion are good for our overall health. If you have compassion for others, he says, your wish will be not to harm but to help them. If you apply your human intelligence, you may also recognize that anger destroys your peace of mind. It ruins the friendly feeling in families and communities. Human beings are social animals, who need close friends. We all want to live a happy life; none of us wants to suffer. So, we need a sense that we all belong to one human family. His Holiness oberserves:

> Sometimes people consider the practice of compassion as a sign of weakness, but this is a mistake. It's anger that is a sign of weakness, while compassion is a sign of strength. Similarly, some people suspect that compassion only results in others' benefit. This too is an error. We are the first to benefit from developing warmheartedness and compassion. It brings peace of mind, which gives rise to self-confidence. This enables us to do what we do transparently, and brings us more friends. Friendship depends on trust, and trust blooms when we show real interest in the well-being of others.

His Holiness contends that people sometimes think warmheartedness, compassion, and love belong only in the realm of religion. He says they are actually crucial to our survival. If we do not take steps to reinforce these qualities now, the twenty-first century will also

Facing page: His Holiness met Richard Moore in Derry, Northern Ireland, in 2001. Derry had been blinded at the age of ten by a rubber bullet fired by a British soldier during "the Troubles."

Not only had he accepted his fate without resentment, but after meeting the soldier who shot him, they befriended each other, in peace. "Forgiveness is a gift primarily to myself," he said. "I have found freedom in it."

The Dalai Lama has called this an example of the power of compassion in action and a true source of hope. "You may be blind, but you can see further than people with eyesight."

end up being an era of violence like the previous one. He is unequivocal that we can't expect change to occur if we don't take action. Prayer is not sufficient; we have to take responsibility ourselves. Problems created by human beings have to be solved by human beings. This is why he campaigns for secular ethics.

Just as he describes compassion, he explains secular ethics in terms of common experience, common sense, and scientific findings. To begin with, we are all born from a mother's womb, and most of us grow up under our mother's care. This is the biological source of our sense of compassion. Our very survival depends on others' care. Those who receive the greatest affection when they were young are happier in later life. Similarly, families bound together by affection and compassion tend to be happier than those who have no such care.

No matter how strong we are, or how educated we are, we cannot survive without others' support—how could we neglect their interests? Warmheartedness and genuine concern for others earns friendship, on the basis of which we can act truthfully and transparently, which in turn is a source of confidence.

Although scientists are mostly concerned with matter and what they can measure, today, increasing numbers are showing more interest in the mind and emotions. They conclude not only that a healthy mind favors sound physical health, but that it is human nature to be compassionate. His Holiness is always quick to clarify that when he uses the word secular as part of "secular ethics," he doesn't wish to imply any disrespect for religious traditions. He uses the word secular according to the Indian understanding of an unbiased respect, not only for those who adhere to religious traditions, but also for those who do not. What he is primarily concerned about is inspiring an interest in basic human values that have a universal appeal to all human beings. "Compassion is the basis of moral principles," he affirms.

> The goodness of an action depends not just on the act itself, but on whether it arises out of concern for others and their rights. If we can instill concern for others in young people, we can create a better world with greater trust and peace of mind—a more equal, more compassionate world.

His Holiness the Dalai Lama with his very dear friend, Archbishop Desmond Tutu, of South Africa, in Oslo, 2002.

Facing page: The blessing, Grosvenor House Hotel, London, 1994.

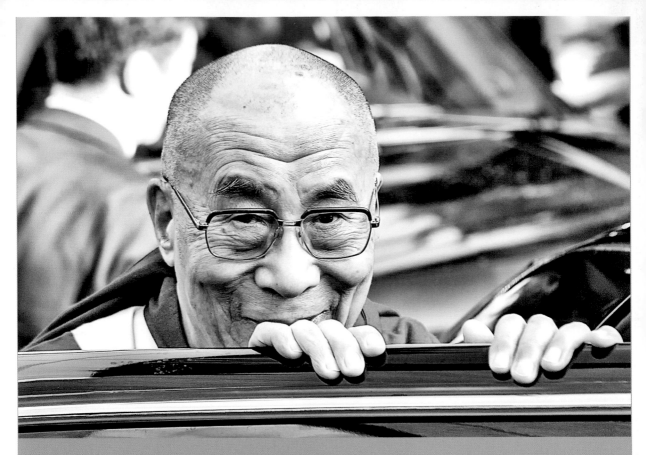

A MESSAGE FOR OUR TIMES

On 6 July 2020, His Holiness the Dalai Lama turned eighty-five years old. Reflecting his spirit of openness, a varied assortment of leaders, friends, allies, and ordinary people from around the globe conveyed their congratulations, well-wishes, tributes, and gratitude. His Holiness later wrote that he was touched by their affection and that he looked forward to living long, to serve humanity. In his official address to the Tibetan people, he said celebrations and gatherings were neither necessary nor advisable due to the Covid-19 pandemic sweeping the world. If they wished to mark the occasion, he said, he would prefer it if they recited the Avalokiteshvara mantra *Om Mani Padme Hum* at least a thousand times, adding, "Avalokiteshvara is my boss and I am his messenger."

Since the beginning of the pandemic, he has addressed the difficulties the world is experiencing. His compassion and prayers have extended to the Chinese people, as well, despite the increasingly strained relations with Communist China. It is a time for the world to unite, he has said. He has taken to technology to attend meetings, conduct teachings, and interact with people the world over. He feels that these hardships are a reminder that compassionate acts, whether they may be by medical staff or by people observing social distancing, can help all of us. But underlining his belief in science along with his spiritual side, His Holiness reiterates that prayers alone will not suffice:

"We should employ science and human ingenuity with determination and courage to overcome the problems that confront us and attain our common goal of a more caring and a more peaceful world."

ACKNOWLEDGMENTS

FROM THE PUBLISHER

We at Interlink Publishing are pleased and honored to publish this portrait of a leader and a people, whose stories are so instructive and inspiring during this time of multiple global perils. The collective efforts of many have made this beautiful volume possible.

My heartfelt appreciation to my colleagues in India, Kapil and Priya Kapoor, for introducing me to Tenzin Geyche Tethong, for fostering the creation and production of this work, and for making this richly detailed account a reality.

Working in tandem with our colleagues at Roli Books, our creative team has collaborated to prepare this edition for a North American readership. Special thanks to production coordinator Pam Fontes-May, edition consultant Anna Sloan, editor John Sobhieh Fiscella, and proofreaders Jennifer McKenna and Jane Bugaeva for their expertise and commitment to this project.

—Michel Moushabeck, Publisher

FROM THE AUTHOR

My immense gratitude to and Priya Kapoor, and to her brother, Kapil Kapoor, the duo behind Roli Books, who made this book possible. Through the entire process, Priya worked very closely on every detail of the book, and many times also helped put my thoughts into words. Neelam Narula, managing editor of Roli Books, worked very hard on the manuscript, and I thank her for her patience and help. Jeremy Russell and the Office of His Holiness the Dalai Lama assisted us with fine details. The beautiful design of the book is a result of Sneha Pamneja's expert creative efforts. The credit for the many and rare photos and image captions goes to my old friend, Jane Moore. She also helped jog my memory and contributed numerous valuable insights to the book. Australian photographer Tim Roodenrys spent weeks photographing people, collections of prints, and special objects in Dharamsala. Without his contribution, many of the rare photo spreads would not have been possible. Several other photographers and institutions, including some I have known for a long time, have been most generous in allowing us to include their material. Above all, I am most grateful to Gautam Pemmaraju who researched extensively and did the bulk of writing.

I am also grateful to my friend, Thupten Tsering Lingtsang, who helped find answers to many queries I had about Tibet before 1959, and to verify names and designations of

many Tibetans featured in the book. He was the personal assistant to Kyabje Ling Rinpoche, the senior tutor of His Holiness, and has lived in the Potala and the Norbulingka palaces. He was with Ling Rinpoche during Dalai Lama's trips to China in 1954 and India in 1956, respectively, and escaped to India with His Holiness in 1959.

The gifts of His Holiness to his people and the world are invaluable, considering that he grew up in an inward looking, materially backward, and conservative country. He was the absolute spiritual and political authority, held in the greatest of awe and devotion. His Holiness was only fifteen years old when China's invasion of Tibet unexpectedly placed the responsibility of the entire nation on his shoulders. Yet, when tragedy struck Tibet and he was compelled to leave the country, he led his people with tremendous calmness, dignity, and farsightedness. While in exile, he traveled the world with a message of compassion and nonviolence, showing deep respect for all religious traditions and to throw light on Tibet's plight—the story we have attempted to narrate through this book.

—Tenzin Geyche Tethong

GLOSSARY

KEY TERMS

Avalokiteshvara	Tibet's patron saint, regarded as the Bodhisattva of Compassion; also referred to as Chenrezig.
Bodhisattva	A realized being, inspired by the wish to attain complete enlightenment, who has vowed to be reborn in the world to help all living beings.
Buddhadharma	Buddhist teaching.
Five-Point Peace Plan	His Holiness' proposal advocating that Tibet become a zone of peace and an environmental sanctuary, with China responsible for defense and foreign policy, delivered in 1987 while addressing the US Congressional Human Rights Caucus, in Washington, DC.
Middle-Way Approach	A proposal that an autonomous region of the three traditional provinces of Tibet be created with meaningful, genuine autonomy.
Seventeen-Point Agreement	The so-called "Agreement on Measures for the Peaceful Liberation of Tibet" that the Tibetan delegation was coerced into signing in 1951, yielding areas of Tibetan autonomy to China.

HIS HOLINESS' FAMILY

Father	Gyalyab Chenmo, the Great Father, (formerly Choekyong Tsering)
Mother	Gyalyum Chenmo, the Great Mother, (formerly Diki Tsering, and Sonam Tsomo)
Brothers	Thubten Jigme Norbu (Taktser Rinpoche), *eldest brother* Gyalo Thondup, *middle brother* Lobsang Samten, *middle brother* Tendzin Choegyal (Ngari Rinpoche), *youngest brother*
Sisters	Tsering Dolma, *eldest sister* Jetsun Pema, *youngest sister*

CHRONOLOGY

▸ **6 July 1935**	In the small village of Taktser in northeastern Tibet, on the border with China, Lhamo Thondup is born to Diki Tsering and Choekyong Tsering. A poor family of farmers and herders, out of 16 children, the child is 1 of 7 who survive.
▸ **1937**	The 2-year-old boy is formally recognized as the reincarnation of the Thirteenth Dalai Lama.
▸ **1939**	Reaches Lhasa, and at the holy Jokhang Temple he is publically declared the Fourteenth Dalai Lama and renamed Jetsun Jamphel Ngawang Lobsang Yeshe Tenzin Gyatso.
▸ **22 February 1940**	At age 4, he is formally enthroned as the Fourteenth Dalai Lama, spiritual leader of Tibet.
▸ **1940–1942**	Residing at Potala and Norbulingka palaces, with his elder brother Lobsang Samten, he begins monastic education, receiving vows of novice monk at the Jokhang Temple.
▸ **1949**	The People's Liberation Army of China (PLA) invades Tibet.
▸ **1950**	At age 15, with his investiture as temporal leader of Tibet, he assumes full political power. He is forced to flee Lhasa for Yatung (Dromo).
▸ **23 May 1951**	The unwilling delegation in Peking is compelled to sign the Seventeen-Point Agreement, yielding areas of Tibetan autonomy to China.
▸ **24 July 1951**	Dalai Lama leaves Yatung and arrives in Lhasa on 17 August.
▸ **9 September 1951**	Approximately 3,000 Chinese troops march into Lhasa, followed by 20,000 more on 26 October.
▸ **1954**	He receives full ordination as monk from his senior tutor Ling Rinpoche and confers his first Kalachakra Initiation, at Norbulingka Palace.
▸ **July 1954–June 1955**	Age 19, the Dalai Lama travels to China for peace talks and meets with Mao Tse-tung, in Peking.
▸ **Nov 1956–March 1957**	Makes his first visit to India, to participate in the 2,500th Buddha Jayanti celebrations.
▸ **1958**	The first Tibetan resistance movement is formed.
▸ **February 1959**	Awarded the geshe lharampa degree as monk, during the annual New Year Prayer Festival.
▸ **10 March 1959**	Tibetan national uprising in Lhasa. Responding to word that the Chinese plan to arrest the Dalai Lama when he attends a performance at the Chinese Army camp in Lhasa, Tibetans converge at Norbulingka Palace to protect him.
▸ **12 March 1959**	Tibetan Women's Uprising Day. Thousands process through the streets of Lhasa and gather in front of Potala Palace, in nonviolent demonstration. Leaders and many others are arrested, imprisoned, beaten, or executed. Their sacrifices would be commemorated as the spark that lit the Tibetan women's movement for independence.
▸ **15 March 1959**	Artillery shells fired by Chinese troops land outside Norbulingka Palace.
▸ **17 March 1959**	Age 23, flees for India, escaping at night from Norbulingka Palace.
▸ **March 1959**	Dalai Lama formally proclaims the Tibetan interim government, at Lhuntse Dzong, and repudiates the Seventeen-Point Agreement.

31 March 1959	Crosses Indian border after a harrowing 14-day escape. Indian Prime Minister Jawaharlal Nehru grants him asylum, which is also extended to Tibetans who accompanied and followed him into exile.
18 April 1959	At his first international press conference, the Dalai Lama formally rejects the Seventeen-Point Agreement: "Wherever I am, accompanied by my government, the Tibetan people recognize us as the Government of Tibet."
20 April 1959	Arrives in Mussoorie and stays at Birla House.
14 November 1959	Now age 24, offers testimony at the International Commission of Jurists hearing in Mussoorie, resulting from an Indian legal inquiry investigating the genocide of the Tibetan people by the People's Liberation Army of China.
30 April 1960	Takes residence at Swarg Ashram in Dharamsala, Himachal Pradesh, a small town partly in ruins after 1904 earthquake.
1960	Launches major drive on education, including the start of the Nursery for Tibetan Refugee Children, run by elder sister, Tsering Dolma.
1961	UN General Assembly resolution passed, urging respect for the rights and self-determination of the Tibetan people.
1963	Age 28, the Dalai Lama presents draft democratic constitution, the Charter of Tibetans in Exile. The first Tibetan Parliament in exile, the Assembly of Tibetan People's Deputies, is established in Dharamsala.
9 September 1965	China formally establishes the "Tibet Autonomous Region" government, incorporating the whole of U-Tsang (Central Tibet) and western Kham.
1965	As UN resolution reaffirming the rights of the Tibetan people is passed, India speaks out for the first time at the General Assembly: "Ever since Tibet came under the stranglehold of China, the Tibetans have been subjected to a continuous and increasing ruthlessness which has few parallels in the annals of the world."
1967	Central Institute of Higher Tibetan Studies is established in Varanasi as a primary university for Tibetans. Dalai Lama takes first visits abroad—to Japan and Thailand.
1968	Moves residence from Swarg Ashram to Thekchen Choeling, previously the Byrne Estate.
1970	The Library of Tibetan Works and Archives (LTWA) is established, which presently houses more than 80,000 manuscripts and resources on Tibetan history, politics, and culture.
1973	Dalai Lama, now 38, makes his first visit to the West—Italy, Switzerland, the Netherlands, Belgium, Ireland, Norway, Sweden, Denmark, UK, West Germany, and Austria.
1979	Makes first visit to the US. The same year, begins initiating dialogue with scientists on the relationship of science and religion.
1979	Reestablishes contact with the government of the People's Republic of China (PRC), for first time since 1959. Deng Xiaoping invites Gyalo Thondup, elder brother of His Holiness, to China.
5 August 1979	Deploys first fact-finding delegation of the Tibetan Government-in-Exile, led by Juchen Thubten Namgya. Two more delegations follow in 1980.

◗ 13 March 1981	In a letter to Deng Xiaoping, the Dalai Lama states that the three fact-finding missions found "sad conditions" in Tibet. He urges that "genuine efforts must be made to solve the problem in accordance with the existing realities in a reasonable way."
◗ 24 April 1982	High-level Tibetan delegation arrives in Beijing to hold exploratory talks with Chinese officials.
◗ 19 October 1984	Second round of talks between the three delegates and Chinese leaders yields no further progress toward substantive negotiations.
◗ 1985	Fourth fact-finding delegation leaves for Tibet.
◗ 1987–1989	Protests in Lhasa are repeatedly crushed by Chinese authorities, resulting in many casualties.
◗ 21 September 1987	Addressing the Congressional Human Rights Caucus, in Washington, DC, His Holiness proposes Five-Point Peace Plan for Tibet. He advocates that Tibet become a zone of peace and an environmental sanctuary, with China responsible for defense and foreign policy.
◗ September 1987	Chinese leadership rejects the Five-Point Peace Plan proposal, and major protests erupt in Lhasa.
◗ 15 June 1988	Delivers the Strasbourg Proposal to European Parliament. For the first time, the Dalai Lama introduces the idea of *association* with China, rather than *separation* from it.
◗ 1989	Death of Tenth Panchen Lama in Tibet. Martial law imposed in Lhasa on 7 March.
◗ 10 December 1989	Dalai Lama awarded the Nobel Prize for Peace in Oslo.
◗ 1989	With funds from the Nobel Prize, establishes Foundation for Universal Responsibility in New Delhi. Its mission is to encourage the practice of nonviolence, improve communication between religion and science, secure human rights and democratic freedoms, and conserve and restore the health of the planet.
◗ 1991	Following a decade of dialogue with scientists, Dalai Lama establishes the Mind & Life Institute.
◗ 10 March 1991	During annual statement on the anniversary of the Tibetan Uprising, declares that unless the Chinese Government responds positively to the Strasbourg Proposal, he would consider himself free from any obligations to abide by concessions he had made.
◗ 25 March 1991	India informs Chinese Embassy in New Delhi that the Dalai Lama wishes to assist in the search for the authentic reincarnation of the Panchen Lama.
◗ 1992	Initiates additional major democratic steps, including the elections of *kalons* (ministers) by the Assembly of Tibetan People's Deputies, and the establishment of a judiciary branch.
◗ 1992	China bans all photographs, tapes, and books containing speeches or teachings of the Dalai Lama in Tibet.
◗ 10 March 1994	During annual statement on anniversary of Tibetan uprising, acknowledges that many Tibetans do not agree on the issue of Tibetan autonomy, rather than independence.

14 May 1995
Recognizes 6-year-old Gedhun Choekyi Nyima (born 25 April 1989) as the Eleventh Panchen Lama of Tibet. On 17 May, he and his family vanish; not seen since.

29 November 1995
Chinese authorities appoint Gyaincain Norbu as Eleventh Panchen Lama, insisting they have the right to choose reincarnation. Vast majority of Tibetan Buddhists reject him.

2001
First democratic elections for the post of *kalon tripa* (prime minister) are held by the Tibetan people.

17 October 2007
Awarded the US Congressional Gold Medal, recognizing His Holiness' role as "one of the world's foremost moral and religious leaders advocating peace."

2007
Named Presidential Distinguished Professor at Emory University in Atlanta, Georgia.

2007
Chinese government passes a law stipulating that all "living Buddhas" be approved by Beijing, effectively asserting that they will choose who becomes the Fifteenth Dalai Lama.

2009
Offers support for the Center for Compassion and Altruism Research and Education at Stanford University.

2009
First self-immolation in Tibet, born of relentless frustration. Many follow during subsequent years.

29 May 2011
Signs into law Amendment to the Charter of Tibetans, formally transferring his temporal power as dalai lama to a democratically elected leader. This ends a 368 year old tradition (since the Fifth Dalai Lama in 1642) of the dalai lamas holding dual responsibility of spiritual and temporal powers. Also draws up guidelines to recognize the next dalai lama.

8 August 2011
Dr. Lobsang Sangay, Harvard-educated lawyer, becomes the newly elected *sikyong*, head of the Central Tibetan Administration.

2012
Awarded prestigious Templeton Prize in London. Donates prize money to Save the Children fund, India, who had helped support young Tibetan children in the early years of exile.

6 July 2015
Celebrations marking His Holiness' 80th birthday are held in Dharamsala and around the world.

2016
Awards the geshe degree to 20 Tibetan Buddhist nuns, in equality with monks—an historical "first."

April 2019
Presides over global launch in Delhi of the Social, Emotional, and Ethical (SEE) Learning curriculum for schools, in association with Emory University.

April 2020
On the 50th anniversary of International Earth Day, delivers message of universal responsibility to save humanity with a spirit of solidarity and cooperation during the global pandemic health emergency.

SELECT BIBLIOGRAPHY

Andrugtsang, Gompo Tashi. *Four Rivers, Six Ranges: Reminiscences of the Resistance Movement in Tibet.* Dharamsala: Information and Publicity Office of His Holiness the Dalai Lama, 1973.

Arpi, Claude, *And Long and Dark shall be the Night: The Karma of Tibet.* Auroville: Pavilion of Tibetan Culture, 2002.

Atisha, Tenzin P. *A Survey of Tibetan History.* Dharamsala: Information and Publicity Office of His Holiness the Dalai Lama, 1984.

Avedon, John F. *In Exile from the Land of Snows.* London: Michael Joseph, 1984.

Bell, Charles. *Portrait of a Dalai Lama.* London: Collins, 1946.

Bell, Charles. *Tibet Past and Present.* Delhi: Motilal Banarsidas Publishers, 1992.

Conboy, Kenneth and James Morrison. *The CIA's Secret War in Tibet.* Lawrence: University Press of Kansas, 2002.

Dalai Lama XIV. *Freedom in Exile: The Autobiography of His Holiness the Dalai Lama of Tibet.* London: Abacus, 1998.

Dalai Lama XIV. *The Universe in a Single Atom: The Convergence of Science and Spirituality.* Danvers: Harmony Books, 2006.

Gould, Basil J. *The Jewel in the Lotus: Recollections of an Indian Political.* London: Chatto & Windus, 1957.

Grenard, F. *Tibet: The Country and its Inhabitants.* London: Hutchinson & Co., 1904.

Halper, Lezlee Brown & Stefan Halper. *Tibet: An Unfinished Story.* London: Oxford University Press, 2014.

Harrer, Heinrich. *Seven Years in Tibet.* New York: Flamingo, 1997.

International Resolutions and Recognition on Tibet (1959 to 2004). Dharamsala: Department of Information and International Relations.

Kuzmin, Sergius L. *Hidden Tibet: History of Independence and Occupation.* Dharamsala: Library of Tibetan Works and Archives, 2011.

Norbu, Dawa. *China's Tibet Policy.* Richmond, Surrey: Curzon, 2001.

Norbu, Jamyang. *Shadow Tibet: Selected Writing 1989-2004.* New Delhi: Srishti Publishers, 2007.

Norbu, Jamyang. *Warriors of Tibet: The Story of Aten and Khampas' Fight for the Freedom of their Country.* London: Wisdom Publications, 1986.

Norbu, Thubten Jigme. *Tibet is My Country—Autobiography of Thubten Jigme Norbu.* As told to Heinrich Harrer. Somerville: Wisdom Publications, 1986.

Peissel, Michel. *The Secret War in Tibet.* London: Little Brown, 1973.

Richardson, Hugh E. *Tibet and its History.* London: Oxford University Press, 1962.

Sadutshang, Rinchen. *A Life Unforeseen: A Memoir of Service to Tibet.* Somerville: Wisdom Publications, 2016.

Samten, Jampa & Nikolay Tsyrempilov. *From Tibet Confidentially—Secret correspondence of the Thirteenth Dalai Lama to Agvan Dorzhiev, 1911—1925.* Dharamsala: Library of Tibetan Works and Archives, 2012.

Sen, Chanakya (Ed.). *Asia: Tibet Disappears.* Bombay: Asia Publishing House, 1960.

Shakabpa, Tsepon W.D. *Tibet: A Political History.* New Haven: Yale University Press, 1967.

Snellgrove, David L. & Hugh E. Richardson. *A Cultural History of Tibet.* Boulder: Prajna Press, 1980.

Speeches of His Holiness the XIVth Dalai Lama (1959–1989) Vol. 1. Translated by Sonam Gyatso. Library of Tibetan Works and Archives, 2011.

Thondup, Gyalo, with Anne F. Thurston. *The Noodle Maker of Kalimpong: The Untold Story of My Struggle for Tibet.* London: Rider, 2015.

Tibet: Human Rights and the Rule of Law. Geneva: International Commission of Jurists, 1997.

Wangdu, Khemey Sonam, Sir Basil J. Gould, and Hugh E. Richardson. *Discovery, Recognition and Enthronement of the 14th Dalai Lama: A Collection of Accounts.* Dharamsala: Library of Tibetan Works and Archives, 2000.

Younghusband, Francis. *India and Tibet.* London: Oxford University Press, 1985.

JOURNAL ARTICLES & REPORTS

Conway, John S. "The Tibetan Community in Exile." *Pacific Affairs* 48, no. 1 (1975): 74-86.

"Dangerous Crossing: Conditions Impacting the Flight of Tibetan Refugees: 2005 Update" Report published by International Campaign for Tibet, Washington, 2006.

Dhondup, Yeshi. "Chronology of Sino-Tibetan contacts from 1978 to 2012." *The Tibet Journal* 38, no. 3-4 (2013): 121-160. Gale

Academic OneFile, Accessed 28 July 2020.

Ernst, Maximilian. "The Tolstoy-Dolan Mission and the Establishment of US-Tibetan Relations: An investigation into the events that unfolded after the first visit of American representatives to Lhasa in 1943." *Seoul National University Journal of International Affairs* 2, no. 1 (2014): 3-13.

Francke, Rev. A.H. "The Kingdom of gNya khri btsanpo, the first King of Tibet." *Journal of the Asiatic Society of Bengal*, March 1910.

Gelek, Surkhang Wangchen. "Tibet: The Critical Years (Part III) 'The Regent Reting Rinpoche,'" *The Tibet Journal* 8, no. 2 (1983): 33-39.

Getzelman, Sarah. "Forbidden Image: The 1996 Chinese Ban on the Fourteenth Dalai Lama's Image." *Stanford Journal of East Asian Affairs*. Winter 2008: 44-55.

Hogendoorn, Rob. "Caveat Emptor: The Dalai Lama's Proviso and the Burden of (Scientific) Proof." *Religions* 5, no. 3 (2014): 522-559.

Jian, Chen. "The Tibetan Rebellion of 1959 and China's Changing Relations with India and the Soviet Union." *Journal of Cold War Studies* 8, no. 3 (2006): 54-101.

Kobayashi, Ryosuke. "Tibet in the Era of 1911 Revolution." *Journal of Contemporary East Asia Studies* 3, no. 1 (2014): 91-113. DOI: 10.1080/24761028.2014.11869072

McGranahan, Carole. "Tibet's Cold War: The CIA and the Chushi Gangdrug Resistance

1956–1974." *Journal of Cold War Studies* 8, no. 3 (2006): 102-130.

Mehra, Parshotam. "Lu Hsing-Chi, The Simla Conference and After." *Journal of Asian History* 10, no. 1 (1976): 49-71. Accessed 28 July 2020. www.jstor.org/stable/41930195.

Michael, Franz. "Survival of a Culture: Tibetan Refugees in India." *Asian Survey* 25, no. 7 (1985): 737-744.

Mullin, Chris & Phuntsong Wangyal. "The Tibetans: Two perspectives on Tibetan-Chinese Relations." Minority Rights Group. Report 49, 1983.

Namgial, Eshey. "Tibetan Language and its Development." *South-Asian Journal of Multidisciplinary Studies (SAJMS)* 4, no. 1: 72-85.

Nashold, James. "The Meeting of East and West: The Dalai Lama's First Trip to the United States." *The Tibet Journal* 5, no 1/2 (1980): 34-41.

Norbu, Dawa. "China's Dialogue with the Dalai Lama 1978-90: Prenegotiation Stage of Dead End?" *Pacific Affairs* 64, no. 3 (1991): 351-372.

Norbu, Dawa. "Refugees from Tibet: Structural Causes of Successful Settlements." *The Tibet Journal* 26, no. 2 (2001): 3-25. Accessed 28 July 2020. www.jstor.org/stable/43302483.

Patterson, George N. "China and Tibet: Background to the Revolt." *The China Quarterly* 1 (Jan-Mar 1960): 87-102.

Relyea, Scott. "Chasing the Butcher's Shadow: The legacy of Zhao Erfeng on Republican Sichuan's policies in Kham." Paper presented at the thirteenth seminar of the International Association of Tibetan Studies, 2013.

Samten, Jampa. "Notes on the Thirteenth Dalai Lama's Confidential Letter to the Tsar of Russia." *The Tibet Journal* 34/35, no. 3/2 (2009): 357-370. Accessed 28 July 2020. www.jstor.org/stable/43302076.

Samuel, Geoffrey. "Songs of Lhasa'" *Ethnomusicology* 20, no. 3 (1976): 407-449.

Shakya, Tsering W. "1948 Tibetan Trade Mission to United Kingdom." *The Tibet Journal* 15, no. 4 (1990): 97-114.

Sinha, Nirmal C. "The Simla Convention 1914: A Chinese Puzzle." *Presidency College Magazine – Diamond Jubilee edition,* republished by The Tibetan and Himalayan Library, 1987.

Sinha, Nirmal C. "Was the Simla Convention Not Signed?" *Bulletin of Tibetology* 3, no. 1: 33-38.

https://2001-2009.state.gov/p/eap/rls/rpt/34266.htm

https://tibet.net/important-issues/sino-tibetan-dialogue/an-overview-of-sino-tibetan-dialogue/sino-tibetan-dialogue-hopes-and-suspicions-1978-1987/

https://www.everycrsreport.com/reports/RL30983.html

http://www.tibetjustice.org/materials/us/us1.html

https://tibet.net/wp-content/uploads/2017/05/The-case-concerning-TIbet.pdf

https://savetibet.org/a-struggle-of-blood-and-fire/

https://www.amnesty.org.ph/wp-content/uploads/2014/11/pol100011975eng.pdf

https://www.tibetwatch.org/30-years-of-resistance

https://tibet.net/wp-content/uploads/2014/10/Dharamsla-and-Beijing.pdf

https://savetibet.org/tibetan-self-immolations/

INDEX

PHOTO CREDITS

*Profound gratitude to the many photographers and
sources who contributed images to this publication. All
photographs are copyright. Permission is strictly required
for further reproduction. Thanks to Diana Gibb, Janet
Millar, Lucy Moore, and Tim Roodenrys for assistance
and support.*

First published in 2021 by

Interlink Books
An imprint of Interlink Publishing Group, Inc.
46 Crosby Street, Northampton, Massachusetts 01060
www.interlinkbooks.com

Originated and published simultaneously in India by Roli Books

Front cover image by Clive Arrowsmith
Back cover image courtesy of Tibet Museum/Jianjup Jinpa
Back flap image [Photo of Tenzin Geyche Tethong and Kelsang
Chukie Tethong] by Tim Roodenrys

Library of Congress Cataloging-in-Publication Data available
ISBN-13: 978-1-62371-877-0 (hardback)

US edition publisher: Michel Moushabeck
Editors: Priya Kapoor, Neelam Narula
US edition editor: John Sobhieh Fiscella
US edition consultant: Anna Sloan
Design: Sneha Pamneja
Photo research and editing: Jane Moore
Production: Pam Fontes-May
Proofreaders: Jennifer McKenna, Jane Bugaeva

Printed and bound in Korea

10 9 8 7 6 5 4 3 2 1